Ingredients for a
Jewish Life

Festivals, Family and Food

Ingredients for a
Jewish Life

Festivals, Family and Food

Compiled by Tammy Russell • Edited by Sarah Manning
With a foreword by Elaine Sacks

ROBSON
BOOKS

united synagogue
ח״ק בנסת ישראל

First published in Great Britain by Robson Books,
The Chrysalis Building, Bramley Road, London W10 6SP

A member of **Chrysalis** Books plc

British Library Cataloguing in Publication Data
A catalogue record for this title is available from the British Library.

ISBN 1 86105 572 2

Typeset by SX Composing DTP, Rayleigh, Essex

Articles written by individuals in this book do not necessarily reflect the views of The
United Synagogue.

Printed in Spain

Dedicated to the memory of

Freda Koppel ז"ל

by her daughter Tammy.

She was an inspiration to all who knew her.

Contents

Introduction

I am delighted to be writing the introduction to this special book, *Ingredients for a Jewish Life*, because a true Jewish life combines home and family. *Shabbat* and Jewish festivals, work and relaxing . . . and, of course, plenty of good, traditional kosher food!

In this diverse book, we are taken through the concept of community and synagogue, and are introduced to the many rituals, prayer books and officiants. No newcomer need feel strange. A fascinating section 'Is Judaism Green?' tells us about Jewish responsibility for guarding the environment: how the *Torah* forbids us from wantonly destroying fruit trees, and indeed it is the custom to plant new trees on the festival of *Tu Bishvat*. We learn about *Shechitah*: the humane slaughter of kosher animals, and also that hunting animals for sport is prohibited by Jewish law.

The laws and customs of *Shabbat* are interspersed with the ideas for creating a special atmosphere, including suggestions for delicious food and customs from many different Jewish traditions. The festivals are also described; what they represent and how they are celebrated, and a wonderful selection from recipes around the world is included. We have all the laws of *Kashrut* clearly explained, and practical suggestions in the splendidly entitled section 'Feng Shui in the Kosher Kitchen'.

In addition, *Ingredients for a Jewish Life* takes us through all the life cycle events, from *Shalom Zachor* and *Brit Milah*, through *Bar* and *Bat Mitzvah* and *Chupah* to the sadder events at the other end of life, with short explanations of the customs and associated terminology. A brief synopsis of *mikveh* laws plus some thoughts on choosing a Jewish school for your children can also be found.

This is a splendidly unusual, informative and positive guide to leading an orthodox Jewish life in the 21st century. Books are listed for further reading, and it is a very well judged balance between Jewish laws, customs, and ways to celebrate a warm Jewish home.

Enjoy!

Mrs Elaine Sacks

1

Home Truths
The Essential Qualities of Jewish Domestic Life

by Chief Rabbi, Professor Jonathan Sacks

The ideal Jewish home is . . . .? A superbly situated ambassadorial-style residence comprising six bedrooms, seven kitchens (three *milchik*, three *fleishik*, one *parev*!), set in undisturbed countryside only five minutes walk from the nearest *shtibl* (near enough for easy *Shabbat* access, far enough away for you not to be woken when they are short of a *minyan*), architect-designed *Pesach* kitchen with turbo-driven double dishwashers, luxury jacuzzi/*mikveh* complex, self-contained *booba*-annexe, and wired throughout to state-of-the-art *Shabbat*-observing microchip technology?

Perhaps not. Ideal homes, Jewishly-speaking, don't come constructed out of estate-agents' hype or float from the pages of glossy dream-magazines. An ideal home is. . .. well, *heimishe*. The outward march of Jewish suburbia has long carried with its changing symbols: in the early postwar years, the interconnecting drawing room-dining room – 'Does this have religious significance?' builders used to ask – then the double-garage, and slowly but surely the swimming-pool/sauna.

Yet in all this spiralling upward-mobility something, surely, is lost. A Jewish home is measured not in property values but in human values. As a *Chassidic* rabbi once said: A home is like a bed on a cold night. First you warm it, then it warms you.

Here, then, is my impromptu check-list for an ideal Jewish home. It is a place where you don't need a written invitation to drop in, where if three visitors call (as they did once on

Abraham) they aren't asked 'What are you collecting for?' Hospitality, said the rabbis, is greater than welcoming the Divine Presence. They also said the Hebrew letter which means home (*bet* or *bayit*) is open on one side to show that a home should always be open to the unexpected guest.

It's a place where the *mezuzot* on the doors don't take second place to the stripped-pine of the doors themselves. The *Torah* is alive to the non-verbal language of furnishing a home. A house can say, 'I am Jewish but I am pretending not to be.' Or it can wear the signs of its identity – the candlesticks, the framed *ketubah*, the sepia-tinted photographs of grandparents – with a certain unselfconscious pride.

It's a place where certain sounds are heard: singing on *Shabbat*, children telling parents what they have learned in this week's Hebrew lessons, a husband telling his wife on a Friday evening: '*Eshet chayil mi yimtsah.*' More than anything else a Jewish home is sensed in its sounds.

And its smells. *Shabbat* announces its arrival through the nose. Chicken soup? *Cholent*? It varies from culture to culture. *Ashkenazi*, *Sephardi*, East European, Oriental, perhaps from family to family. Food is part of a Jewish home, in its special way. It says: what we eat is not a function of appetite alone. But the *Torah* was generous. It chose to sanctify rather than frustrate desire. In eating, through *Kashrut* and the blessings over food; in sexuality, through *mikveh* and the code of husband-wife relations, it takes us always through a route of affirmation rather than denial. Rav[1] said – in a Talmudic aphorism that never ceases to amaze – that we will be judged for every legitimate pleasure we denied ourselves.

A Jewish home has its rhythm of time. Like a well-structured symphony, you can hear the coming allegro or adagio long before it arrives. Before *Pesach*, the flurry of cleaning and cooking; before *Purim*, getting the children's costumes ready; before *Succot*, the sound of hammer hitting nail or thumb; before *Shabbat*, the rush to beat the Jewish Parkinson's Law which says that getting ready takes just longer than the time available for it. Time is patterned, in a Jewish home, by something other than the '*TV Times*' or '*Time Out*'.

A Jewish home is: a place where you say '*Mazel Tov*' if someone breaks a plate, instead of pretending not to notice. A place where husbands help – on good ancient, rabbinic insistence – in the *Shabbat* preparations. Where children share a common language with parents. Where no guest feels that his footprints are an affront to the flawless white-pile Wilton. Where what is most valuable can't be stolen.

[1] Rav: 3rd century Talmudic sage.

Somewhere in London, not far from where we live, is a house outwardly indistinguishable from all the others in a row of Edwardian semis of which it is a part. What makes it special is that the family who lives there has taken it on themselves to invite home every new or lonely or unattached person they meet in *shul* on *Shabbat* morning. Perhaps there are many such homes, direct descendants of Abraham's and Sarah's.

Once a week, in such a house, one can almost feel the Divine Presence, welcomed in, made to feel part of the family. That is my ideal Jewish home.

Reprinted with the kind permission of the Jewish Chronicle.

2

A Unique *Kehillah*

'To be a member of an outstanding synagogue, to be part of a community's celebrations and study and prayers, is to be glad to be alive and to be a Jew.'

Chief Rabbi, Professor Jonathan Sacks

The United Synagogue is a unique organisation in the Jewish world – no similar institution exists in Israel, America or any of the other large Jewish communities. Together its individual communities constitute a single *'Kehillah Kedosha'* – a holy community of synagogues with shared aims and objectives, adhering to the tenets of centrist Orthodox Judaism. As such, it provides the mainstream Anglo-Jewish community with recognised standards of religious observance and a consistent approach to matters of personal status.

Anyone who marries under the auspices of the United Synagogue can rest assured that their marriage will be recognised by every *Beth Din* in the world. Membership of a United Synagogue is the passport to a lifelong support network, extending literally from the cradle to the grave, embracing mother and toddler groups, nurseries, day schools, Sunday schools, youth groups, summer camps, Israel trips, university chaplains, social groups for single people, *mikvaot*, friendship clubs for old people, hospital visitation, welfare support and burial services, as well as synagogue services, kosher food and religious guidance.

In contrast with its patrician beginnings, the United Synagogue today is energetic and modern, in touch with local concerns and focused on clear communal objectives, led by a team of professional managers and experienced lay leaders. Traditional values are still important, but innovations, like communal websites and e-mail newsletters, enable synagogues to stay up-to-date with the needs of their 21st-century membership. In accordance with its mission statement, everything undertaken by the United Synagogue is in accordance with the principles of *Torah* and *Halachah* (Jewish law), and inclusive of every Jew.

3

Belonging to a Community of Faith

by Leonie Lewis, Director of Community Development, United Synagogue

For many people, the word 'community' conjures up warm, caring and friendly images. The idea of a community can describe either a tangible location or a group of people, and it may be rather an amorphous concept embracing both. One might say that community is about feeling part of something bigger than ourselves, which provides us with a sense of pride, identity and togetherness.

Being part of a community means being 'in'. Being outside the community is the opposite, suggesting social isolation. In a society in which the maxim is 'every man for himself' and Robert Putnam's concept of 'Bowling Alone' is considered the norm, Jewish people tend to place a greater value on the importance of the community and people's ability to be inside it.

It is often hard to know when one is part of a community. Sometimes the all-inclusive label – 'the community' – may not reflect any personal involvement at all. For example, the Anglo-Jewish community is generally reckoned to comprise approximately 280,000 people, without their actually doing anything to merit inclusion in it. It would be difficult to argue that these 280,000 individuals share common values and common goals. And yet, the existence of our community was confirmed to me recently by two defining communal moments. These occasions have helped me to understand that I am part of a community and have demonstrated how it contributes to my wellbeing. Both experiences were positive and convinced me that being 'in' is a truly wonderful thing.

The first of these experiences confirmed my belief that members of a community nurture and sustain each other as part of the fundamental rubric of Judaism. If it did not exist, we would have to invent it. On the death of my beloved father, I remember my brother, not noted for his strong religious beliefs or communal involvement, being overwhelmed by the large number of well-wishers who came to visit our family. He was especially amazed by the meals that appeared on our table for the entire week of *shivah* and even several months later. He marvelled at the support we received from our local synagogue and from the wider Jewish community, which helped us through our bereavement. I realised then that this support was an integral part of our belonging to a community.

My second confirming experience was the rally in support of the people of Israel, held in Trafalgar Square in May 2002. I literally stood up to be counted alongside with 50,000 Jewish souls. It seemed that the entire Anglo-Jewish community was represented there. The sense of communal pride that swelled up in me and in so many others was immense. On that day, the Jewish community was one community. In caring for both the welfare of the individual in times of need, and the welfare of the Jewish people as a whole, we experience the power of community. It is about feeling loved and feeling needed, helping and being helped.

Margaret Thatcher once said that there is no such thing as society. The national outcry that greeted her assertion proved it false. If it were true – if we were to close ourselves off in our homes and ignore the wellbeing of our neighbours, the state of our neighbourhoods, the interests of future generations and the concerns of the rest of humanity – the world would be a much poorer place. As the great 1st century Rabbinic leader Hillel said in the 'Ethics of the Fathers' (1:14): 'If I am not for myself, then who will be for me? And if I am only for myself, what am I?'

The Chief Rabbi has said: 'Communities are an essential part of our wellbeing. They bridge the gap between family and society. They are the human face of the common good, they are where we learn to be citizens, carrying our share of the collective weight.'[1] Every individual needs a community and the community needs every individual. The opportunity to involve oneself in one's community, in whatever way one can, should not be missed. It is only by being part of something bigger and more worthy than ourselves that we can express our humanity and our purpose on this planet.

[1] *'Celebrating Life'* by Jonathan Sacks, Fount/HarperCollins, 2000.

4

Stress-free Synagogue Services

Walking into a synagogue for the first time on *Shabbat* morning can be an intimidating experience. Whether it is your first time visiting a new *shul*, or the first time in a while that you have been to a service, it is natural to worry about sitting in the wrong seat or doing the wrong thing. The service is all in Hebrew, which sometimes sounds like Chinese, especially at the speed that it is often read, but there are usually prayer books provided with an English translation. If one doesn't understand Hebrew, it is considered better to pray quietly in one's own mother-tongue, but with the long-term goal of learning to understand and join in the prayers of the community.

The Development of the Synagogue

As with any ritual event, there are rules and customs to be observed. It is often comforting to note the similarities between the synagogues that one can visit all over the world, but there are differences too. The United Synagogue and similar orthodox congregations follow the mainstream customs of Anglo-Jewry, known as *'Minhag Anglia'*, based on the *Ashkenazi* tradition and influenced by the customs of 19th century German Jewry.

The Hebrew for Synagogue is *Bet Knesset*, literally 'House of Assembly'. This recognises the social function that a synagogue plays in Diaspora communities. The whole idea of the synagogue grew out of the necessity for communal prayer when the Jewish people were sent into exile after the destruction of the First Temple in Jerusalem. The Men of the Great Assembly in the 4th century BCE (Before the Common Era) developed the daily *Shabbat* and festival services to fulfill the needs of the exiled Jewish people to gather together to praise G-d, to read from the *Torah* and to pray for their personal and communal concerns, including the rebuilding of the Temple.

The concept of the synagogue as a place of prayer, and the fixed forms of prayer, became a pivotal part of Jewish life after the destruction of the Second Temple in the first century CE (Common Era), when the Jewish people were scattered all over the world and had to learn to live as a minority in their host country, held together by their religious traditions. Jews living in northern and southern Europe developed different modes of prayer, and the *Ashkenazi* and *Sephardi* traditions retain differences to this day. In modern Israel we find these traditions existing side-by-side, and cross-fertilisation between them, with influences from the Eastern European *Chassidic* movement and even today from modern Jewish folk music, such as the popular tunes of the sixties singer Rabbi Shlomo Carlebach.

The Layout of the Synagogue

The layout of the synagogue echoes the contents of the Temple, and the Tabernacle which predated it. The cupboard or ark containing the *Torah* scrolls, which is known as the *Aron Kodesh*, replicates the Ark of the Covenant that was carried through the desert by the Children of Israel and placed in the Holy of Holies in Jerusalem. It originally contained the two tablets from Sinai and the first *Sefer Torah* written by Moses. Today the *Aron Kodesh* is the focal point of the *shul*, situated at the eastern end of the hall, so that when we face it we are praying towards Jerusalem. Like the Holy of Holies, a *parochet* curtain hangs in front of the *Aron*, and this is usually embroidered with Hebrew verses and traditional images of the two tablets, lions with crowns, or the tree of life.

Above the Ark hangs the *Ner Tamid*, a perpetual light that serves as a reminder of the lamp, in the Tabernacle and later in the Temple, that was never allowed to be extinguished. The *Sifrei Torah*, or *Torah* scrolls, kept inside the *Aron* are each hand-written on parchment, rolled on wooden poles, covered with embroidered covers and adorned with silver crowns, bells and breastplates. They are taken out for the reading of the weekly portion of the Five Books of Moses each *Shabbat* and festival, and on Monday and Thursday morning services, and carried to the *Bimah*, the central dais with the table from which they are read, and from which most of the service is conducted.

Service Styles

The atmosphere in the synagogue is usually one of informality. Worshippers pray both individually and collectively, and may enter and leave at various times during the service. This may appear strange to anyone expecting the decorum and silence found in the houses of prayer of some other faiths, but our synagogues are really an extension of our homes. In fact, new communities often start by holding their services in the homes of their members until there are enough Jews living in an area to found a synagogue. Many of the United Synagogue communities started in this way. Such communities may continue to hold informal services in their synagogues, led by lay members, if they are unable to employ or choose not to have a professional *chazan* to lead the singing.

The purpose of the *chazan* is to assist the congregation in their prayers, to direct their thoughts with inspiring melodies and to pronounce the prayers on behalf of those who are unable to do so for themselves, who should answer 'Amen' at the appropriate junctures. Modern tastes differ and synagogues today choose whether to have choral services or ask trained members of the community to lead more informal communal singing, or indeed to have a mixture of the two.

It should be noted that wedding ceremonies and the High Holy Day services of *Rosh Hashanah* and *Yom Kippur* tend to be the most formal choral-style services in most synagogues, while *Shabbat* prayers are more participatory and considerably shorter. Weekday services are often led by a member of the congregation who is a mourner and needs to say the *Kaddish* prayer, during the first year of his bereavement of a parent (thirty days for another relative) or on the *Yarzheit* anniversary, to give him the maximum number of opportunities to commemorate and honour his deceased relative.

Men, Women & Children

Orthodox Jewish services are led by men. Men and women worshippers do not sit together as each would be liable to distract the other from their prayers. It is helpful to bear in mind that prayer is meant to be a personal experience, not a family event, and indeed that one should not really sit with anyone who might distract you from the business in hand, namely communication with the Creator of the World and Master of the Universe. The separate seating areas provided for men and women are either on different levels, if there is a women's gallery, or they are divided by a *mechitzah*, which may be a grille or a semi-transparent curtain to prevent interaction.

Young children are permitted to cross the *mechitzah*. Some communities provide children's services in another room as this enables their parents to participate more fully in the service while also providing for the children's needs. Other communities are more relaxed and encourage a family atmosphere, as long as the service is not disrupted by noise. Parents have to find their own balance in deciding how much of the service their children are able to sit through quietly, using whatever suitable inducements and distractions they can. There is often a box of books or a pocketful of sweets provided; the education and encouragement of our children being key to our tradition. As they approach the age of *Bar Mitzvah*, boys may be invited to play a minor role in the service, such as reading the *Anim Zemirot* song of praise at the end.

Married men are required to wear, and unmarried men and boys may choose to wear, a prayer shawl, known as a *Tallit*. This is a rectangular cloak of white wool or silk adorned with fringes at each corner, known as *Tzitzit*. By wrapping himself in this garment during the service, a man symbolically surrounds himself in the commandments of Judaism, and he may drape it over his head from time to time to screen out the outside world and focus more deeply on his prayers.

Women who are, or have been, married and all men and boys are required to cover their heads during the service, albeit for different reasons. The skull-cap worn by Jewish men, known variously as a *kippah, kapul* or *yarmulke*, is a constant reminder of God's existence above our heads, as it were. Prayers and blessings cannot be said without wearing one, and it has become normal in Israel and in most Diaspora communities for men to wear a head covering all the time.

It is appropriate for everyone to dress smartly in synagogue because they are in 'G-d's house' – not because His presence is confined there, but because it is felt more directly there. We are instructed to behave in the synagogue as we would in the palace of a king or queen. Appropriate standards of formality vary between different communities, and people tend to dress up more for festivals and family occasions for social rather than religious reasons, but men are expected to wear trousers rather than shorts, and jackets are usually worn.

The Shabbat Morning Service

Saturday morning services usually start between 9.00 a.m. and 9.30 a.m. and end at around noon. They are conducted in Hebrew, which can be followed using a *Siddur* and a *Chumash*. The *Siddur* is a prayer book which contains the order of service for almost every occasion. It opens from right to left because Hebrew is written and read from right to left, and most *Siddurim* give an English translation opposite each Hebrew page. The *Siddur* is a compilation of psalms, blessings, extracts from the *Torah* and prayers composed by rabbis down the ages.

The service starts with preliminary blessings in which we praise and thank G-d for the things we would otherwise take for granted each morning. The morning service is known as *Shacharit* and consists of *Pesukei de Zimra* (psalms and songs of praise), the *Shema* prayer and its blessings and an *Amidah*, or 'standing prayer', which is read silently and repeated publicly. In fact, every one of the daily *Shabbat* and festival services follows this fundamental structure, with variations and additions.

After the morning service the *Torah* scroll is brought out for the Reading of the Law, which can be followed in the *Chumash*. A portion, known as a *Sidra,* comprising of a few chapters from one of the Five Books, read in order during the year, is chanted aloud from the *Sefer Torah* by a skilled *Ba'al Kore*. This is followed by a related extract called *Haftarah,* read from one of the books of the Prophets by a male from the community.

During the Reading of the Law seven men, plus one for *Maftir,* are chosen for the honour of being called up to stand next to the reader during the recitation of one of the *Aliyot* (call-ups), to recite certain blessings and to receive blessings for himself and his family. The first man to be called up has to be a *Kohen,* a member of the priestly tribe, and the second a *Levi,* from a different group of the same tribe. After that anyone besides a *Kohen* or *Levi* can be given an *Aliyah,* and the last man called, the one for *Maftir,* will be the one who also reads the *Haftarah.* Each man is called up by his Hebrew name and recites blessings before and after his portion of the *Torah* has been chanted. These honours are often reserved for people who are celebrating a family event or commemorating a *yahrzeit* during that week. Fathers of new babies are called-up for an *Aliyah* and the name of a newborn baby girl will be announced at the end of her father's *Aliyah.*

When the *Torah* has been read, the *Sefer Torah* is opened and lifted up for all the congregation to see, before being carefully rolled up and dressed in its mantle and silverware. Before it is returned to the *Aron Kodesh* the Rabbi will recite special prayers for the welfare of the British Royal Family and the State of Israel. After it has been put away, the Rabbi may give a sermon relating to that week's *Torah* reading and any relevant issues of current concern.

On *Shabbat,* festivals, intermediate days of a festival and celebrations for the new moon, we recite an Additional Service known as *Musaf,* which is not said on weekdays. This includes another version of the *Amidah* standing prayer, which is first read silently and then sung aloud by the *Chazan.* The service usually ends with the *Anim Zemirot* song of praise, often sung by a young boy, followed by communal announcements and the concluding song *Adon Olam.*

Male visitors to the synagogue may be given honours during the service, either by opening the *Aron Kodesh,* being called up for an *Aliyah,* for which they will be asked their Hebrew name, or by being asked to lift up the heavy *Sefer Torah* scroll, or to roll it up and dress it. It may be possible to request an *Aliyah* by speaking to the rabbi, *Shamash* (beadle) or warden in advance. In each case one should ask for a *Tallit* to put on if you are not wearing one. Declining these honours does not cause offence, and may be preferable to doing the wrong thing. Anyone who wishes to say *Kaddish* during the service should feel free to do so at the appropriate moments in the service when it is said collectively by mourners.

After the service, the congregation is often invited to participate in a *Kiddush.* This is the Sanctification of the Sabbath day and it enables the congregation to enjoy a glass of wine and a piece of cake or a biscuit together. A more lavish spread may be provided by a family celebrating a special occasion, such as a *Bar Mitzvah* or forthcoming wedding. The traditional greeting on *Shabbat* is 'Shabbat Shalom' – a peaceful sabbath – or in Yiddish, 'Gut Shabbos'.

5

Charity Begins at Home

'Love your neighbour as yourself' is a fundamental precept of the *Torah*. As children of G-d, we are all responsible for one another's wellbeing. There are a host of ethical and legal principles which stem from this precept, and which form the basis of the charitable instinct for which the Jewish community is renowned.

In Jewish law there are guidelines for giving to charity within which one will be able to choose one's priorities. One of the rules laid down by Maimonides in his guide to *tzedakah* is that charity begins at home, with one's extended family, with the priorities for giving radiating outwards to one's immediate community, to the wider community, to Jewish people in other countries, and to the world at large, in ever-increasing circles. It is a well-known Jewish custom that we should give a tenth of our disposable income to charity, as it belongs to G-d by rights. In fulfilling this practice it is therefore important to remember that we are returning to G-d what is His, through the medium of the recipient, who is actually enabling us to do the *mitzvah*.

One of the fundamental principles of charitable giving is to respect the dignity of the recipient. The highest level of *tzedakah* is to assist someone before they become in need of charity by providing them with business or work. The next level of *tzedakah* is where the recipient does not know from whom the money comes, and the donor does not know who is receiving it. Local synagogues often operate *Gemillut Chassadim* funds, known as *Gemachs*, which offer interest-free loans or grants to members who are experiencing short- or long-term financial difficulties. Help is given on a totally confidential basis, and enables those who donate to these funds to know that they are helping their neighbours directly, but in a private and dignified fashion.

Gemillut chassadim, acts of kindness, are another way of loving our neighbour. The time and effort we spend helping other people makes us better people, and increases the sum of human happiness. In our disconnected society, connecting with others, especially those who are lonely, disadvantaged and housebound, can make a real difference to their lives. It can also make us appreciate our own circumstances, putting our personal problems into perspective.

The United Synagogue is one of the many communal institutions which deploy volunteers to help provide support for its members. Each local synagogue has a 'US Cares' team to co-ordinate local care activities. This can include befriending individuals, helping those who are housebound with their shopping, visiting the sick, at home or in hospital, helping to run *Shivah*s for the bereaved and providing emotional support to mourners.

Tzedakah literally means 'righteousness', which can be expressed in many different ways. Sending a cheque to any of the large institutional charities is an obvious and easy form of charity, which enables their staff to help others on our behalf. But the act of helping other people face-to-face – by giving some of our money or our time – enables us to share our humanity with other people, putting ourselves into the *mitzvah* and putting the merit of the *mitzvah* back into ourselves.

Is Judaism Green?

Environmental causes may have come to public attention towards the end of the 20th century, but 'green' ideas are not new to Judaism. Preserving our world for future generations is certainly a concept which finds much support in Jewish sources. When G-d created the world and gave control of nature to humankind, it was given entrusted to us on condition that we guard and look after all His wonderful creations. This custodianship gives rise to a host of responsibilities and commandments, which are perhaps only today being recognised as 'environmentally-sound'.

The agricultural society described in the Bible was governed by laws which our ancient ancestors understood as being essential to the continued wellbeing of the land and those who depend on it. One of the benefits of the *shmittah* system – leaving the land to lie fallow for one year every seven – is to allow the soil to rest and recover its nutrients so that it does not become over-farmed. Similarly there are restrictions on the cultivation of orchards, such that trees have to be allowed to reach maturity before their fruit can be eaten. Even in our era of intensive farming, farmers in Israel are still required to follow these commandments, to preserve the fertility of the Holy Land.

The *Torah* forbids us from the wanton destruction of fruit trees and even sets strict instructions for armies who besiege enemy cities not to cut down their fruit trees. It is customary to plant trees on *Tu Bishvat*, a minor festival which is designed to teach us an appreciation of fruit trees and nature in general, and the planting of trees has become an important way of developing the land of Israel. Sustainability has always been a priority for the Jewish people and we find in the *Talmud* a story which expresses the importance of preserving the world for future generations. An old man was asked why he was planting a carob tree, which would surely not produce fruit in his lifetime. He replied that he was planting it for the sake of his grandchildren, just as his own ancestors had planted the trees whose fruit he now enjoyed.

Respect for nature can also be seen in the early planning restrictions set out in the *Torah*, which required towns to preserve their 'green belt' of undeveloped land for the grazing of animals and aesthetic pleasure. Today we can clearly see the importance of these natural 'lungs' in helping to balance our cities' CO_2 emissions and counter the 'greenhouse' effect. Early cases of environmental pollution are discussed by the Rabbis in the *Talmud*, with penalties set for tradesmen, such as tanners, who spill or dump harmful substances into rivers and public areas.

Just as the *Torah* requires us to respect the land, it contains many commandments for the protection of animals. While we could not be said to grant animals 'rights', we are clearly required to respect their needs. For example, any person who keeps domestic animals – either on a farm or as pets – must feed them before they eat their own meals. Because cows must be milked regularly, so that they do not suffer discomfort, we are allowed to milk them on *Shabbat* and festival days, but only for their sake – we are not allowed to use the milk. Animals are also supposed to be allowed to rest on *Shabbat*. Farmers are not allowed to harness two different animals to pull their plough, because of the discomfort that would be caused if they walk at different speeds. These restrictions do not only apply to those who own and use animals; anyone who sees that a donkey is struggling with its heavy load has an obligation to go and unload it to reduce the weight it is carrying. We are even required to respect the vulnerability of animals, by shooing away the mother bird before collecting eggs from its nest, and by not slaughtering a cow and its calf on the same day, which teaches us not to be cruel to animals or to human beings.

The whole issue of eating meat is dealt with in the *Torah*. Vegetarians will find sources for their preference in the fact that Adam and Eve were meant to eat only fruit and vegetables. Animals and humans were both created on the sixth day of Creation, and they were all given permission to enjoy the same vegetarian diet. But mankind was endowed with a spiritual potential which animals lack, which gives us not only a superior intellect but also the ability to make moral choices. This freedom of choice led to man's fall from grace and expulsion from the ideal world of the Garden of Eden, and later to the destruction of almost all living creatures in the flood.

When Noah and his family emerged from the ark, G-d gave them dominion over all creatures including the right to eat them, albeit with restrictions to prevent unnecessary cruelty to animals. We can therefore understand the permission to eat meat as a Divine concession to human weakness, based on the fact that ours is an imperfect world. The prophecy of Isaiah predicts that in the Messianic era, when we return to the perfection of Eden, the eating of meat will again be forbidden – lions will eat straw and lambs will lie peacefully with wolves, and we will all become vegetarians.

Far from understanding the *Torah*'s permission for mankind to eat and enjoy meat as a mere dispensation, we see that the Children of Israel were given implicit instructions as to what meat was permitted to be eaten and used in Temple sacrifices, and how to kill animals humanely. Although it is true that there is no commandment to eat meat, there are specific *mitzvot* which require animal slaughter, such as the *Korban Pesach* meal just before the Children of Israel left Egypt, and all the various sacrifices that they were instructed to bring in the Tabernacle and Temple.

The procedure for humane animal slaughter, known as *shechitah*, is designed to cause minimum pain to the animals that we kill. It can only be carried out by a specially trained person, who must be a pious person of good character who takes his responsibilities seriously. He must check that this knife is perfectly sharp so that his swift stroke to the animal's jugular vein will be accurate and instantly fatal. He must recite a blessing before performing *shechitah*, to concentrate his mind on the responsibility of taking an animal's life as painlessly as possible. Some lobbying groups argue against the efficiency and painlessness of *shechitah*, insisting that animals should be stunned first, but there is considerable scientific evidence that the stunning procedure they recommend is less efficient than the swift method of slaughter set out in the *Torah*, which we believe to be G-d's own manual for the ideal operation of His world.

The fact that we are allowed, and in some cases even required, to eat meat should be seen in the context of the other commandments which require us to protect animals from unnecessary suffering. Hunting animals for sport, for example, is understood as prohibited by Jewish law. But having been specifically given permission to eat meat by G-d, with careful rules to ensure that we do not abuse this privilege, the Rabbis encourage us to enjoy meat, as we enjoy G-d's other creations. What's more, we are encouraged to eat meat on *Shabbat* and festivals, and to celebrate any *simchah*, because by doing so we fulfil a natural human urge.

Vegetarianism may be seen as a valid lifestyle choice for anyone who is uncomfortable with the idea of eating meat, especially if doing so would give them no pleasure. However, it would be wrong to describe meat-eating as immoral, because this would imply that G-d allows and encourages us to do something immoral – a clearly inconsistent position.

Many modern farming methods differ greatly from those envisioned in the *Torah*. It may be true to say that the production of battery chickens, the livers of force-fed geese, and veal calves transported in crowded crates, for example, are not in harmony with the spirit of Jewish law. There is certainly scope to recommend considerate farming practices. Animal rights should be respected by everyone, although not at the expense of our human right to eat and enjoy them as permitted by G-d.

So Jews can be said to be green, and proud to be so. Every time we say a *berachah* (blessing) before we eat, whether a salad or a steak, we thank G-d for creating it for us and we elevate it to a higher spiritual level by utilising it in His service. There are also blessings to be said when smelling fragrant flowers, when first seeing the spring blossom on a fruit tree, and when witnessing the wonders of nature – oceans, mountains and waterfalls. We recognise that the bounty of nature has been given to us to enjoy and to respect, to use responsibly and to preserve for future generations.

7

Decorating a Jewish Home

If you were to look 'through the keyhole' of a house, you would probably be able to tell if it was a Jewish home. There are certain tell-tale signs in any house that show the ethnicity of its occupants and the traditions that they keep. Even an amateur detective would notice the *mezuzah*, not only on the front door but on almost every doorway inside the house as well. A *mezuzah* is a small box containing a handwritten parchment inscribed with two paragraphs of the *Shema* prayer – our fundamental statement of Jewish belief and practice. G-d's name is shown on the outside of the box, which is attached two-thirds of the way up the right-hand doorpost, with its top pointing inwards. Whether it guards a Jewish home or acts as a 'spiritual air-freshener' depends on your point of view, but in some communities a person who is experiencing bad luck will often be advised to have his/her *mezuzot* checked by a scribe to ensure that the parchment has not become damaged.

There is a myth that every Jewish house needs a through-room and at least one extension. In fact, some builders who work in Jewish neighbourhoods seem to think that knocking down walls to make rooms bigger is part of our religion! This has more to do with our enthusiasm to invite large numbers of people into our homes for festivals and celebratory meals. Food, as we know, plays an important part in Jewish life, so it is unusual to find a Jewish home without a well-furnished kitchen and dining room. In a society where meals are increasingly eaten alone and in front of the television, family dining is still *de rigueur* in most Jewish families, especially on *Shabbat*. When the festivals come around, so does the whole extended family, so an extendable table is often a good investment.

Entertaining family and friends is one of the purposes of a Jewish home, so homebuyers will often put special emphasis on the lounge, dining room and kitchen, expecting to spend time and entertain there. Furnishing to suit your own taste and budget is usually more important than following the fashions set in interiors magazines, whose recommendations do not always suit a Jewish family home. For example, clutter-free living is generally difficult for Jewish people. Storage space in the kitchen is clearly a must, as the requirement for the separation of meat and milk necessitates twice as many pots, pans and dishes as non-kosher kitchens might contain. You may also find that you need extra wardrobe space for formal clothes, as Jewish people traditionally dress smartly for *Shabbat*, festivals and family celebrations. As any Jewish woman will tell you, hats and shoes can take up a lot of room!

There are some Jewish traditions and superstitions that may be worth bearing in mind when you decorate your home, if only to keep your grandmother happy! There is a well-established custom not to position one's bed with its foot pointing directly towards the door, because coffins are carried out this way. Blue is a very traditional colour, often used to paint the walls of synagogues, because it represents the heavens. There is also a tradition to leave a small part of one wall undecorated, to remind us that while there is no Temple standing in Jerusalem, G-d has no home, so our homes should not be perfect. Another Jewish custom within the home is to hang one's *ketubah*, the marriage certificate, which is often a beautifully illuminated manuscript, in a prominent position on the wall. Pictures of Israel are also traditional, as a reminder of our spiritual homeland as well as of happy holidays spent there. Some people like to hang a picture of Jerusalem on the wall of the home which faces eastwards, which is the direction we face during prayer, and there are special pictures produced for this purpose showing the word '*mizrach*', meaning east.

Family photos are a must in a Jewish home – not just of children and family gatherings, but often including a couple of faded pictures of our grandparents and great-grandparents, to show where we have come from and whose traditions we are perpetuating. They often provide a talking point and prompt that favourite Jewish game '*Mishpachology*' – spotting connections between families and recognising people we know. Books are generally on display but not just for show. The mandatory *siddur* (prayer book) and *chumash* (Bible), festival prayer books and Passover *haggadah* are often part of a much wider collection of books, because we are 'The People of the Book' and we love to read, to educate ourselves and our children about our heritage and the world we live in. Also on display are the symbols and artefacts used in Jewish rituals – the *kiddush* cup, *havdalah* candle and spice box, *Chanukah menorah* and *Shabbat* candlesticks, *challah* board and cloth. These may be traditional family heirlooms, or modern pieces designed by contemporary Israeli craftsmen. Either way they symbolise our past as well as our present, our traditions and our Jewish lifestyle, and they are often prominently displayed within the home.

Last but not least, no Jewish home is complete without at least one *tzedaka* box. The *Torah* mandates us to give a tenth of our income to charity and we remind ourselves and our children of the obligation to be generous to those less fortunate than ourselves by putting spare coins in collecting boxes, as well as giving donations to charity and attending charity fundraising events. The charities we support may be local or national, Jewish or general, but there is a particularly strong tradition of giving money to Israel, dating back before the establishment of the Jewish state. The *pushka* or charity box in our homes reminds us that, whatever we spend on decorating the house, we must always remember the world outside our front door and our obligations to other people.

8

Achieving Work–Life Balance

by Diana Wolfin

It may not come as a surprise to learn that in the UK today we work the longest hours in the European Union, and our workforce suffers the greatest work-related stress. These statistics impact even more on the Jewish household, where achieving a work–life balance carries with it the added burden of juggling both the calendar of the working world and the calendar of Jewish festivals. Whatever your level of observance, there will most probably be at least some occasions when you will have to negotiate space in your secular calendar for Jewish activities.

The good news is that the workforce is generally becoming more flexible, with a greater willingness by employers to offer working hours in a different way, such as allowing employees to work from home. This new flexibility lends itself to a way of life which considers family, community and spirituality as much as workplace and pay packet.

Far from being a recent consideration, the concept of work–life balance goes back to Creation itself: 'By the seventh day G-d finished His work which He had done, and He abstained on the seventh day from all His work which He had done' (Genesis 2:2). The premise of balancing work and rest begins in the book of Genesis and brings us right up-to-date with contemporary work practices. Our template comes from the *Torah*, as relevant now as it was when we were first given it. The value and benefit of observing *Shabbat* can be clearly seen today, where both the secular and the religious worlds agree that too much work is not good for you!

Away from our working lives, we have families, communities, friends, recreation, spirituality and general wellbeing to consider, all of which are of equal – if not greater – significance. Money is, after all, just a means to an end. It is perhaps in the rest of our lives that we learn its true value and appreciate the enjoyment it affords us. In celebrating the festivals and taking a day off to observe *Shabbat*, we are allowing ourselves the opportunity to rest, relax and renew our tired minds and bodies. Even for those who are not religious, the concept has a great deal to commend it. By trying to balance the amount of time we spend at work with other aspects of our lives, we enrich that which we bring to the workplace, as we are not tired or burnt-out from constantly doing the same things with no break. Sitting with one's family, eating, debating, even arguing, with no interruptions from phone or television, develops a side of us which is strangely at odds with the current climate. Mobile phones, fax machines, text messages all have an air of urgency about them which creates a pressured atmosphere.

Research shows that parents and children, as well as couples, spend surprisingly little time each week talking to each other, and many families never eat together. Time away from life's stringent demands can give us that relaxed approach to meals and communication which is lacking the rest of the week, and a chance for the generations to talk to each other and communicate in more than the usual rushed way. Putting something back into the community, in whatever way one is able, and spending time with children, parents and friends, are activities which enrich our lives and make us feel good about ourselves. The Jewish way of life gives us a structure which, once we are committed to it, makes it easy for us to look at work–life balance. When we are able to distinguish between quantity and quality of work, we will realise that the regular recharging of our batteries will, in fact, make us more, not less productive.

Brian Dyson, Chief Executive of Coca Cola, puts it like this: 'Imagine life as a game in which you are juggling some five balls in the air. You name them: work, family, health, friends and spirit – and you are keeping all of these in the air. You will soon understand that work is a rubber ball. If you drop it, it will bounce back. But the other four balls – family, health, friends and spirit – are made of glass. If you drop one of these, they will be irrevocably scuffed, marked, damaged or even shattered. They will never be the same. You must understand that and strive for balance in your life.'

Whether we see ourselves as jugglers of life, or guardians of the *Torah*, or even both, there is much to be said for getting the balance right and acquiring a different perspective on our priorities. And we may just become less stressed in the process!

9

Making Shabbat Special

Shabbat
The Sabbath
Source: *Exodus 31:17*

In six 'days' G-d created a world. It was a wondrous home for humanity, with all life beautifully balanced and interwoven to form a perfect synthesis, the symphony of Creation. On the seventh day He rested, and He told mankind to do likewise, to recreate His world of perfection by making *Shabbat* into an ideal living space in which to reflect on the deeper values of life.

Shabbat living is dramatically different to weekday living. On *Shabbat* no work needs doing, there are no troubles to worry about and there is no pressure. Through observing the laws of *Shabbat*, we leave the world of *becoming* and concentrate on *being*. Ideally, the warmth and intensity of *Shabbat* creates a feeling of fulfilment and an appetite for life that lasts throughout the week until the next *Shabbat* comes around.

Shabbat does not arrive in a home, but has to be created – ideally it should be the focus of the whole week, so that our preparations engender excitement and anticipation. Creating *Shabbat* involves observing both positive and negative regulations – there are *mitzvot* (commandments) to perform, and activities to abstain from.

Food customs

The *Shabbat* meals are central to the celebration of *Shabbat*. They should be special events, with favourite foods set aside to be shared with family and friends. The paradox is that this must be achieved without any cooking being done on the *Shabbat* day itself, because Jewish law states that all food to be consumed during the twenty-five hours of *Shabbat* must have been cooked before it commences on Friday night.

To understand how *Shabbat* meals work, it is worth remembering that many of the traditional *heimishe* dishes were chosen by our ancestors with these rules in mind. *Cholent*

– meaning 'slow heat' in French – is designed to sit in the oven for hours without drying out. *Gefilte* fish is minced because removing fish bones on *Shabbat* can be problematic. *Kugels* of every kind are easy to warm through and keep better than many vegetable dishes.

Modern technology offers some simple and elegant solutions to the challenge of serving hot food on *Shabbat*. As well as the *blech* – a metal sheet which covers the gas flame of a cooker – we now have the electric hotplate, the slow-cooker, and the hostess trolley to keep the food hot. A *Shabbat* urn is another boon – either a metal urn on a low light on the gas hob or, more commonly now, a large plastic electric kettle.

Nothing can beat the weekly treat of freshly baked *challah*. In years gone by, our mothers would stand for hours and knead, pummel and work hard to provide beautiful plaited loaves for the *Shabbat* table. Nowadays many of us have Jewish bakeries nearby, but it is still a special treat to bake our own *challah*. Today we have special food processor attachments and even a domestic breadmaker, a most wonderful invention for those in a hurry, who still want the personal touch for their bread. There is even a unique *mitzvah* to perform as part of the baking process.

Dina's *Challah* – page 169
Breadmaker *Challah* – page 17136

On *Shabbat*, extra effort is made to make everything look special. Traditionally the dinner table is covered with a white tablecloth and laid with fine crockery and cutlery. For busy people, these meals provide valuable 'quality time' with one's children and one's friends, and there is an extra dimension to the offering of hospitality to out-of-town visitors and lonely friends, so that everyone in the community has a place to eat the *Shabbat* meals.

Friday Night

The art of welcoming *Shabbat* begins on Friday night. Fifteen minutes before the sun sets, candles are lit in the Jewish household to honour *Shabbat* and to ensure that there is light and harmony in the home. After the synagogue service, which nowadays many women attend as well as men, the evening begins with the singing of two beautiful songs: '*Shalom Aleichem*' (Welcome), a salute to the mystical angels of peace who grace the world on *Shabbat*, and '*Eshet Chayil*' (A Woman of Worth), a chapter from the book of Proverbs acknowledging the crucial role of women in Jewish life. On Friday night, parents traditionally bless their children, in a moment of family togetherness.

The ceremony of *Kiddush*, a blessing of sanctification, is recited over a cup of wine or grape juice by the head of the family to affirm the holiness of *Shabbat*. The cup of wine is shared between those at the table. Before eating bread, Jewish law requires us to wash our hands, not because they are dirty but in order to spiritually cleanse them. Bread is singled out for this because of its special place in the Temple service, and to remind us how the *Kohanim* used to wash their hands as part of their ritual duties. Water is poured from a cup over each hand once, and a blessing is recited while we dry our hands. Then we return to the table, without speaking to one another, to make the second blessing over the two *challot*. These plaited loaves of bread are eaten to commemorate the double portion of *Manna* that our ancestors collected every Friday while travelling through the desert.

There are no set rules regarding the Friday night menu – the most important thing is to eat special foods and to enjoy G-d's bounty. Historically, meat and chicken were reserved for *Shabbat* consumption. A traditional menu might start with chopped liver or *gefilte* fish, the famously Jewish chicken soup, followed by roast chicken or a good cut of meat, and a delicious dessert. Between courses it is traditional to sing *zemirot*, *Shabbat* songs, and to discuss ideas from the *Torah* which have modern relevance, in particular the themes of the week's *Torah* reading. As well as special tastes, the *Shabbat* meal involves special sounds – the sounds of people talking to each other (and not on the telephone), arguing and laughing together (and not at the television), sharing food and singing songs together. By the end of the evening, an atmosphere of comfort and closeness has descended on the Jewish home.

This atmosphere of *Oneg Shabbat*, literally '*Shabbat* delight', may continue after the Friday night meal, with more singing, a glass or two of whisky, some chocolates, cakes and biscuits, playing games with the children, the intimate relations of a husband and wife, and the feeling of relaxation and enjoyment that come with the freedom from life's daily stresses. The idea of *Oneg Shabbat* is not 'do what you feel', but 'feel what you do'. It is a reminder of how great life can be.

Traditional menu ideas:
Chopped Liver – page 82
Chicken Soup with Knaidlach– page 80
Roast Chicken – page 126
Hot Chocolate Cake – page 145
Peaches.Cardinal – page 148

Shabbat Day

In addition to fulfilling the religious requirement to pray with the community, Jews go to their local synagogue on *Shabbat* morning for a number of reasons – social, spiritual, pedagogical and communal. The service includes the reading of the weekly portion of the Five Books of Moses from a *Sefer Torah* scroll, a sermon on its contemporary relevance by the rabbi, and tuneful melodies praising G-d's greatness, the sanctity of *Shabbat* and the commitment of the Jewish people. There is usually a communal *Kiddush* reception, often to celebrate a family event, and people wish each other '*Shabbat Shalom*' – a peaceful *Shabbat* – or in Yiddish, '*Gut Shabbos*'.

Lunch is the second of the three *Shabbat* meals, starting with the preliminary rituals of *Kiddush*, hand-washing and the blessing over *challot*. In many homes this second *Shabbat* meal features fresh salads and cold meats, but there should also be a hot dish. The most famous dish for *Shabbat* day is the hot stew, whose name and ingredients vary from one household to another depending on family tradition. *Ashkenazi* Jews of German or East European descent will cook a *Cholent* with meat, beans and barley, while *Sephardi* Jews of Spanish or North African descent will cook *Hamin* using chicken, chickpeas, eggs, rice and potatoes. Whatever the ingredients, the idea behind this dish is the same – to demonstrate that one can and should enjoy a hot meal without contravening the laws prohibiting cooking on *Shabbat*.

Again, to accompany the nourishment of the body, *zemirot* are sung to nourish the soul. The table conversation may focus on the issues raised in the rabbi's address, or local and world news, because the atmosphere of meditation created on *Shabbat* allows scope for discussion of the deeper issues of life. One should, of course, be careful to abstain from the kind of derogatory conversations about individuals which transgress the restrictions of *Lashon Hara* – evil speech – on *Shabbat* as every day. Instead it is praiseworthy to discuss the weekly *Torah* portion and perhaps to catch up with what the children have been learning at school or Hebrew lessons, so that they know that their education is important to us. *Shabbat* also frees up time to go for walks, to sleep and to catch up with our reading.

Traditional menu ideas:
Gefilte Fishballs – page 85
Cholent – page 135
Potato Kugel – page 102
Pineapple Pudding – page 143

Alternative menu ideas:

Chilled Lemon Grass & Coriander Vichyssoise – page 76

Turkey Schnitzels – page 127

Spinach & Popped Rice Salad – page 91

Chocolate Mousse Cake – page 144

Seudah Shlishit

The third *Shabbat* meal, *Seudah Shlishit*, takes place in the late afternoon, before sunset. In the Jewish literature of *Kabbalah*, *Seudah Shlishit* is described as the time when G-d is especially close to the Jewish people and, with *Shabbat* nearly over, there is a sadness at the loss of this paradise island in time. Wistful songs that speak of the deep relationship between us and our Creator are sung, including Psalm 23, which expresses the young King David's feelings of trust in G-d while on the run from King Saul.

Ideally, *Seudah Shlishit* should be a proper meal including bread, but if *Shabbat* is short and people are not so hungry, it may be a simple meal of rolls and dips, or a light snack of cake. In the summer months, when *Shabbat* lasts late into the night, a more extensive evening meal may be appropriate.

Summer menu ideas:

No-Crust Asparagus Tart – page 107

Stuffed Tomatoes – page 100

Tiramisu – page 142

The End of Shabbat

When the stars come out on Saturday night, *Shabbat* is over. To signify this, the *Havdalah* prayer is said over a cup of wine or grape juice, along with blessings over fragrant spices and the light of a plaited candle. Before we extinguish the candle's flame, we inhale the uplifting fragrance in the hope of carrying some of the inspiration of *Shabbat* into the week ahead. During *Shabbat* we were blessed with an extra dimension of spirituality and when this leaves us we need the restorative scent of the *Havdalah* spices to lift our spirits.

There is a custom to eat another meal later on Saturday night, which is called *Melaveh Malkah*, 'escorting the Queen'. *Shabbat* is compared to the presence of a queen, who visits Jewish homes for the duration of *Shabbat*. Just as on Friday night her arrival is celebrated with the song 'Lecha Dodi', so after Havdalah we escort her as she leaves. One can either eat leftover food from Shabbat or cook something special for the Melaveh Malkah, and invite guests for another relaxing and uplifting meal. There are many special spiritual songs associated with this meal which mention the prophet Elijah, the herald of the Jewish Messiah, whose arrival can be anticipated once Shabbat is over. The hope is that when the Mashiach (Messiah) arrives, the beauty and spiritual quality of life on Shabbat will become an everyday experience.

Menu suggestions:
Almond & Broccoli Stir-Fry – page 99
Roasted Red Peppers – page 96
Florentines – page 161

10

The Jewish Year

The cycle of the Jewish year is the rhythm of Jewish life, with celebrations of freedom in the spring, commitment in the autumn and light in the dark winter months. The historical meanings of the festivals are matched by their modern significance, so that each time they come around we are able to draw fresh inspiration from their relevance to our lives, as individuals and as a community.

Whether celebrated with our immediate or extended family, with local friends or with guests from far away, Jewish festivals are an opportunity to share what we have with others. The traditions that we bring to the table may differ, but this sharing too is part of the richness of Jewish life.

Most people who visit communities around the world are struck by the similarities rather than the differences in styles of celebration. Most of the Jewish world follows the same codified system of laws for the Sabbath and festivals. Some of the laws are positive instructions and others are prohibitions, and it is the combination of the two which makes both *Shabbat* and *Yom Tov* (festivals) special.

The Festivals

The festivals, other than *Yom Kippur*, differ from the Sabbath in some of their laws – basically the cooking of *Yom Tov* meals using an exisiting flame is allowed on *Yom Tov* but not on *Shabbat*, and objects which are needed for the celebration of *Yom Tov* can be carried in public areas. If festivals fall on Saturday, the *Shabbat* rules apply. When festivals last for a week, their first and last days (one day in Israel and two days in the Diaspora) are celebrated as *Yom Tov,* and the intermediate days are called *Chol Hamoed*, when some work is allowed.

Jewish festivals follow the Jewish calendar, based largely on the lunar system, which explains why the festivals can fall in different solar or secular months in different years. The celebration of most festivals, like *Shabbat*, starts shortly before sunset on the evening before, with the lighting of candles in the home before sunset, followed by *Kiddush* over

wine, blessings over bread, and a festive meal. The special day lasts until nightfall at the end of the next day, when three stars are visible in the sky, and its end is marked by the *Havdalah* ceremony.

The festivals decreed by G-d in the Bible are *Shabbat*, *Rosh Chodesh*, *Rosh Hashanah*, *Yom Kippur* and the pilgrimage festivals of *Pesach*, *Shavuot*, *Succot* and *Shemini Atzeret*. To these our Rabbis have added post-Biblical festivals – *Purim* and *Chanukah*, *Tu Bishvat*, *Lag Ba'Omer* – and special days to commemorate more events in Jewish history – the Three Weeks of Mourning leading up to *Tishah B'Av, Yom Ha'atzma'ut, Yom HaShoah*, *Yom HaZikaron* and *Yom Yerushalayim*. Their reasons, customs and food traditions are set out briefly in this chapter.

It is customary to reserve even better foods for *Yom Tov* than we eat on *Shabbat*, and to expend extra effort and money to make the festivals feel really special.

Eruv Tavshilin
The Mixing of Foods

One of the main differences between *Shabbat* and the Biblical festivals is that cooking is permitted on *Yom Tov* but only for that day. When one of these festivals falls on a day or days immediately preceding *Shabbat*, this creates difficulties in preparing food for *Shabbat*. It is therefore necessary to make an *Eruv Tavshilin* before *Yom Tov*, by setting aside food which has been prepared for *Shabbat* and declaring our intention to continue with further *Shabbat* preparations during *Yom Tov*.

The food to be set aside should be one cooked or roasted dish (such as a boiled egg or piece of fish), and one baked dish (usually bread or *matzah)*. A special blessing and declaration are recited before *Yom Tov*, and the *Eruv Tavshilin* foods set aside and eaten at one of the *Shabbat* meals. Further food for *Shabbat* can then be prepared on the Friday, using a pre-existing flame or heat source.

Rosh Chodesh
The Beginning of the Month

Since the Jewish calendar is largely based on the cycles of the moon, the start of each month, *Rosh Chodesh*, is celebrated in some respects as a minor festival. It can last for one day or two, embracing the last day of one month and the first day of the next. *Hallel* psalms are recited in the morning service and a special *Torah* portion is read. Some families have a special meal on *Rosh Chodesh* and, if eating bread, the 'Ya'ale veyavo' paragraph is added into the Grace after Meals and *Amidah* prayer.

Rosh Chodesh is traditionally a special holiday for women, in recognition of their refusal to participate in the making of the Golden Calf at Mount Sinai. The concept of monthly renewal is also particularly relevant to women, and *Rosh Chodesh* has been adopted by many women's groups as an opportunity for spiritual renewal, through meetings for study, discussion, song and celebration. It is also customary for women to abstain from non-urgent housework and to make the *Rosh Chodesh* day, or days, special.

Rosh Hashanah
New Year
Date: 1st and 2nd Tishri

During the month of *Ellul* the shofar horn is blown in synagogue each weekday morning except the last day to remind us that *Rosh Hashanah* is coming and awaken us to reflection and repentance.

Rosh Hashanah is a time for personal spiritual stock-taking. To prepare ourselves for a fresh start and a New Year, we are encouraged to review our behaviour and reflect on our real priorities. This is the time to pray for blessing and success for ourselves and our families and, although each of us faces Divine scrutiny and judgment at this time, there is an underlying mood of optimism and family celebration as we look forward to a better new year.

Food customs:

The wish for a sweet New Year is marked by eating *challah* dipped in honey on *Rosh Hashanah* and, according to some traditions, until *Hoshana Rabba*. Similarly, the traditional food for New Year is Honey Cake. There is also a custom on the first evening of the festival to eat certain foods, called *Simanim*, which are symbolic of our wishes for the year ahead, either because of their names or their inherent qualities, and to pronounce our wishes over them.

Some traditional *Simanim* are:

Apple dipped in Honey – for a good and sweet year.

Pomegranate – for our merits to be as many as the seeds of a pomegranate.

Carrots (Yiddish, *mehren*) – derived from 'many' – we ask that our merits be many.

Head of Lamb or Fish – *rosh* meaning 'head' in Hebrew – that we be likened to the head, not the tail.

Fish – that we may multiply like the fish of the sea.

Dates (Hebrew, *tamar*) – similar to the word *tamah* – 'eliminated' – that G-d eliminate our enemies, especially the enemy within us, the *yetzer hara* (evil inclination).

Spinach (Aramaic, *silka*) and Beetroot (Hebrew, *selek*) – 'to remove', alluding to the hope that our enemies be uprooted and removed.

If you want to add some modern puns, additional *Simanim* might perhaps include:

Sardines (Hebrew, *sar din)* – 'remove the harsh judgment'.

Bananas (French, *bonne année*) – 'good year'.

Lettuce, Raisins & Celery – 'let us have a raise in salary!'.

The blessing '*Shehechiyanu*' is said during *Kiddush* on both evenings of *Rosh Hashanah*, and many people have the custom to eat a new fruit or wear a new garment on the second evening to reinforce the need to say the *Shehechiyanu* blessing again.

Menu ideas:
Carrot Soup – page 79
Honey Citrus Chicken – page 121
Easy Honey Cake – page 162

Yom Kippur
Day of Atonement
Date: 10th Tishri

On *Yom Kippur*, the holiest day of the Jewish year, we try to express true repentance and pray for justice and mercy, in the belief that G-d will forgive our sins if we are sincere. The Rabbis teach that we receive Divine assistance on this day, so that our prayers have a greater chance of success, and *Yom Kippur* should be seen as a happy rather than a sad occasion.

We do not eat, drink, wash, wear leather shoes or have marital relations during the twenty-five hours of *Yom Kippur*, and all the prohibitions of *Shabbat* also apply. Many people do not wear gold jewellery, as this is linked to the worship of the Golden Calf. It is customary to wear white clothes, and some men wear a *kittel* (white robe) in synagogue as a sign of purity. Unlike other fast days we are not in mourning, our task is to cleanse ourselves spiritually and focus on the prayers, which deepen our connection to G-d.

It is traditional to gather for a full *Yom Tov*-style meal before the fast commences, starting with *Challah* dipped in honey, but without saying *Kiddush*. There is a particular custom to bless one's children on this special night of the year. *Yom Kippur* commences with the lighting of candles, after the meal and just before the *Kol Nidrei* service. Almost the entire day of *Yom Kippur* is spent in synagogue, until the *shofar* is blown triumphantly at nightfall and we return home to break our fast.

Food customs:

Some people have the custom to serve soup with *kreplach* (dumplings filled with meat), symbolising G-d's strictness enveloped by His loving kindness. Practicality suggests that the meal before the fast on *Erev Yom Kippur* be substantial but not too salty or spicy, to make the fast easier. Similarly, it is a good idea to prepare food for the next evening before *Yom Kippur* so that people can break their fast straight away. It is an Anglo-Jewish tradition to break the fast on a cup of tea and a slice of honey cake from *Rosh Hashanah*.

Menu ideas for *Erev Yom Kippur*:
Minestrone Soup – page 81
Cola Brisket – page 129
Date, Walnut & Apple Cake – page 157

Menu ideas for after the Fast:
Carrot Soup – page 79
Smoked Fish Niçoise – page 115
Easy Honey Cake – page 162

Succot
Feast of Tabernacles and Festival of Ingathering
Date: 15th–21st Tishri

The spiritual intensity of *Yom Kippur* is followed by the physical festival of *Succot*, which gives us the opportunity to put our good intentions into practice. We celebrate *Succot* for seven days and it is followed by the separate festival of *Shemini Atzeret* and *Simchat Torah* – two further days which are combined as one day in Israel.

For seven days we are commanded to live, or at least eat our meals, in a *Succah*, a temporary structure with a roof made of *S'chach* (bamboo canes or cut tree branches). This fragile tabernacle reminds us that we are dependent on the protection of G-d, just as we were during the forty years of wandering in the desert. People make particular efforts to eat in the *Succah* especially on the first night of the festival.

The other special *mitzvah* (commandment) on *Succot* is to take and wave the *Arba'ah Minim* (four species): *Lulav* (palm), *Hadass* (myrtle) and *Aravah* (willow) branches and the *Etrog* (citron), every day except on *Shabbat*. Each of these plants represents Jews of different characters and levels of observance, and their being bound together is a symbol of Jewish unity, shared destiny and our mutual responsibility towards one another.

The last day of *Succot*, *Hoshana Rabba*, is the last opportunity for repentance and the end of the process which started fifty days before at the beginning of the month of *Ellul*. There are special prayers and rituals in the synagogue, but this is otherwise a *Chol Hamoed* day.

As the Festival of Ingathering, *Succot* is associated with seasonal fruits, in particular the seven species special to the Land of Israel, which were brought as first-fruit offerings in Temple times. These are: dates, grapes, pomegranates, figs, olives (or olive oil), wheat and barley.

Food customs:

As befits a harvest festival, it might be appropriate to use the fruits and vegetables which are in season at this time of year. If one is eating outdoors, hot soups, stews and puddings are particularly appreciated, Other traditional *Succot* foods include *holishkes* – cabbage-wrapped meat parcels – and *kreplach*.

Shemini Atzeret
Eighth Day of Gathering
Date: 22nd Tishri

We celebrate *Succot* for seven days and then, according to a *Midrash*, G-d says: 'Stay (*Atzeret*) *and celebrate for an extra day with Me.*' *Shemini Atzeret* corresponds to the 'eighth day' following the seven-day festival of *Succot* and it is regarded as a separate festival in its own right. Although the *Lulav* is not taken, some families continue to eat their meals in the *Succah*. In synagogue the *Yizkor* prayer for departed relatives is said.

Simchat Torah

Rejoicing with the Torah
Date: 23rd Tishri

Simchat Torah represents the climax of all the *Tishri* festivals, and the completion and recommencement of the annual cycle of weekly readings from the *Sefer Torah*, comprising the Five Books of Moses. *Simchah* denotes joy, as we display our love, excitement and great rejoicing at the completion of yet another year of *Torah* reading, studying and observance.

All the *Sefer Torah* scrolls are taken out on the evening and the morning of *Simchat Torah* and everyone sings and dances around the synagogue to celebrate the fact that *Torah* and all its teachings are part of every Jew's inheritance and life. Two men – called *Chatan Torah* and *Chatan Bereshit* – Bridegrooms of the Law and Bereshit – are chosen for the honour of reading the last and first portions of the *Torah* respectively. Many communities also honour selected women with the title *Eshet Chayil* – woman of worth – on this day.

Children are given flags to wave and sweets and apples to eat in the synagogue, so that they always associate *Torah* with sweetness and enjoyment. Grown-ups celebrate with *kiddush* and a *l'chaim* or two with whisky or other alcoholic drinks, making it a lively festival of celebration and fun before winter sets in.

Menu ideas:
Curried Butternut Squash Soup – page 77
Holishkes – page 133
Chicken with Artichokes – page 125
Plum Pudding – page 149
Apple Cake – page 163

Chanukah

Festival of Lights and Dedication
Date: 25th Kislev – 2nd or 3rd Tevet (first candle 24th Kislev evening)

Chanukah lasts for eight days and is, perhaps, one of the most popular festivals in the Jewish calendar. A post-Biblical festival, it celebrates the victory of the Maccabees over the Syrian-Greek oppressors and the rededication of the Temple in Jerusalem. The one small jar of oil which was found to light the holy *Menorah* lasted miraculously for eight days and we light an increasing number of candles on each of the nights of *Chanukah* to commemorate this.

Food customs:

Pancakes, doughnuts and *latkes* (a.k.a. hash browns) fried in oil are all traditional on *Chanukah*. These are usually eaten near the candles during the first half-hour that the candles are alight, as it is customary to relax and not work during this time.

Menu ideas:
Potato Latkes – page 95
Fabulous Chocolate Fudge Cake – page 168

Tu Bishvat
New Year for Trees
Date: 15th Shevat

The idea of a New Year for Trees relates to the start of the fiscal year for the tithing of fruit, which is a Biblical requirement for fruit grown in Israel. It also marks the beginning of spring and the renewal of growth. Just as on *Rosh Hashanah* G-d grants us a good year, on *Tu Bishvat*, G-d grants the trees a year of fruitfulness.

In Israel, schoolchildren mark the day by planting new trees, a custom initiated by the pioneers in pre-State of Israel in the early 20th century. It is also customary to celebrate this day by eating fifteen tree-grown fruits because it falls on the 15th of the month.

Fun on *Tu Bishvat*

The *Tu Bishvat Seder*, a ritual established by the 16th-century *kabbalists* in Tzfat, is an enjoyable way to mark this minor festival. Rabbi Isaac Luria (known as the *Arizal*), and his followers would gather to feast on fruit, drink wine and read a book of extracts from the *Torah*, *Talmud* and *Zohar,* which refer to G-d's presence in nature, trees and agricultural produce. This *Seder* is modelled on the *Pesach Seder*.

The *Tu Bishvat Seder*

Cup One – This is drunk in pure white wine and represents the cold winter months. It is symbolic of how vulnerable and fragile our lives are. A blessing is made over fruits with hard, inedible skin or shell (the protective cover for the fragile fruit inside), such as melons, almonds and bananas.

> **Cup Two** – Pour a glass of light rosé, or white wine with a few drops of red wine. Spring holds the promise of new growth and the transition from cold to warmth. Fruits with inedible stones or seeds are eaten, like dates, plums, olives, mangos or apricots. Through these seeds, we see the miracle of birth.
>
> **Cup Three** – A glass of mostly red with some white wine is poured. Here we see the fullness of life revealed in the summer months and we eat entirely edible fruits such as figs, raisins, grapes and berries.
>
> **Cup Four** – A full-bodied red wine is drunk, symbolic of the autumn of life and of 'The World to Come', a world that transcends the physical and reaches the true essence of our being. Here we make a blessing over fragrant flowers and spices (cinnamon and cloves). Herbal teas may be served with dessert at this point.

Purim
Feast of Lots
Date: 14th Adar

Purim is one of the most joyous festivals in the Jewish calendar. We commemorate the courage of Queen Esther and her role in saving the Jewish nation, in the Persian kingdom of King Ahashverosh. His Prime Minister Haman planned to kill all the Jews on a day chosen by lottery but the intervention of the Jewish Queen Esther and her relative Mordechai led to the miraculous salvation of the Jews from his decree of genocide. First we fast, on 13th *Adar,* to commemorate the fast undertaken by our ancestors and their prayers for Divine assistance, and then on *Purim* itself, 14th *Adar,* we celebrate with parties, gifts, fancy dress and fun.

The story of *Purim* is read from a *Megillah* (scroll) in synagogue, both in the evening and the morning of *Purim.* We celebrate the solidarity of the Jewish people by sending *Mishloach Manot* food gifts to one another, giving charity to the poor, and enjoying a festive *Purim Seudah* meal with family and friends. Children dress up in costumes and visit friends, and some communities produce *Purim* plays and sketches.

The *Mishloach Manot* should include at least two ready-to-eat foods and often comprise parcels of sweets, *Hamentashen* cakes and alcoholic drinks. *Hamentashen* are three-cornered pastries, filled with poppy seeds, jam, chocolate or cheese, which remind us of Haman's hat. *Hamantashen*, with their hidden fillings, and the wearing of masks and costumes, allude to the hidden aspect of the *Purim* miracle.

Special *challah* containing raisins is often made for the *Purim Seudah, a* meal on the afternoon of *Purim,* which is meant to include a great deal of alcohol. This is because it is a *mitzvah* to drink and feel merry on *Purim*, to celebrate escaping Haman's evil decree.

Menu ideas:
Slow-cooked Lamb Shanks – page 132
Garlic Mash – page 98
Queen Esther's Salad – page 93
Bread & Butter Pudding – page 147

Pesach
Passover
Date: 15th–22nd Nisan

Pesach celebrates the Jewish people's deliverance from slavery in the land of Egypt, as narrated in the book of Exodus. Not only does it mark the birthday of the Jewish nation, but it also stands as an eternal reminder of G-d's special involvement in our people's fate throughout history.

Egypt also symbolises a state of mind and on *Pesach* the exodus from Egypt can be relived in a personal sense as each individual's personal departure from anything that interferes with the true expression of their spiritual self. The *Matzah* (unleavened bread), which must be eaten by everyone on *Seder* night, and is the main alternative to bread throughout the festival, symbolises selflessness and humility. By removing *chametz* (leavened foods) from our home before the festival, we symbolically also remove the inflated egotism and arrogance from ourselves.

Food customs:

The celebration of *Pesach* centres around food – both the removal of what is forbidden in the days before the festival, so that we neither eat nor own any *chametz*, and the preparation of *chametz*-free *Pesach* food, in special utensils kept only for this week of the year. In addition, *Ashkenazim* (Jews originating from northern Europe) are prohibited to eat anything containing *kitniot* (pulses) – foods such as rice, peas, beans, chickpeas and soya products. *Sephardim*, however, permit their consumption for historical reasons. Leftover *chametz* may be donated to the poor or symbolically sold through a rabbi to a non-Jewish person, and placed in a separate sealed place in the home. The house is searched for *chametz* on the night before *Seder* night and any last morsels are burnt next morning.

The *Pesach Seder*

On the first two nights of *Pesach* in the Diaspora, the miraculous story of the Exodus is told at the *Seder* from the *Haggadah* book. It is brought to life with 'show and tell' symbolic foods, which encourage the children to ask questions of their parents and grandparents. Thus the Jewish story is passed down the generations, as it has been for millennia, but not just as a historical tale but as a continuing saga, in which each person is inspired to see themselves as if they have personally 'gone out of Egypt', and to leave the *Seder* table feeling liberated.

The *Haggadah* story is told over four cups of wine with the following foods on the special *Seder* plate.

Matzah – The unleavened bread eaten by the slaves and baked on the backs of the departing Jews when they did not have time to let their dough rise into bread. Three *Matzot* are required for the *Seder* and these are traditionally super-supervised *Shemurah Matzot*.

Zeroah – The shank bone represents the *Paschal* lamb eaten on the eve of the exodus.

Betzah – The roasted egg represents the festival offering in the Temple.

Maror – The bitter herbs remind us of the bitterness of the slavery. Usually a combination of *Chazeret* (romaine lettuce) and horseradish is used.

Salt Water – A dish of cold water with salt added, symbolising tears.

Charoset – The mixture of apples, nuts and wine resembles the mortar made by the Jews for Pharaoh. (See recipe on page 86.)

Karpas – A vegetable to be dipped in salt water. Celery, parsley, potato and onions are used in different traditions. By symbolising both an hors d'oeuvre usually eaten by noblemen and the tears wept by the Jewish slaves, this combination represents the transition from slavery to freedom and inspires the *Ma Nishtanah* questions.

The meal within the *Seder* ritual is a festive meal and can comprise almost anything which is permissible on *Pesach*, except that roasted meat should not be eaten at the *Seder*, because of the *Korban Pesach* (paschal lamb) which was roasted, and which we are unable to eat in the absence of the Temple.

Seder menu ideas:
Chicken Soup with Knaidlach – page 80
Chicken Passata – page 119
Roasted Vegetables – page 97
Parev Ice Cream – page 152

Chol Hamoed Pesach is traditionally a time for outings and *matzah* picnics. The last two days of *Yom Tov* commemorate the crossing of the Red Sea, which finally freed the Jewish people from the clutches of the Egyptians. *Yizkor*, the prayer for departed relatives, is said in the synagogue on the last day of *Pesach*.

Other *Pesach* menu ideas:
Courgette & Pepper Bake – page 104
Cold Fish with Lemon Sauce – page 116
Salt Beef – page 131
Sponge Cake – page 167

Yom Ha'atzma'ut
Israel's Independence Day
Date: 5th Iyar

Yom Ha'atzma'ut is Israel's Independence Day, which celebrates the creation of the State of Israel and its miraculous victory in the 1948 War of Independence. On the eve of *Yom Ha'atzma'ut*, *Yom Ha'Zikaron* Remembrance Day is observed across Israel as a day set aside to the memory of Israel's fallen soldiers. At the conclusion of *Yom Ha'Zikaron*, a formal remembrance service marks the transition between the sombre and the festive moods, followed by celebrations, concerts, Israeli folk dancing and, in Israel, public firework displays. *Yom Ha'atzma'ut* is a national holiday in Israel, celebrated with food, family and friends.

Menu ideas:
Melanzana Ripieno – page 138
Green Salad with Orange Mustard Dressing – page 92

Lag Ba'Omer
Date: 18th Iyar

Beginning on the second night of *Pesach*, we count forty-nine days until *Shavuot*, the festival of the giving of the *Torah*. This period is called the *Omer*, because an *omer* measure of barley was brought to the Temple on each day. During this period around 130 CE a harsh plague annihilated the 24,000 students of Rabbi Akiva. In the Medieval period, the *Ashkenazi* Jewish Community was decimated during the Crusades at this time of the year. Thus, certain days of the *Omer* have become days of mourning, when no major celebrations or weddings are held, nor the sound of music heard.

Lag Ba'Omer is the 33rd day of the *Omer*, marked as a festive day for a number of reasons. The disciples of Rabbi Akiva ceased dying on this day, so the customs of mourning are suspended. It also marks the *Yahrzeit* (anniversary of death) of Rabbi Shimon bar Yochai, on which we rejoice and celebrate this great scholar's life and accomplishments. The *Talmud* relates that Rabbi Shimon bar Yochai and his son had to flee Roman persecution and hide in a cave for thirteen years. During this time, they devoted themselves entirely to *Torah* study, and their nourishment was provided by G-d. According to tradition, a carob tree and a spring of water miraculously sprouted at the entrance to their cave.

Some people eat carobs on *Lag Ba'Omer* to commemorate this miracle. In Israel this is a special date to visit the tomb of Rabbi Shimon bar Yochai in Meron, near Tzfat, and to celebrate the *Opshiren* – first haircut – of 3-year-old boys (page 178). In Israel, in particular, *Lag Ba'Omer* is an occasion for barbecues, picnics and outings.

Menu ideas:
Indian Aubergine – page 89
Sea Bass Cooked in Foil – page 118
Crème Brûlée – page 141

Yom Yerushalayim
Jerusalem Day
Date: 28th Iyar

Yom Yerushalayim marks the date of the reunification of Jerusalem in 1967, when regaining sovereignty over the Jewish Quarter and the Western Wall from Jordanian hands had an invigorating effect on the whole of the Jewish world. In Israel, it is a popular day for excursions exploring the visible history of Jerusalem through its many archaeological layers, or for discussions and seminars examining the centrality of Jerusalem in Jewish thought and experience.

Some people eat a special noodle *kugel* called, aptly, *Yerushalmi kugel*, to celebrate this event.

Shavuot
Feast of Weeks
Date: 6th and 7th Sivan

Seven weeks after the second night of *Pesach*, we celebrate *Shavuot*, the Feast of Weeks. This *Yom Tov* commemorates the bringing of the *Bikurim* (first fruits) from all over Israel to the Temple in Jerusalem for the harvest festival, and also the most significant event in the history of the Jewish people – the giving of the *Torah* at Mount Sinai.

Shavuot is the day on which we, as a nation, received the Ten Commandments and accepted the *Torah* in its entirety. Included, of course, were the laws of keeping *kosher* – which animals we can eat, how they must be slaughtered, the separation of meat and milk, and more. When the Jewish people accepted the *Torah* they were bound by these laws, but needed time to learn them in detail and make the appropriate changes to their lifestyles. To avoid unwittingly transgressing the laws of *kashrut* the Jews simply prepared dairy dishes and avoided meat. For this reason it is customary to eat dairy products on *Shavuot*. There is yet another beautiful message in this custom. Just as a newborn baby is nourished by milk, so the *Torah* gives spiritual nourishment to those who 'drink' from it.

Shavuot is a two-day festival in the Diaspora and on the first evening it is customary to stay up all night learning *Torah* texts, to show our enthusiasm to receive the *Torah*, and the account of what happened on Mount Sinai is read early in the morning (although there is usually a later morning service in the synagogue for those who prefer to sleep at night!).

Menu ideas:
Cream of Artichoke Soup – page 75
Mock Chopped Liver – page 83
Vegetable Lasagne – page 106
Mandarin Cheesecake – page 165

Three Weeks of Mourning
Date: 17th Tammuz – 9th Av

These three weeks are a period of gradually intensified mourning, during which we commemorate the various tragedies which the Jewish nation has suffered throughout our history, and particularly the destruction of both the First and Second Temples in Jerusalem. During these days we do not hold big celebrations such as weddings, and we do not wear new clothes or have our hair cut.

During the Nine Days from *Rosh Chodesh Av* until the Fast of the 9th *Av*, we do not wash ourselves luxuriously, but just enough to keep clean. The wearing of new or newly laundered clothes is avoided, apart from on *Shabbat*, when the laws of mourning never apply. During the Nine Days we further limit our rejoicing by abstaining from meat and wine, again with the exception of *Shabbat* meals, as a reminder that the offerings of meat and wine ceased with the destruction of the Temples.

The days of 17th *Tammuz* and 9th *Av* – known as *Tishah B'Av* – both are fast days, 17th *Tammuz* from dusk to dawn and 9th *Av* for twenty-five hours. On *Tishah B'Av* there are special sombre services, with the Book of Lamentations read in a darkened synagogue in the evening, and special *Kinnot* prayers said in the morning. We pray to G-d for forgiveness, in particular for the sins of communal disunity, in the hope that we can earn the merit to see the Temple rebuilt in our generation and that the ideal world of the Messiah will come about soon.

Food customs:

During the Nine Days we do not eat meat or poultry, or drink wine or grape juice, except for *Shabbat* meals. This presents a challenge to the chef to provide fish or vegetarian meals for a whole week!

Menu ideas:
Oven-baked Salmon stacked with Potato and Courgette Fritters – page 112
Vegetable Lasagne – page 106

11

Jewish Food

'You are what you eat' is a saying well endorsed by Rabbinic teachings. Eating kosher food enhances the spiritual and religious sensitivity of the soul – as G-d says in Leviticus Chapter 11: 'Keep the laws of *Kashrut* and you will be a holy people to Me.' Conversely, eating non-kosher food stops-up the pores of the soul (according to the *Talmud*). We are, it seems, spiritually allergic to forbidden foods, and their consumption impairs our performance as Jews.

The main principles of *Kashrut* are laid down in the Five Books of Moses and are classified as 'statutes' – no reason is given for keeping them, other than being commanded to do so. Nevertheless, our Sages have always stressed their essential role in preserving Jewish life.

When Jews lived in closed communities and made their own food from basic ingredients, there was no need for products to carry a *hechsher* symbol to prove their *Kashrut*. You knew the butcher and the baker, and trusted the grocer. The butcher, however, was under the direct authority of the local rabbi. Today food manufacture is a great deal more complicated, and the science of kosher food has kept pace with developments. Mainstream food manufacturers now invite rabbinical authorities into their factories so that they can put kosher symbols onto the packaging of their products.

Ethnic influences and cosmopolitan attitudes to food, as well as tolerance of food allergies and special diets, have made it easier for Jews to keep kosher at home and away. Using the Internet it is often possible to find kosher food when you travel the world. Kosher meals can be requested from many airlines.

Kosher Ingredients

Twenty years ago kosher food meant a handful of traditional restaurants and caterers, thick syrupy *kiddush* wine, meat that needed koshering at home, a few Israeli products imported at great expense, and a lot of hard work in the kitchen. Now the kosher consumer's choice encompasses sushi, pizza, *shwarma*, Chinese, Indian and other international flavours, organic meat and poultry, dozens of supervised cheeses and hundreds of quality kosher wines.

Certain kosher products can only be obtained from reliable kosher suppliers, but these can be found in most cities with a sizeable Jewish population. Look for a certificate of kosher supervision on the wall of the butcher, and it may also be worth checking that the meat has been *kashered* (made kosher by salting), as this may not be the norm in every country.

Kosher Meat

The basic rules about which animals, birds and fish are kosher are set out in Leviticus Chapter 11. Pig meat is specifically prohibited and the rule for red meat is that the animal must have cloven hooves and chew the cud – such as goats, sheep, cattle and deer. Kosher venison is not generally available in the UK only because, according to agricultural regulations, deer must be shot in the open field, not brought into an abattoir.

The *Torah* lists only those birds which Jews are forbidden to eat, such as ostriches, owls and vultures. We cannot be sure of the true identity of the species listed but, by tradition passed down through the generations, we know we *can* eat poultry, such as duck, chicken, goose and turkey. Pigeon, pheasant and partridge are also kosher, while a Germanic tradition also allows sparrow, but you would have to catch them without shooting or hurting them to prepare them for *shechitah*.

Kosher meat and poultry must be prepared by the traditional method of *shechitah* – a swift cut across the throat with a razor-sharp knife – which we believe is the most painless means of slaughtering an animal. After *shechitah*, the animal must undergo a thorough inspection (*bedikah*) to check if there are any blemishes or disease symptoms which would make it unkosher. This is one of the ways in which kosher butchers can guarantee the quality and safety of the meat they sell.

The lungs of cattle and intestines of chickens are always checked, and this is where the term '*glatt kosher*' comes in. If a cow's lungs are free of adhesions, they are termed '*glatt*', meaning smooth. If there are adhesions which leave no holes when removed, the animal may still be kosher but not *glatt*. Before the meat reaches the shop counter it must be porged. This process, called *nikur,* involves the removal of a number of veins and forbidden fats. Because porging the hindquarters of an animal is so tricky, it is not carried out in most diaspora communities. The hindquarters, incidentally, contain the sciatic nerve, which the Bible mentions as being prohibited to the Children of Israel because this was where Jacob was wounded in his wrestling match with the angel.

To be fit for kosher use, meat must then be drained of any remaining blood, the consumption of which is strictly forbidden by the *Torah*. That is why it must be soaked in water and salted before food preparation. Nowadays in the UK most meat is koshered by the butcher before sale, sparing the consumer the need.

Liver sold by kosher butchers may need to be koshered at home. Since it is full of blood, it has to be roasted over a naked flame. All the utensils required to do this will be rendered non-kosher and should be kept for this purpose and treated as *treif* when washing-up, etc. First, the liver is scored with a special knife, rinsed with cold water and sprinkled with a little salt. Then it is placed on a wire grid, so that the blood can drip freely into a pan or other container. It must be roasted over a naked flame, under an electric or gas grill, or in an oven, until the outer surface has turned brown and is dry. It should be washed and it is then ready for use.

Fish

To comply with kosher requirements, a fish must have fins and easily detachable scales, as mentioned in the verses of Leviticus Chapter 11. All shellfish, eels, shark, monkfish, huss and catfish fail the kosher test. Fresh or frozen fish should always be bought with some skin attached, so that you can check for scales. It is recommended that you buy only from a kosher fishmonger, but if you do not have access to one, you should wash all fish carefully when you get home. If possible, ask your fishmonger to keep a separate knife for cutting the kosher varieties to avoid getting shrimp on your salmon steak.

The types of fish that are kosher vary from country to country, depending on the locally available species names. You might try to ask to inspect the fish for fins and scales before you decide whether or not you can eat it, or ask a member of the local Jewish community.

Checking Eggs & Vegetables

Because of the strictures against blood, it is customary to check eggs that have been opened before cooking, so as to reject any with blood spots. There is no requirement to check them before hard-boiling. Eggs should be opened individually into a glass so that the yolk can be inspected for any red spots, which renders the egg *treif*. Any brown material floating in the white of the egg should be removed. Free-range eggs are more likely to contain blood spots. White eggs commonly have fewer blood spots than brown ones, because white eggs with blood spots are easier to detect and reject in the factory 'candling' process.

All fruit and vegetables are kosher, but insects and bugs are strictly forbidden. While eating pork involves a single transgression, eating a fly, worm or other creepy-crawly involves several. The *Torah* is very explicit in its ban on insects, so any fruit and vegetables liable to be infested with them have to be thoroughly scrutinised and cleansed. Lettuce is problematic and other tricky customers include parsley, asparagus, spring greens, cauliflower, broccoli and watercress. Look out for insects which might be lurking inside dried fruit (dates in particular), as well as in rice and beans.

Dairy Products

Since it is not possible to distinguish kosher milk (i.e. milk from a kosher animal) from non-kosher milk, rabbinical law requires that milk be supervised from the point of milking until it is bottled, in order to guarantee that it comes from a kosher animal. In countries where the source of milk offered for sale is guaranteed by civil law (such as the UK), some authorities rule that all milk is guaranteed as kosher and need not be supervised. Supervised – so-called 'kosher milk' (*Chalav Yisrael*) – is widely available nowadays in the major centres of Jewish life, in fresh or long-life formats.

When it comes to cheese the rules are tighter. All cheese must be rabbinically certified. This is because the curdling agent – rennet – is often derived from an animal source, usually a calf's stomach. The rabbis in the *Talmud* ruled that all cheese must come from a supervised source, even when the rennet is made artificially. Thus vegetarian cheeses may not be used unless they have a kosher symbol. Fromage frais is also made with rennet and requires rabbinical supervision.

Wine & Grape Juice

Wine and grape juice, and any grape-based liqueur or drink, must come only from a rabbinically-approved source. The Sages put a ban on non-Jewish wine primarily as a safeguard against intermarriage. In fact, non-kosher ingredients also occur in the manufacture of non-Jewish wines, including bull's blood used for colouring some red wines, and isinglass, a fining agent derived from sturgeon. Wine derivatives, like brandy, wine vinegar and balsamic vinegar, must likewise also carry a kosher symbol, and one should take care when buying fruit drinks and canned fruit, which may contain grape juice.

Processed Foods

When people bought all their food from local farmers and shops, you could trust the people you knew not to adulterate it with anything suspicious. Nowadays, many of the food products we buy have hidden, or coded, ingredients which can present problems to the kosher consumer. Many seemingly innocent products, such as yoghurt, may contain gelatine; spices may contain stearic acid salts, and even breakfast cereals may contain glycerine, all of animal origin. Edible fats and oils should be avoided, together with

shortenings, emulsifiers and stabilisers, as they may be derived from animal fats. Rennet and gelatine are derived from cows' stomachs and cochineal is derived from the cochineal beetle – enough to put anyone off!

But even if the ingredients look fine, the product may still be non-kosher because of other unlisted agents used in its manufacture – such as release agents used to grease the production line. Even when a product claims to be 'vegetarian', it may have been prepared using equipment previously used for a meat product. So before any processed food item can be regarded as kosher, it has to be thoroughly investigated by food technology experts, who are able to apply the laws of *Kashrut* to modern production methods.

The *hechsher* stamp on packets of food is there to show that someone has checked the contents of that package and the process by which it was made, to ensure that there is nothing spiritually harmful inside. From cereals to crackers, pickles to peanuts, international ice cream and confectionery brands – thousands of products can now be purchased in supermarkets nationwide in complete confidence that every ingredient has been checked by *Kashrut* experts.

Food Additives

Kosher consumers should be aware that some food additives are derived from non-kosher sources. These may be listed by name on the ingredients panel of the product, or referred to by an E-number. For example, emulsifiers and stabilisers are very often used in food manufacture, to extend the shelf-life of the product, with E471 the most common one to avoid. It should also be noted that whey and lactose are milk derivatives, so that products containing them are dairy. The main non-kosher additives to watch out for are:

- Casein and Caseinates
- Cochineal and Carmine (E120)
- Diacetin and Triacetin
- Edible Bone Phosphate (E542)
- Edible Fat, Edible Oil, Fish Oil
- Emulsifiers and Stabilisers (E432–E436, E470, E471, E472–E477, E481–E483)
- Gelatine
- Glycerol (E422) and Glycerides
- Polysorbates
- Shortening and Rennet
- Stearic Acid (E570) and Magnesium Stearate (E572)
- Wine Vinegar, Wine and Brandy

Despite all the high-tech processes, chemical additives and European food directives which apply nowadays to food manufacture, Jews still try to adhere to the original food standards set down in the Bible, and that's what makes kosher food special.

The London Beth Din's *Really Jewish Food Guide* contains a full listing of kosher products which are widely available. For details, see the London Beth Din website: www.kosher.org.uk.

12

Feng Shui for the Kosher Kitchen

by Sandy Littman

A bit like feng shui, the kosher kitchen reflects arrangements of physical objects, space and liquids according to rules which, when followed properly, will prove pleasing, providential and practical, and which are subservient to a higher spiritual force.

'Basic to *Kashrut'* is the complete separation of milk and meat foodstuffs. By foodstuffs, we mean that milk and cheese are milk, and rice cooked with milk is also regarded as milk, as well as rice cooked in a 'milky' saucepan. Meat and poultry are meat, and anything cooked in a 'meaty' saucepan is also treated as meat. Thus the terms 'meaty' and 'milky' refer not just to the actual meat and dairy products, but also to anything prepared with them or in their designated utensils.

Meanwhile, *'parev'* (neutral) refers to foods such as fruits, vegetables, eggs, fish and grains which are intrinsically neither meat nor milk. The term *'treif'* includes anything which has become contaminated through the mixing of milk and meat, and to anything which is intrinsically not kosher, such as commercial pet food. Cats and dogs need their own bowls, mats, spoons, etc., which may not be washed in your kosher washing-up bowls or sinks.

In a kosher kitchen the main objective is to keep meat and dairy totally separate for the purposes of storage, preparation, cooking, eating, and washing-up. With thought and planning this can be achieved in even the smallest of kitchens, and it need not call for two of every major appliance. The key concepts are clutter control and colour-coding. Clutter control means having a place for things, and keeping the minimum on kitchen worktops. Just like feng shui, it is easier to do things with as much light and space as possible. This also means that you are less likely to reach for and use a milky spoon to stir chicken soup (for example) if it's not to hand.

Colour coding means having different colours and patterns for meat and dairy. Two distinctly separate sets of cooking utensils, pots, pans, crockery and cutlery are necessary;

similarly, two sets of washing-up equipment, including tea towels, are needed. It is a good idea to use very different patterns and styles for crockery and cutlery to help remember which is which. It also helps to store dishes and utensils in different cupboards or, if space is really limited, on different shelves, labelling what's what. Another handy tip is to line the drawers and cupboards with shelf-paper corresponding to the meat and milk colours.

Traditionalists often prefer red for meat, blue for dairy and green for *parev*. The manufacturers of kitchen sponges and cloths seem to concur. But there's no reason not to use purple and yellow if you prefer. A lot depends on what colour washing-up bowls are available. Nail varnish of the appropriate colour can be used to mark wooden spoons, chopping boards and plastic containers, for example, as an instant visual reminder for cook and consumer.

When storing milky and meaty utensils separately, think about how you will be using your kitchen for cooking a meat dinner, for making a cup of tea, for making a cheese sandwich: most kitchens have optimum places for kettles and toasters. Have tea and coffee, sugar and mugs, bread board, bin and knife and the like near to each other to save pacing the kitchen at breakfast time (unless pacing the kitchen at breakfast time helps start your day!). Similarly, keep all meat implements together.

Washing-up, draining and drying need to be separate too: two separate sinks and drainers provide one way of achieving this, but not all kitchens have or can accommodate two sinks. Two washing-up bowls (in different colours) are quite adequate, and offer the practical advantage that only one sinkful of dirty dishes need be visible at a time! (Stow the bowl that's not in use under the sink.) Different drainers, tea towels, dish cloths, kitchen brushes, etc. are needed for meat and milk. If you have a dishwasher, you may use it for either meat or milk but not both. If you move in somewhere that already has a dishwasher, it can under some circumstances be made kosher (i.e. *kashered*). Ask your rabbi.

If you can handle a three-dimensional kitchen, utensils such as knives used only for vegetables, your bread knife and board, salad bowls and the like may be kept *parev* and used at both meat and milk meals, as long as they are not contaminated with meat or milk, and are washed up separately from both meat and milk items. It may also be worth keeping your baking equipment, pans, measuring cups, and trays *parev*, by ensuring that only *parev* ingredients are used. The same applies to mixers and food processors. Alternatively, separate bowls, blades and other attachments can be bought for meat and milk, and clearly marked to avoid any chance of mix-up.

Non-porous glass containers, such as salad bowls or drinking glasses, which are not used for hot food, may be used during meaty or milky meals and washed up accordingly, because they are non-absorbent. However, Pyrex and other heat-proof glass is porous or absorbent and becomes meaty or milky according to the foodstuffs first used in it, just like china.

Meat and milk foods should be prepared on different work surfaces. The easiest system is to use geographically separate areas of the kitchen. If work-top space is insufficient, restrict the surfaces to milk and cover them with plastic, aluminium foil, boards or mats, when meat meals are being prepared.

Cooking separately is more than not using the same pan for meat and milk. It also means that meaty and milky dishes should not be cooked in the oven at the same time, to avoid cross-contamination of steam. When cooking on the hob, stove or cooker, saucepans should be covered and placed sufficiently far apart to prevent splashes from one reaching the other. Particularly when frying, keep meat utensils away from milk and vice versa – droplets of fat travel farther than you'd think. When refrigerating anything, cover carefully and beware of potential spills, drips, overflows or leaks.

And now, after all that, there's separate eating. Meat and milk are not eaten together at the same meal, nor is milky coffee or tea served after a meat meal; there is a waiting time of three hours (some people wait six) after eating meat and before eating dairy foods. This also applies to eating meat after the consumption of certain types of cheese. Meat foods may be eaten after other dairy foods and you should seek a ruling from your Rabbi as to the exact *halachah* regarding this.

Meat and fish should not be cooked together or eaten together at the same time, but can be part of the same meat meal in separate courses. In other words, if you have a smoked salmon starter, you must wash or change the cutlery before the chicken course. Watch out for sauces which contain fish extracts (e.g. Worcester Sauce, Thai Nam Pla Sauce), which may not be used with meat.

You'll need to use different table mats, cloths or coverings for meat and milk meals. If two people are eating together, but one's got the meat leftovers and the other has milk, it is important to use different mats and put some visual barrier as a reminder not to reach over and taste your dining companion's meal.

Special care is taken with *parev* foods that may be used at different meals. For example, when spooning mustard from the jar on to the edge of the plate, be careful to avoid contact between the spoon and the plate. Also, beware normally *parev* foods, like breads, cakes or biscuits, which may have been baked with dairy ingredients.

And if any mix-ups occur anywhere along the food chain, or any aspect of *Kashrut* is unclear or confusing, don't hesitate to ask someone who knows what's what. Even in the best regulated houses things walk to the wrong part of the kitchen and jump into the wrong bowls or pans! But before throwing anything away it is always worth phoning your rabbi – rabbis like being asked and much prefer to say 'yes' wherever possible.

13

The Recipes

Introduction

The recipes on the following pages were selected and tested by a team from the United Synagogue Community Development Department from recipes submitted by members of the Association of United Synagogue Women. Last year the Chairwomen of Ladies` Guilds at United Synagogues all over London asked their members to recommend their favourite recipes. Staff at the United Synagogue, including one or two of the men, also raided their recipe files, and two of Anglo-Jewry's leading cookery writers – Evelyn Rose and Denise Phillips – contributed. A selection was made which gives a cross-section of styles and tastes – old and new, formal and informal, for *Shabbat*, festivals and celebrations, and for simple midweek meals. Some are traditional dishes, tested by generations of Jewish cooks and their families, and others are more exotic and contemporary, adapted to comply with the rules of *kashrut*.

These recipes are presented largely as they were submitted, reflecting the tastes and cooking styles of their contributors. Every attempt has been taken to standardise measurements and to give alternative ingredients where necessary, without altering the original recipes, which in some cases have been handed down from mother to daughter.

We have included a dairy carton symbol to show where a dish includes milky ingredients, a letter 'M' to highlight meaty recipes, a leaf to indicate *Parev* or neutral dishes, and a *matzah* symbol to indicate which recipes are suitable for *Pesach*. However, it may also be possible to adapt other recipes by substituting ingredients. Soups and other dishes which are shown as meaty, for example, may be made *parev* by the substitution of vegetable stock for chicken stock.

We hope that you will enjoy trying out the recipes suggested here, and sharing them with your family and friends.

soups
&
starters

Cream of artichoke soup with hazelnuts

2 × 425g (15oz) tins of artichoke hearts, drained
120g (4oz) butter
75g (3oz) shallots, finely chopped
475ml (17fl oz) hot vegetable stock
750ml (1¼ pints) milk
2 tablespoons cornflour
18 grinds of black pepper
1½ teaspoons salt
75g (3oz) ground hazelnuts
150ml (¼ pint) half milk and half single (light) cream

Serves: 8
Storage: Refrigerate 3 days
Freeze: 2 months

DAIRY

Drain the artichokes, then set 2 aside and slice the rest into a pan with just under half the butter. Cover and cook gently for 10 minutes, making sure they do not brown.

Meanwhile, in a large soup pan cook the shallots in the remaining butter until they are golden. Add the hot stock and 600ml (1 pint) of the milk. Mix the remaining milk with the cornflour and add to the pan. Season, then bring to the boil and simmer for 4 minutes.

Add the artichokes and 50g (2oz) of the hazelnuts, stirring them in well. Remove from the heat, purée in a blender and return the soup to the pan – still off the heat. Leave to stand for 4 hours for flavours to develop fully.

To serve, cut the remaining artichokes into pieces and add them to the soup with the milk and cream mixture. Reheat and sprinkle over the remaining hazelnuts before dividing between soup bowls.

Chilled
lemon grass
& coriander
vichyssoise

50g (2oz) fresh coriander

4 stems thick lemon grass

4 spring onions (scallions), finely chopped

salt and freshly ground black pepper

50g (2oz) butter

2 medium onions, chopped

300g (10oz) new potatoes, scraped and
chopped

150ml (¼ pint) milk

lemon slices to garnish

Serves: 4

Storage: Refrigerate 3 days

Freeze: Not suitable

DAIRY   PESACH

Strip the coriander leaves from their stalks, reserving the stalks. Trim the lemon grass stems, removing and reserving the outer skins, before chopping the stems finely. Do the same with the spring onions, then set them aside to use later as a garnish.

Gather together these trimmings and the coriander stalks, wash them and place them in a saucepan with a little salt and 900ml (1½ pints) of water. Cover and simmer for 30 minutes to make a stock.

Melt the butter in a large saucepan and add the chopped lemon grass, onions and potatoes. Let them sweat, uncovered, for 10 minutes, then pour in the stock through a strainer.

Add the milk, together with 40g (1½oz) of the coriander leaves and the seasoning. Bring to simmering point, then lower the heat and cook very gently for 25 minutes.

After the soup has cooled, blend and strain into a container. Cover and chill thoroughly.

Serve garnished with the remaining coriander leaves, finely chopped, the spring onions and slices of lemon.

Curried
butternut
squash
soup

2 tablespoons vegetable oil

2 teaspoons margarine

1 large onion, chopped

450g (1lb) butternut squash or pumpkin,
   peeled, deseeded and cubed

1 medium potato, peeled and cubed

2 apples, peeled and cubed

½ teaspoon turmeric

½ teaspoon ground cinnamon

½ teaspoon ground ginger

1 teaspoon curry powder

1 litre (1¾ pints) chicken stock

½ teaspoon salt

1 bay leaf

small pinch of sugar

2 tablespoons brandy (optional)

paprika to garnish

Serves: 6–8

$\mathcal{M}$

MEAT

Heat the oil and the margarine in a large saucepan, then add the onion and sauté until golden.

Add the butternut squash, the potato, the apples and the spices, and toss over a low heat for about 2 minutes until well coated.

Pour in the stock, then add the salt, the bay leaf and the sugar. Allow to boil before lowering the heat and simmering gently for 25 minutes.

Cool, remove the bay leaf and purée in a blender. Return the soup to the pan and add the brandy if using. Heat through without boiling.

Garnish with paprika and serve with garlic croutons.

Broccoli
soup

2 tablespoons vegetable oil

15g (½oz) margarine

1 small onion, chopped

3 large leeks, sliced

300g (10oz) broccoli florets, chopped

2 apples, peeled and cubed

1 litre (1¾ pints) chicken stock

2 bay leaves

½ teaspoon salt

¼ teaspoon nutmeg, plus extra to garnish

120ml (4fl oz) water

parsley to garnish

Serves: 6

$\mathcal{M}$

MEAT   PESACH

Heat the oil and the margarine in a large saucepan, then add the onion and leeks and sweat over a low heat.

Add the broccoli and the apple cubes. Toss to mix, then add the stock, the bay leaves, the salt and the nutmeg. Cover and simmer gently for 20 minutes.

Remove the bay leaves and add the water. Stir well, then purée in a blender till smooth. If you intend to serve the soup cold, refrigerate overnight.

Garnish with a few tufts of parsley and a sprinkling of nutmeg.

Carrot
soup

margarine or vegetable oil for frying
450g (1lb) carrots, peeled and sliced
1 large potato, peeled and sliced
1 onion, chopped
900ml (1½ pints) chicken stock
salt and pepper to taste
1 tablespoon parsley, chopped, plus extra
   sprigs to garnish
1 teaspoon sugar

Serves: 4–6
Freeze: 2–3 months

MEAT   PESACH

Melt the margarine or heat the oil in a large saucepan, then add the sliced and chopped vegetables and cook gently for about 5 minutes.

Pour in the chicken stock and bring to the boil. Season and add the chopped parsley and the sugar.

Simmer gently for 30 minutes until the vegetables are soft, then remove from the heat and allow to cool. Blend and reheat when required.

Serve with toasted croutons (if not for Pesach) and sprigs of parsley.

Chicken soup with knaidlach

½ large or 1 small boiling chicken
1.8 litres (3 pints) water
1 teaspoon salt
black pepper
1 teaspoon soy sauce
1 chicken stock cube
1 whole onion, not peeled
1 leek, trimmed and sliced
1 parsnip, 1 swede, 2 carrots and 2 celery sticks, trimmed and sliced
2 parsley sprigs
1 squashed tomato

for the knaidlach
1 large egg
1 tablespoon margarine
2 tablespoons warm chicken soup or water
½ teaspoon salt
pinch of white pepper
50g (2oz) matzah meal
2 tablespoons ground almonds

Serves: 4–6
Storage: Refrigerate 3 days (soup), 2 days (knaidlach)
Freeze: 3 months (soup), 1 month (knaidlach)

M MEAT   PESACH

Place the chicken in a large heavy saucepan and add the water, the seasoning and the stock cube. Cover and bring to the boil. Uncover and remove the scum with a large wet metal spoon. Add all the remaining ingredients and bring back to the boil. Cover and simmer for 3 hours until the chicken feels very tender.

Strain the soup into a container, reserving the carrots, and allow to cool. Refrigerate. The next day, remove the congealed fat.

To make the knaidlach, whisk the egg until fluffy, then stir in all the other ingredients. Mix well – the consistency should be stiff but still allow you to stir. Refrigerate for at least 1 hour, then wet your hands with cold water and roll the mixture into walnut-sized pieces. At this point the knaidlach can be frozen.

To cook, place the knaidlach in a large pan half full of salted, bubbling water. Cover and simmer gently for 40 minutes without looking in. Then remove the lid and lift out the knaidlach with a slotted spoon. Add gently to the simmering soup.

Minestrone soup

2–3 tablespoons vegetable oil

1 small onion, chopped

2 garlic cloves, crushed

2 celery sticks, diced

2.3 litres (4 pints) parev vegetable stock

225g (8oz) lima beans

4 carrots, diced

2 medium potatoes, diced

1 teaspoon basil

1 teaspoon oregano

½ teaspoon salt

¼ teaspoon pepper

450g (1lb) tinned tomatoes, chopped

120g (4oz) pasta

Serves: 6–8

PAREV

Heat the oil in a large saucepan, then add the onion, the garlic and the celery. Let them sweat, then pour in the stock and the beans. Simmer for 1½ hours.

Add the carrots and the potatoes with the herbs, the seasoning and enough water to cover. Simmer, uncovered, for a further hour.

Add the tomatoes and simmer for 20 minutes, then, 10 minutes before serving, stir in the pasta.

Chopped liver

1 large onion, sliced
2 tablespoons chicken fat
225g (8oz) koshered chicken livers
6 large eggs, hard-boiled

Serves: 4–6
Storage: Refrigerate 2 days
Freeze: Not suitable

MEAT   PESACH

Fry the sliced onion in 1 tablespoon of the chicken fat. When golden brown, add the chicken livers and fry for about 5 minutes until cooked through.

Combine the onion, the livers, 4 of the eggs and the remaining chicken fat in a food processor. Use the pulse button so that the liver retains some texture rather than becoming too smooth.

When serving, grate the remaining egg yolk over the centre and egg white over the outside to garnish.

Mock chopped liver

2 tablespoons vegetable oil for frying
3 medium onions, chopped
1 garlic clove, crushed
3 large eggs, hard-boiled
3 × 400g (14oz) tins of green peas, drained
1 teaspoon **parev** chicken soup powder
salt and pepper for seasoning
120g (4oz) chopped walnuts

Serves: 4
Storage: Refrigerate 3 days

PAREV

Heat the oil and fry the chopped onions and the crushed garlic until golden brown.

Mince or blend together the hard-boiled eggs, the fried onions and garlic, the peas and the chicken soup powder. Season to taste, then add the chopped nuts.

Serve on a bed of lettuce with bread.

Salmon
mousse

2 × 175g (6oz) tins of salmon

4–5 spring onions (scallions), finely chopped

1 sachet vegetarian gelatine

120ml (4fl oz) cold water

120ml (4fl oz) tomato ketchup

50ml (2fl oz) wine vinegar

220ml (8fl oz) mayonnaise

Serves: 10

Storage: Refrigerate 3 days

Freeze: Not suitable

PAREV

Drain and flake the salmon, reserving the liquid, then mix in the spring onions.

Sprinkle the gelatine onto the cold water.

Put the salmon liquid, the tomato ketchup and the vinegar into a saucepan and bring to the boil. Add the gelatine and stir until it has dissolved. Pour the liquid into the salmon mixture and blend gently, then stir in the mayonnaise.

Grease a large plastic mould with a little oil, pour in the salmon mousse and chill overnight.

Gefilte
fishballs

1 large onion

3 tablespoons oil

1 tablespoon sugar

1 tablespoon salt

½ teaspoon white pepper

3 large eggs

5–6 tablespoon medium matzah meal

2 tablespoons ground almonds

1.5kg (3lb 2oz) mixed fish, chopped

sunflower oil

Makes: 18–20 balls

PAREV   PESACH

Using a food processor, blend all the ingredients except the fish and
the sunflower oil until smooth, then fold thoroughly into the chopped fish.
Shape the mixture into small balls.

Heat the sunflower oil in a deep pan (deep enough to cover the balls) until it is hot.

Carefully place the balls in the hot oil and fry for 5–6 minutes until they are a rich brown.

Lift out with a slotted spoon and dry on kitchen paper.

Charoset

3 medium apples, peeled, cored and
   coarsely grated
120g (4oz) chopped walnuts or almonds
¼ teaspoon ground ginger
¼ teaspoon cinnamon
1½ tablespoons sugar
3 tablespoons sweet kiddush wine

Serves: 6–8 people at one *Seder*
Storage: Refrigerate 3 days
Freeze: Not suitable

PAREV   PESACH

Combine the grated apples and the nuts.

Mix in the ginger, the cinnamon and the sugar.

Stir in the wine and adjust the flavourings to taste, then cover and refrigerate until the start of the *Seder*.

Serving suggestion: Leftover Charoset is delicious for breakfast served on *Matzah*.

salads
&
vegetables

Cabbage
& almond
salad

for the salad

225g (8oz) flaked almonds
50g (2oz) sunflower seeds
75g (3oz) sesame seeds
1 medium cabbage, shredded
6 spring onions (scallions), sliced

for the dressing

120ml (4fl oz) vegetable oil
120g (4oz) granulated sugar
120ml (4fl oz) water
65ml (2½fl oz) vinegar
1 tablespoon soy sauce
1 teaspoon **parev** soup powder

Serves: 8
Storage: Refrigerate 2–3 days
Freeze: Not suitable

PAREV

Toast the almonds and seeds in the oven at 180°C (350°F/gas mark 4) or under a hot grill until golden and then allow to cool.

Combine all the salad ingredients and toss well to mix.

Blend the dressing ingredients and pour over the salad just before serving.

Indian
aubergine

350g (12oz) tomatoes, skinned and seeded

2.5cm (1in) fresh ginger, peeled and chopped

4 large garlic cloves, peeled

60ml (2fl oz) water

875g (1¾lb) aubergines (eggplants)

350ml (12fl oz) vegetable oil

1 teaspoon fennel seeds

½ teaspoon kalonji or whole cumin seeds

1 tablespoon ground coriander

¼ teaspoon ground turmeric

½ teaspoon cayenne pepper

1 teaspoon salt

coriander leaves to garnish

Serves: 6

Storage: Refrigerate 3 days

Freeze: Not suitable

PAREV

Place the tomatoes in boiling water and leave for 1 minute, after which time the skins should be easy to remove.

Put the ginger and garlic into a food processor, add the water and blend until smooth.

Cut the aubergines into slices 2.5cm (1in) thick and heat 120ml (4fl oz) of the oil in a large, deep frying pan or wok. When hot, add a layer of aubergine slices and fry them on both sides until they are reddish brown. Continue until all the aubergine slices are done, adding fresh oil as necessary. Leave them in a sieve for an hour to drain off the oil.

Put 3 tablespoons of the oil in the frying pan or wok over a moderate heat, then add the fennel and kalonji or whole cumin seeds. Let the seeds darken (this will take only a few seconds) before adding the chopped tomatoes, the ginger and garlic paste, the spices and seasoning.

Cook for 6 minutes, stirring to break up the tomatoes, then increase the heat a little and continue stirring until the mixture thickens.

Add the drained aubergine slices and mix gently. Allow to simmer, covered, for 5–10 minutes until cooked through. Drain off the oil.

Serve garnished with coriander leaves.

Serving suggestion: A contemporary dish for a mixed Mediterranean hors-d'oeuvre, this can be served with other starters such as hummus and tahina. They all go well with grilled pitta triangles brushed with olive oil and garlic or bread sticks.

Spinach & popped rice
salad

for the salad
120ml (4fl oz) oil
120g (4oz) white rice
225g (8oz) spinach
3 celery sticks, sliced
6 spring onions (scallions), chopped
3 hard-boiled eggs, grated
2 avocados, sliced

for the dressing
120ml (4fl oz) vegetable oil
120ml (4fl oz) white spirit vinegar
4 tablespoons mayonnaise
4 tablespoons sugar or to taste
salt and pepper

Serves: 6
Storage: 2 days (preferably without dressing)
Freeze: Not suitable

PAREV

Heat the oil in a small pan and add 1 tablespoon of rice at a time. The rice will pop almost immediately. Drain on kitchen paper as soon as it does.

Assemble the salad ingredients in large bowl, then add the rice.

Blend the dressing ingredients and pour over just before serving.

Green salad
with
orange
mustard
dressing

for the salad

½ large iceberg lettuce, shredded or torn into
   small pieces

150g (5oz) spinach leaves, chopped

1 large avocado, cubed

½ cucumber, sliced

½ red pepper, sliced

for the dressing

120ml (4fl oz) vegetable oil

50ml (2fl oz) orange juice

1 garlic clove, crushed

¼ teaspoon orange rind

½ teaspoon salt

½ teaspoon mustard powder

4 spring onions (scallions), chopped

½ teaspoon sugar

Serves: 6

Storage: 2 days (preferably without dressing)

Freeze: Not suitable

PAREV

Assemble the salad ingredients in a large salad bowl or on a flat platter, then blend the dressing ingredients and pour over just before serving.

Queen
Esther's
salad

BY EVELYN ROSE

for the salad

175g (6oz) brown rice

½ teaspoon salt

50g (2oz) toasted cashew nuts

2 tablespoons toasted sunflower seeds

4 tablespoons toasted sesame seeds

6 spring onions (scallions)

1 red pepper, cored,
   deseeded and diced

1 green pepper, cored,
   deseeded and diced

1 yellow pepper, cored,
   deseeded and diced

50g (2oz) currants

3 tablespoons chopped parsley

1 × 325g (11oz) tin of sweetcorn,
   drained

for the dressing

2 tablespoons sunflower oil

6 tablespoons soy sauce

2 tablespoons lemon juice

1 large garlic clove, crushed

good pinch of sea salt

8 grinds of black pepper

1 tablespoon fresh ginger, peeled and finely
   chopped

1 green (hot) chilli pepper, deseeded and
   finely chopped (optional)

Serves: 6–8

Storage: Refrigerate 2 days

Freeze: Not suitable

PAREV

Combine the dressing ingredients in a screw-top jar and shake well.

Rinse the rice, then cook in boiling salted water for 30 minutes.

Toast the nuts and seeds in the oven at 180°C (350°F/gas mark 4) until golden and then allow to cool.

Transfer the rice to a bowl while still warm and stir in the dressing.

An hour before serving, add all the remaining ingredients. Toss thoroughly and transfer to a serving dish.

Potato
latkes

450g (1lb) potatoes, peeled and grated

1 tablespoon fine matzah meal

1 onion, peeled and grated

1 egg, whisked

salt and pepper

oil for frying

Serves: 6–8

Storage: Refrigerate 3 days

Freeze: Not suitable

PAREV   PESACH

Drain the grated potatoes and add the matzah meal, the onion, the egg and the seasoning.

Heat the oil in a large frying pan, then fry flattened spoonfuls of the mixture steadily for about 3 minutes on each side or until brown and crisp.

Drain well on kitchen paper and serve.

Roasted
red peppers

4 large red peppers with their stalks on

4 medium tomatoes, skinned

8 tinned anchovy fillets, drained

2 garlic cloves

4 tablespoons extra virgin olive oil

grinds of black pepper

basil leaves to garnish

Serves: 4

Storage: Eat same day

Freeze: Not suitable

PAREV   PESACH

Preheat the oven to 180°C (350°F/gas mark 4).

Cut the peppers in half, removing the seeds but leaving the stalks intact. Lay them on a shallow roasting tin 40 × 30cm (16 × 12in).

Place the tomatoes in boiling water and leave for 1 minute, after which time the skins should be easy to remove. Cut the tomatoes into quarters and place a couple of quarters in each pepper half.

Snip the anchovy fillets into little pieces and sprinkle these over the peppers.

Peel the garlic cloves, slice thinly and divide between the peppers, then spoon over the olive oil.

Season with black pepper and place the tin on a high shelf in the oven and roast for between 50 minutes and an hour.

Serving suggestion: Pour the juices over and garnish with basil leaves as a starter, or as a vegetable accompaniment to a vegetarian or fish meal. Omit anchovies if serving with meat.

Roasted
vegetables

1 red pepper, cored and deseeded
1 orange pepper, cored and deseeded
1 yellow pepper, cored and deseeded
1 medium aubergine (eggplant)
1 large red onion
2 fat garlic cloves, finely chopped
salt and freshly ground black pepper
2 tablespoons olive oil
handful of fresh basil leaves

Serves: 4
Storage: Refrigerate 4 days
Freeze: Not suitable

PAREV   PESACH

This dish can be modified to include a variety of different herbs and a vegetables – try mushrooms, fine beans or mangetout, baby corn, carrots and courgettes (zucchini).

Preheat the oven to 230°C (450°F/gas mark 8).

Cut the vegetables into even-sized pieces about 2.5cm (1in) square and place on a large baking tray.

Sprinkle with the chopped garlic and season. Pour over the olive oil and add some of the basil leaves, torn into pieces.

Cook on the second highest shelf for 40 minutes until the edges are slightly blackened.

Serve sprinkled with more basil leaves. A dressing of balsamic vinegar and extra virgin olive oil could be added if desired.

Garlic mash

4 large potatoes
2 garlic cloves, crushed
4 tablespoons extra virgin olive oil
knob of margarine
sea salt and black pepper

Serves: 4
Storage: Refrigerate 2 days

PAREV   PESACH

Cut the potatoes into even-sized pieces and boil in salted water until tender.

In the meantime, fry the garlic very slowly in the oil (alternatively use the microwave, which is good for this – cook on the lowest heat for 2–3 minutes).

Mash and whisk the cooked potatoes, gradually adding the hot garlic oil and margarine. Continue until smooth and creamy. Add sea salt and freshly ground black pepper to taste.

Serving suggestion: For a milky meal, butter and milk could be added if preferred.

Almond & broccoli stir-fry

450g (1lb) broccoli florets, frozen or fresh

4 tablespoons olive oil

2 tablespoons flaked almonds

1 garlic clove, crushed

1 teaspoon fresh ginger, finely shredded

2 tablespoons red wine vinegar

1 tablespoon soy sauce

2 teaspoons sesame oil

1 teaspoon toasted sesame seeds

Serves: 6

Storage: Refrigerate 3 days, but best eaten fresh

Freeze: Not suitable

PAREV

Wash the fresh broccoli thoroughly and drain on kitchen paper.

Heat the olive oil in a wok or a large heavy-based frying pan. Add the almonds and stir quickly over a medium heat for 1 minute or until golden.

Add the garlic, the ginger and the broccoli to the wok and stir-fry over a high heat for 2 minutes. Remove from the heat.

Combine the vinegar, the soy sauce and the sesame oil and pour into the wok. Toss until the broccoli is well coated.

Serve warm or cold, sprinkled with toasted sesame seeds.

Stuffed
tomatoes

4 large tomatoes

1 tablespoon onion, chopped

1 garlic clove, crushed

1 teaspoon butter

150g (5oz) white breadcrumbs

1 teaspoon parsley, chopped

2 tablespoons Cheddar cheese, grated

salt and pepper

Serves: 4

Storage: Refrigerate 2 days

Freeze: Not suitable

DAIRY

Preheat the oven to 200°C (400°F/gas mark 6).

Cut a small round lid from the top of each tomato. Scoop out the seeds and flesh and set aside.

Fry the onion with the garlic in the butter for 5 minutes, then stir in the remaining ingredients and the tomato pulp.

Spoon the mixture into the tomatoes and replace their lids. Bake for 10–15 minutes.

Golden spiced rice

300g (10oz) basmati rice

shake of dried onion flakes

¼ teaspoon turmeric

½ teaspoon ground cumin

¼ teaspoon ground cardamom or the seeds
from two pods

2.5cm (1in) cinnamon stick

1 bay leaf

½ teaspoon salt

10 grinds of black pepper

600ml (1 pint) stock

Serves: 4–6

Storage: Refrigerate 3 days

Freeze: 2 months

PAREV

Soak the rice for 15 minutes, then rinse.

Add the onion flakes, the spices and the seasoning to the hot stock, pour into a casserole with the rice and cover.

Cook in the microwave on high for 5 minutes, then 10 minutes on 80 per cent power.

Potato
kugel

2 eggs, separated

6 medium potatoes, grated

1 onion, finely grated

2 tablespoons vegetable oil

1 teaspoon baking powder

½ teaspoon sugar

1 teaspoon salt

¼ teaspoon pepper

2 tablespoons flour

Serves: 6

Storage: Refrigerate 3 days

Freeze: 3 months

PAREV

Preheat the oven to 180°C (350°F/gas mark 4).

Beat the egg whites until stiff.

Combine all the other ingredients in a large bowl, then fold in the whites.

Pour the mixture into a 20cm (8in) square greased ovenproof dish and bake for 45 minutes.

main
courses

Courgette
& pepper
bake

3 tablespoons vegetable oil

1 large red pepper, cored, deseeded and sliced

1 large green pepper, cored, deseeded and sliced

1 onion, sliced

1 garlic clove, crushed

450g (1lb) courgettes (zucchini), sliced

120g (4oz) mushrooms, chopped

200ml (7fl oz) milk

2 eggs

120g (4oz) Cheddar cheese, grated

salt and freshly ground black pepper

2 large tomatoes, sliced

Serves: 4

Storage: Refrigerate 3 days

Freeze: Not suitable

DAIRY   PESACH

Preheat the oven to 190°C (375°F/gas mark 5).

Heat the vegetable oil in a pan and lightly fry the peppers, the onion and the garlic for 7–10 minutes, until the vegetables begin to soften.

Add the courgettes and the mushrooms to the pan. Stir, then cook for 10–15 minutes, until all the vegetables are tender.

Transfer the prepared ingredients to a 23cm (9in) square greased ovenproof dish and smooth the top.

Whisk together the milk, the eggs, the grated cheese and the seasoning, then pour over the vegetables, spreading evenly. Garnish the top with the tomato slices.

Bake for 35–40 minutes or until set.

Spanish lentil pasties

3 tablespoons vegetable oil, plus a little for shallow-frying
1 onion, finely chopped
1 green pepper, cored, deseeded and finely chopped
1 garlic clove, crushed
1 × 400g (14oz) tin of tomatoes
2 tablespoons tomato purée
salt and freshly ground black pepper
2 teaspoons oregano
200g (7oz) split red lentils
combination of wholemeal flour and matzah meal to coat

Serves: 4
Storage: Refrigerate 3 days
Freeze: Not suitable

PAREV

Heat 3 tablespoons of vegetable oil in a saucepan and add the onion and the green pepper. Cook gently until they begin to soften, then add the garlic.

Chop the tomatoes and add them to the pan with the juice from the tin, the tomato purée, salt and pepper, the oregano and the lentils. Bring to the boil and simmer, stirring frequently, until the lentils can be mashed to make a thick purée (you may need to add a drop of water).

Leave the mixture to cool, then shape into small patties and coat with flour and matzah meal.

Shallow-fry in hot vegetable oil until the patties are golden on both sides. Drain on kitchen paper.

Vegetable
lasagne

2 tablespoons olive oil

2 onions, finely chopped

1 garlic clove, crushed

350g (12oz) mushrooms, sliced

350g (12oz) courgettes (zucchini), sliced

1 tablespoon oregano

450g (1lb) tomatoes, skinned and chopped

1 tablespoon tomato purée

salt and freshly ground black pepper

10–12 strips of lasagne

for the sauce

25g (1oz) butter

1 tablespoon flour

300ml (½ pint) milk or single (thin) cream

50g (2oz) grated cheese

Serves: 4

Storage: Refrigerate 3 days

Freeze: 1 month

DAIRY

Preheat the oven to 180°C (350°F/gas mark 4) and lightly grease a 2.3 litre (4 pint) ovenproof dish.

Heat the oil in a saucepan and fry the onions and the garlic. Add the mushrooms and the courgettes, continuing to fry on a medium heat.

Add the oregano, the tomatoes, the tomato purée and the seasoning, then cover the pan and cook for a further 10 minutes.

To make the sauce, melt the butter, stir in the flour and cook for 2–3 minutes on a medium heat. Take the pan off the heat and pour in the milk or cream, stirring to combine. Return the pan to a gentle heat and simmer for 5 minutes, stirring continuously to ensure that the sauce is smooth.

Place a layer of vegetables on the bottom of the dish, followed by a sheet of lasagne, a layer of sauce, then more lasagne. Repeat, ending with a layer of lasagne, and top with the grated cheese.

Bake for 35–40 minutes and serve hot.

No-crust asparagus tart

1 × 400g (14oz) tin of asparagus

3 medium eggs, beaten

4 tablespoons flour

½ teaspoon salt

3 or 4 grinds of black pepper

1 tablespoon vegetable oil

1 large onion, chopped and lightly fried

225g (8oz) Cheddar cheese, grated

Serves: 8

Storage: Refrigerate 2 days

Freeze: Not suitable

DAIRY

Preheat the oven to 180°C (350°F/gas mark 4) and grease a 23cm (9in) diameter pie dish.

Drain the asparagus and mix together with the eggs, the flour, the seasoning, the oil and the onion. Arrange the mixture in the dish and sprinkle with the grated cheese.

Bake for 30 minutes or until lightly browned.

Note: A similar tart can be made with mushrooms or sweetcorn if you prefer.

Tammy's
pasta
sauce

olive oil for frying

2 onions, sliced

2 garlic cloves, crushed

2 large green peppers, cored, deseeded
and sliced

1 × 400g (14oz) tin of chopped tomatoes

120ml (4fl oz) water (or dissolve a vegetable
stock cube into the small amount of boiling
water)

1 × 325g (11oz) tin of sliced mushrooms,
drained

1 × 175g (6oz) tin of tuna, drained and flaked

1 teaspoon oregano

½ teaspoon salt

½ teaspoon pepper

Serves: 6

Storage: Refrigerate 2–3 days

Freeze: Not suitable

PAREV

Heat the oil in a large frying pan, then add the onions, the garlic and the peppers. Allow to sweat until soft.

Add the chopped tomatoes and the water or stock. Cook for 2 minutes. Mix well, then transfer to a large bowl and blend with a hand-blender until smooth. Return the mixture to the frying pan on a low heat.

Add the mushrooms, the tuna and the oregano to the sauce and season to taste.

Serving suggestions: Mix with penne or corkscrew pasta that you have already cooked and place in an oven-to-table serving dish. For a dairy meal, cover with grated cheese (Parmesan or Cheddar) and put under the grill for 5 minutes. The sauce can also be used in a lasagne.

Pesto
sauce

½ garlic clove, chopped

3 handfuls of fresh basil leaves

1 handful of lightly roasted pine nuts

1 handful of grated Parmesan cheese

extra virgin olive oil

juice of 1 lemon

Serves: 6–8

Storage: Refrigerate 3 days

Freeze: Not suitable

DAIRY

Blend the garlic and the basil leaves in a food processor. Add the pine nuts and continue to blend.

Put the mixture in bowl and add half the Parmesan cheese.

Gently stir this in and add the olive oil, 2 tablespoons at a time, so that the mixture binds into a sauce. It should be semi-wet but firm.

Add the lemon juice, the remaining cheese and more oil to taste.

Serving suggestions: This can be served with pasta, mixed with new potatoes or used as a topping for roast salmon fillets.

Thai
pancakes

2 green chillies, deseeded and chopped

1 small onion, chopped

2 garlic cloves, chopped

2.5cm (1in) fresh root ginger, peeled and grated

rind of 1 lime, finely grated

2 tablespoons fresh coriander, chopped

2 × 325g (11oz) tins of sweetcorn, drained

1 large egg, beaten

3 tablespoons coconut milk

3 tablespoons plain flour

salt and pepper

vegetable oil for frying

Serves: 4

Storage: Refrigerate 2 days

Freeze: Not suitable

PAREV

Blend the chillies, the onion, the garlic, the ginger, the lime rind and the coriander in a food processor.

Add half the sweetcorn, the egg, the coconut milk and the flour, then process to make a batter.

Pour the batter into a bowl, add the rest of the sweetcorn and season.

Heat a little oil in a frying pan and fry large tablespoons of batter for about 3 minutes on each side until golden. Drain on kitchen paper.

Seared
tuna steaks
with
Thai-style
vegetables

4 × 200g (7oz) fresh tuna steaks
120ml (4fl oz) light soy or teriyaki sauce for
    marinade
1 red pepper, cored and deseeded
1 green pepper, cored and deseeded
1 large leek
2 courgettes (zucchini)
sunflower oil for frying
2 tablespoons coconut milk
juice of 1 lime
1 teaspoon fresh coriander
salt and freshly ground black pepper
olive oil

Serves: 4
Storage: Refrigerate 2 days
Freeze: Not suitable

PAREV

Lightly marinate the tuna in the soy or teriyaki sauce for 15 minutes.

Meanwhile, slice the vegetables into narrow strips for stir-frying.

Heat the sunflower oil in a wok or a deep frying pan and add the vegetable strips, stirring continuously for 3 minutes to make sure they do not burn.

Add the coconut milk, the lime juice and the coriander.

Stir-fry for a few more minutes until the vegetables are softened. Taste for seasoning and then set aside, keeping warm.

Lightly coat a griddle pan with olive oil and pan-fry the tuna steaks for 4–5 minutes on each side (thick steaks take a bit longer).

Place the vegetables on a plate and lay the tuna steaks on top.

Oven-baked
salmon
stacked with
potato & courgette
fritters

BY DENISE PHILLIPS

4 × 175g (6oz) fresh salmon fillets, skinned
   and pin-boned
150ml (¼ pint) dry white wine
sea salt and freshly ground black pepper
4 tablespoons sesame oil
4 bunches of pak choi (Chinese cabbage)
4 tablespoons extra virgin olive oil for drizzling

for the fritters
450g (1lb) potatoes, grated
450g (1lb) courgettes (zucchini), grated
4 eggs, beaten
4 tablespoons plain flour
3 garlic cloves, peeled and finely chopped
2 tablespoons fresh coriander, finely
   chopped, plus 15g (½oz) to garnish
2 teaspoons dried coriander
150g (5oz) Cheddar cheese, grated
sea salt and freshly ground black pepper
approximately 8 tablespoons vegetable oil for
   frying

Serves: 4

DAIRY

You can make these fritters in advance and reheat them in the oven for
15 minutes at 180°C (350°F/gas mark 4).

Preheat the oven to 180°C (350°F/gas mark 4).

Start by making the fritters. Remove excess water from the grated potato and the
courgettes by squeezing them dry in a clean tea towel or kitchen paper (this is best done
in batches), then place them in a large mixing bowl.

Add the eggs, the flour, the garlic, the fresh and dried coriander, salt and black pepper
and the cheese.

Heat the vegetable oil in a large frying pan, then place a heaped tablespoon of mixture into
the pan, flatten with a palette knife and cook for 4–5 minutes. Turn over and cook for a

further 4 minutes. Try not to disturb the fritters while they are cooking so that a good crust forms. (Change the oil and clean the pan out if it starts to burn and leaves black crumbs.)

Remove the fritters once cooked and place on kitchen paper before completing the cooking in the oven.

Place the salmon in a deep casserole dish that has a lid (or make a cover with aluminium foil). Season, then pour over the wine and cook for approximately 20 minutes, until the flesh is no longer bright pink and firm to touch.

Line a baking tray with baking parchment paper and place the fritters in the preheated oven for a final 10 minutes to crisp up.

Heat the sesame oil in the frying pan and cook the pak choi for 3 minutes or until softened.

To serve, place some pak choi in the middle on a warmed plate. Stack on top a fritter, then a salmon fillet and then another fritter. Drizzle over olive oil and garnish with coriander leaves.

Roast
salmon
fillets with warm
tomato
& olive
vinaigrette

4 × 175g (6oz) fresh salmon fillets
olive oil
salt and freshly ground black pepper
juice of ½ lemon

for the vinaigrette
1 × 400g (14oz) tin of tomatoes or 4 buffalo
    tomatoes
6 tablespoons extra virgin olive oil
1 tablespoon white wine vinegar
2 tablespoons green olives, chopped
1 garlic clove, crushed

Serves: 4
Storage: Refrigerate 2 days once cooked
Freeze: Not suitable

PAREV   PESACH

Preheat the oven to 220°C (425°F/gas mark 7).

Brush the salmon fillets with a little olive oil and season with salt, pepper and lemon juice.
Place them on a preheated baking tray, loosely cover with foil and bake for 10–15 minutes.

Meanwhile, make the vinaigrette. Cut the tomatoes into quarters, remove the seeds and
dice. Mix with the olive oil, the vinegar, the olives and the garlic. Season to taste.

A minute or so before the fillets are due out of the oven, gently heat the tomato vinaigrette
until just warm.

When they are ready, place the fillets on warmed plates and spoon over the vinaigrette.

Smoked fish niçoise

350g (12oz) new potatoes, thickly sliced
175g (6oz) fine green beans
175g (6oz) cherry tomatoes
1 small red onion, sliced
2 × 150g (5oz) salmon fillets
150g (5oz) smoked haddock fillet
15g (½oz) butter, melted
½ teaspoon dried crushed chillies
sea salt
1 tablespoon good-quality salad dressing
chives to garnish

Serves: 4
Storage: Refrigerate 2 days once cooked
Freeze: Not suitable

DAIRY

Preheat the oven to 200°C (400°F/gas mark 6).

Cook the potatoes in boiling salted water for 8 minutes. Add the beans and cook for a further 2 minutes. Drain well.

Place the potatoes and the beans in a bowl with the tomatoes and the onion slices.

Place the fish on baking sheets and brush with the melted butter. Sprinkle over the chillies, together with a little sea salt, and cook for about 4–5 minutes.

Add a tablespoon of water to the salad dressing to give the consistency of single (thin) cream, then spoon three-quarters of the dressing over the vegetables and toss well, seasoning if necessary.

Flake the fish over the vegetables and cover with the rest of the dressing.

Garnish with chives.

Cold fish
with
lemon
sauce

2 medium-sized carrots, sliced

2 celery sticks, sliced

1 medium onion, sliced

4 × 225g (8oz) cod or haddock steaks or
    900g (2lb) fillet

6 egg yolks

juice of 3 lemons

5 tablespoons sugar

handful of flaked almonds

Serves: 4

Storage: Refrigerate 4–5 days

Freeze: Not suitable

PAREV   PESACH

Boil the vegetables in salted water for 15 minutes.

Add the washed fish and boil for a further 15 minutes.

While the fish is boiling, beat the egg yolks with the lemon juice and sugar, add the almonds and transfer to a pan. Bring to the boil with a little cold water, stirring all the time until the mixture begins to thicken.

Add some of the water the fish cooked in, a ladleful at a time. Continue to stir until the sauce is smooth and creamy, then pour into a fairly deep serving dish and set aside to cool.

Using a slotted spoon, remove the fish from the remaining water, together with the vegetables, and add to the creamy sauce. Gently combine.

Creamy poached
cod
with
spicy mash

2 × 175g (6oz) cod fillets

300ml (½ pint) full-fat milk

20g (¾oz) butter, cut into small pieces, plus
  a little extra

salt and freshly ground black pepper

2 large potatoes, peeled and halved

½ red chilli, deseeded and finely chopped

several parsley sprigs, finely chopped

½ red onion, finely chopped

Serves: 2

Storage: Refrigerate 2 days once cooked

Freeze: Not suitable

DAIRY   PESACH

Preheat the oven to 180°C (300°F/gas mark 4).

Place the cod in an ovenproof dish and cover with the milk and the small pieces of butter. Season well, then cover the dish with foil and bake for 20 minutes. Reserve the sauce.

Put the potatoes in a saucepan of cold salted water and bring to the boil over a medium heat. Simmer for 20–25 minutes until they are soft.

Mash the potatoes until they are creamy, with no lumps. Add the chilli, most of the parsley (keep a little aside for garnish), the red onion and a knob of butter.

Place the mashed potatoes on warmed plates, making a bed in the middle for the fish. Lay the fish on top, pour over some of the creamy sauce and sprinkle with parsley.

Sea bass cooked in foil

4 whole sea bass
2 lemons, sliced
2 onions, sliced
8 tablespoons lemon juice
salt and freshly ground black pepper

Serves: 4
Storage: Refrigerate 2 days once cooked
Freeze: Not suitable

PAREV   PESACH

Preheat the oven to 200°C (400°F/gas mark 6).

Wash the fish and dry thoroughly.

Tear off pieces of foil large enough to wrap each fish individually.

Pour a tablespoon of lemon juice on a piece of foil and scatter over a few slices of lemon and onion. Sprinkle with salt and pepper and lay the fish on top.

Add another tablespoon of lemon juice, more slices of lemon and onion, and seasoning inside and on top of the fish, then bring up the sides of the foil and fold closed, creating a loosely wrapped parcel.

Place the foil parcels on a baking tray and cook for 30–40 minutes, until the fish is no longer translucent in the middle.

Chicken
passata

3 tablespoons olive oil

1 garlic clove, chopped

225g (8oz) shallots, peeled and halved

2.5kg (5½lb) roasting chicken, cut into
  4–6 portions

500g (1lb 2oz) jar of passata or tinned
  chopped tomatoes

2–3 tablespoons fresh thyme, chopped

1 yellow pepper, cored, deseeded and sliced

1 red pepper, cored, deseeded and sliced

12 pitted black olives

Serves: 4–6

Storage: Refrigerate 3 days

Freeze: 2 months

$\mathcal{M}$

MEAT   PESACH

Preheat the oven to 180°C (350°F/gas mark 4).

Heat the oil in a casserole dish, add the garlic and the shallots, and fry until soft and golden.

Add the chicken portions, skin-side down.

Pour over the passata, add most of the thyme, and stir well. Cover and cook in the oven for 35 minutes.

Remove and stir in the pepper slices and olives, then return to the oven and cook, uncovered, for a further 35 minutes.

Before serving, sprinkle over the remaining thyme.

Chinese
spiced
chicken
kebabs

2.5cm (1in) fresh ginger, peeled and grated

2 garlic cloves, peeled and crushed

2 tablespoons dark soy sauce

2 tablespoons dry sherry or rice wine

4 teaspoons caster sugar

1 teaspoon Chinese five-spice powder

450g (1lb) skinned chicken breasts, sliced
    into 12 strips

12 wooden skewers

1 tablespoon vegetable oil

300g (10oz) beansprouts

225g (8oz) fine rice or egg noodles, cooked
    and drained

fresh coriander to garnish

Serves: 4

Storage: Refrigerate 2–3 days

Freeze: 2 months uncooked

M

MEAT

Combine the ginger, the garlic, the soy sauce, the sherry or rice wine, the sugar and the Chinese five-spice powder in a bowl, then add the chicken strips. Cover and chill for 2 hours in the refrigerator.

Soak wooden skewers in water for approximately 10 minutes (this will prevent them burning) and preheat the grill.

Remove the chicken strips from the marinade and thread them onto the skewers, working over a roasting tin so as to collect the juices. Lay the skewers on a rack and grill for 10–15 minutes on a medium heat, turning occasionally and basting with the marinade.

Heat the oil in a large frying pan or wok. Stir-fry the beansprouts for 2–3 minutes. Add the noodles and toss for another 3 minutes.

Serve the chicken skewers with the noodles and vegetables, garnished with coriander.

Honey
citrus
chicken

1 large roasting chicken

2 lemons

1 large orange

2 teaspoons ground ginger or small piece of
  fresh ginger, grated

2 tablespoons honey

salt and freshly ground black pepper

Serves: 4

Storage: Refrigerate 3 days

Freeze: Not suitable

$\mathcal{M}$

MEAT   PESACH

Preheat the oven to 180°C (350°F/gas mark 4).

Place the chicken in a roasting dish. Squeeze a lemon and half an orange, reserving the skins to place in the chicken later, and pour the juice over. Sprinkle with the ginger and place the chicken in the refrigerator to marinate for at least 2 hours.

Remove the chicken and place the lemon and orange skins in the cavity. Pour half of the honey over the skin, season and roast for 40 minutes.

Turn the chicken, pour the remaining honey over the other side, season again and roast for another 45 minutes.

Before serving, garnish with orange and lemon slices.

Moroccan
chicken

6 garlic cloves, crushed

1 teaspoon salt

1 teaspoon ground black pepper

1 teaspoon ground ginger

½ teaspoon ground cumin

½ teaspoon paprika

4 skinless chicken breast fillets

150ml (¼ pint) fresh orange juice

rind of 1 orange rind, pared

150g (5oz) dried apricots

¼ teaspoon saffron threads

150ml (¼ pint) sherry

3 tablespoons balsamic vinegar

2 tablespoons vegetable oil

1 onion, sliced

3 tablespoons plain flour

300ml (½ pint) chicken stock

parsley to garnish

Serves: 4

Storage: Refrigerate 5 days

Freeze: Not suitable

M

MEAT

Preheat the oven to 180°C (350°F/gas mark 4).

Place the crushed garlic in a large bowl with the seasoning and spices. Stir well to combine.

Slash the surface of the chicken breasts with a sharp knife and place in the same bowl. Pour in the orange juice and rind. Stir well to coat. Cover the bowl with cling film and refrigerate for at least 4 hours or preferably overnight.

Place the apricots, the saffron, the sherry and the sherry vinegar in a separate bowl. Cover and leave at room temperature to marinate for at least 4 hours or overnight.

Heat the oil in a frying pan. Remove the chicken from the marinade with a slotted spoon, reserving the marinade, and brown both sides over a high heat.

Drain the chicken of excess oil and place in a casserole.

Add the onion to the frying pan and fry for about 5 minutes or until soft.

Add the flour to the hot pan, stir well and cook for 1 minute. Pour in the marinade, the stock and the apricots, along with their soaking liquid. Stir well and bring to the boil, then pour over the chicken.

Cover the casserole and cook in the oven for 30–40 minutes.

Sweet & sour chicken
mince

450g (1lb) chicken mince

1 egg

2 tablespoons oil

1 garlic clove, crushed

½ medium Spanish onion, roughly chopped

1 tablespoon fine matzah meal

25g (1oz) ground almonds

salt and freshly ground black pepper

1 × 400g (14oz) tin chopped tomatoes

1 tablespoon sugar

juice of 1½ lemons

1½ teaspoons mixed dried herbs

1 bay leaf

Serves: 4–5

Storage: Refrigerate 5 days

Freeze: 1 month

$\mathcal{M}$

MEAT   PESACH

Place the chicken mince in a large bowl.

Blend the egg, the oil, the garlic and half of the onion in a food processor or liquidise. Add to the chicken mince, together with the matzah meal, the ground almonds and the seasoning. Mix thoroughly and leave to rest in the refrigerator for 2 hours (this can be done a day in advance if you wish).

Liquidise the tomatoes and the remaining onion, then pour into a good-quality non-stick saucepan and simmer together with the sugar, the lemon juice, more seasoning and the herbs for 15–20 minutes. Taste the sauce and adjust the seasoning if necessary.

When the tomato sauce is ready, take the chicken mince from the refrigerator, wet your hands in a bowl of water and roll the mixture into walnut-sized balls. Gently drop them into the simmering sauce and poach for approximately 45 minutes.

Chicken
with
artichokes

225g (8oz) plain flour

2 tablespoons dried oregano

2 tablespoons dried basil

1 tablespoon dried parsley

garlic powder to taste

salt and freshly ground black pepper

8 chicken breasts

5 tablespoons olive oil

450g (1lb) mushrooms

1 × 400g (14oz) tin of artichoke hearts,
drained

120ml (4fl oz) white wine

Serves: 6–8

Storage: Refrigerate 5 days

Freeze: Not suitable

$\mathcal{M}$

MEAT

Preheat the oven to 180°C (350°F/gas mark 4).

Mix the flour, the herbs, the garlic powder and the seasoning together and coat the chicken breasts.

Heat the olive oil in a large skillet and sauté the chicken over a medium heat until lightly browned. Remove with a slotted spoon and place in a casserole dish.

Sauté the mushrooms and the artichokes in the same pan with the remaining oil, then add the wine. Pour this sauce over the chicken.

Bake uncovered for approximately 35 minutes.

Roast
chicken

2.25kg (5lb) roasting chicken

2 garlic cloves

2 large parsley sprigs or 1 teaspoon dried parsley

2 bay leaves

1 tablespoon vegetable oil

4 fresh thyme sprigs or 2 teaspoons dried thyme

salt and freshly ground black pepper

1 large carrot, sliced

1 small onion, sliced

225ml (8fl oz) hot chicken stock

Serves: 4–6

Storage: Refrigerate 5 days

Freeze: 2 months

MEAT   PESACH

Preheat the oven to 220°C (425°F/gas mark 7).

Clean the chicken thoroughly, especially the cavity, and dry with kitchen paper.

Peel and slice the garlic cloves in half and place in the cavity, together with the parsley and the bay leaves. Brush the skin with oil, sprinkle with thyme and season well.

Put the carrot and the onion in a roasting tin and place the chicken on top.

Roast for 15 minutes, then add the stock and continue to roast at 180°C (350°F/gas mark 4) for a further 20 minutes per 450g (1lb).

For easier carving, let the roast chicken rest in a low oven for at least 15 minutes.

Turkey
schnitzels

BY EVELYN ROSE

6–8 × 150–175g (5–6oz) turkey escalopes
2 tablespoons lemon juice
1 teaspoon salt
15 grinds of black pepper
6 tablespoons groundnut, sunflower or olive oil
lime or lemon wedges to garnish
parsley sprigs to garnish

for the coating
1 heaped tablespoon plain flour
2 eggs, beaten to blend with 1 tablespoon
    cold water
75g (3oz) each of matzah meal and fine matzah
    meal or 175g (6oz) fine dry breadcrumbs
½ teaspoon salt
15 grinds of black pepper
good pinch of paprika

Serves: 6–8
Storage: Refrigerate 2–3 days
Freeze: 2 months

$\mathcal{M}$
MEAT

Lay the escalopes between 2 pieces of greaseproof paper and pound until half the original thickness.

Combine the lemon juice and the seasoning in a shallow dish. Add the escalopes and turn, so both sides are wet. Allow to stand for 30 minutes.

For the coating, place the flour, the beaten eggs with water and the seasoned matzah meal or breadcrumbs in 3 separate shallow dishes, side by side.

Dip the escalopes first into the flour, then into the egg mixture and finally into the seasoned matzah meal or breadcrumbs. Leave them covered in the refrigerator for 30 minutes to set.

Heat the oil in large, heavy-bottomed frying pan and cook the escalopes steadily for 5 minutes on each side, or until crisp and brown. Season.

Serve garnished with lime or lemon wedges and parsley.

Roast
English
shoulder
of
lamb

1.8–2.25kg (4–5lb) whole shoulder of lamb
1 fat garlic clove, sliced
1 rosemary sprig or 2 teaspoons dried
   rosemary
sea salt and freshly ground black pepper
½ bottle of red wine
1 tablespoon redcurrant jelly
1 tablespoon cornflour mixed with 1
   tablespoon water

Serves: 6–8
Storage: Refrigerate 3–4 days
Freeze: 2–3 months

M

MEAT

Preheat the oven to 220°C (425°F/gas mark 7).

Make small cuts in the lamb, then push the garlic slices and the rosemary in. Season.

Place the lamb in a roasting tin and roast for 15 minutes.

Add the wine and continue to roast at 180°C (350°F/gas mark 4) for a further 20 minutes per 450g (1lb) and then an additional 20 minutes.

Remove the lamb from the gravy, cover and let it rest in a very low oven for 15 minutes.

Add any additional gravy from the dish in which the meat has been resting to the gravy left in the roasting tin and warm on a low heat. Stir in the redcurrant jelly until it has melted and add the cornflour paste so that the gravy thickens. Season to taste.

Cola
brisket

475ml (17fl oz) Coca-Cola or Diet Coke

425ml (15fl oz) chutney

225ml (8fl oz) tomato ketchup

1 × 400g (14oz) tin of tomatoes

120ml (4fl oz) water

1 tablespoon prepared French mustard

1 large onion, chopped

2 tablespoons vegetable oil

2kg (4¼lb) fresh brisket

1 packet of onion soup mix

Serves: 6–8

Storage: Refrigerate 3–4 days

Freeze: 2–3 months

$\mathcal{M}$

MEAT

Preheat the oven to 180°C (350°F/gas mark 4).

Combine the Coca-Cola, chutney, tomato ketchup, tomatoes, water, French mustard and the chopped onion to make a sauce.

Place the oil in a roasting tin and brown the brisket on both sides. Sprinkle the onion soup mix over the meat, then pour in the sauce.

Cover with foil and roast for 2 hours, basting and turning until almost soft.

When the brisket is cool, uncover it, remove it from the sauce and slice. Return the slices to the sauce and heat for 1 hour before serving.

Spiced
lamb
curry

5 teaspoons vegetable oil

3 large onions, sliced

3 garlic cloves, crushed

1 tablespoon curry powder

2 teaspoons turmeric

2 teaspoons ground coriander

1 teaspoon ground cumin

1 cinnamon stick

small piece of fresh ginger, peeled and grated

4 cardamom pods, split

2 bay leaves

3 cloves

1.5kg (3lb 4oz) cubed lamb

3 tomatoes, skinned and chopped

2 teaspoons salt

2 teaspoons sugar

200ml (7fl oz) hot water or stock

Serves: 4–5

Storage: Refrigerate 3–4 days

Freeze: 2 months

$\mathcal{M}$

MEAT

Heat the oil in a large saucepan and brown the sliced onions.

Add the garlic and the spices. Fry them together for a few minutes, taking care not to let them burn.

Add the lamb to the pan and coat it with the curry mixture, then tip in the tomatoes and the other remaining ingredients.

Cover the lamb and simmer slowly, stirring occasionally for 1½ hours until it is tender.

Remove any whole spices from the sauce before serving.

Salt
beef

1.5kg (3¼lb) pickled brisket
1 carrot, sliced
1 onion, peeled but left whole
2 bay leaves
4 peppercorns
75g (3oz) fresh parsley

Serves: 6–8
Storage: Refrigerate 1 week
Freeze: 2–3 months

$\mathcal{M}$

MEAT   PESACH

Wash the meat thoroughly, place in a large saucepan, cover with cold water and bring to the boil.

Skim the top and add the vegetables and seasoning. Cover and gently simmer for approximately 1½ hours.

Allow the meat to cool in the saucepan. Reserve 225ml (8fl oz) of strained liquid for reheating purposes, then drain and slice the meat.

When ready to serve, reheat the sliced brisket in the liquid.

Slow-cooked lamb shanks

plain flour for dusting
sea salt and freshly ground black pepper
6 small lamb shanks
2 tablespoons olive oil
6 small red onions, peeled and finely sliced
handful of chopped rosemary leaves
4 garlic cloves, peeled and chopped
175ml (6fl oz) balsamic vinegar
300ml (½ pint) red wine

Serves: 6

MEAT   PESACH

Preheat the oven to 200°C (400°F/gas mark 6).

Season the flour with salt and pepper, then lightly dust the lamb.

Heat the oil in a heavy-bottomed sauté or frying pan and brown the meat, then remove it and set aside.

Lower the heat, add the onions to the pan and cook for 10–15 minutes.

Add the rosemary and the garlic, and cook for a further 2 minutes.

Raise the heat again and add the balsamic vinegar and the red wine. Cook for a couple of minutes so that the liquid reduces.

Return the lamb to the pan, reduce the heat again and cover with moistened greaseproof paper and the lid.

Cook in the oven for approximately 2½ hours.

Holishkes

1 large cabbage

1 potato

1 onion

1kg (2lb 2oz) minced beef

2 eggs

½ teaspoon salt

3 tablespoons tomato ketchup

2 teaspoons chicken stock

120ml (4fl oz) boiling water

for the sauce

1 onion, chopped

1 carrot, chopped

1 × 400g (14 oz) tin of chopped tomatoes

4 tablespoons golden syrup

4 tablespoons water

2 tablespoons lemon juice

1 teaspoon vinegar

Serves: 8–10 (20–24 parcels)

Storage: Refrigerate 4–5 days

Freeze: 3 months

M

MEAT

Preheat the oven to 160°C (325°F/gas mark 3).

Remove the core of the cabbage and boil the rest whole in salted water for 15 minutes. Separate the leaves and return to the boil for a further 10 minutes.

Finely chop the potato and the onion in a food processor.

Add the meat, the eggs, the salt, the tomato ketchup and the chicken stock diluted with the boiling water.

Wrap the meat mixture in the cabbage leaves by turning in the sides first. Set aside.

To make the sauce, combine the ingredients in a large ovenproof saucepan. Bring to the boil on the stove and gently simmer to reduce.

Place cabbage blintzes in the sauce, cover and cook in the oven for 1½ hours. Remove the lid and brown for 30 minutes.

Cholent

1.75kg (3½lb) chuck steak, cubed

4 tablespoons vegetable oil

2 large onions, chopped

1 tablespoon paprika

225g (8oz) tinned red kidney beans, washed

5 tablespoons pearl barley

450g (1lb) carrots, coarsely chopped

4 garlic cloves, peeled

1kg (2lb 2oz) potatoes, cubed

salt and pepper

Serves: 8

Storage: Refrigerate 2 days

Freeze: 2 months

M

MEAT

Wash and dry the meat, then heat the oil and brown the meat in a large pan. Add the onions and the paprika and cook until soft.

Place in a large ovenproof pot, add all the other ingredients and cover with cold water.

Bring to the boil and simmer gently for 2 hours.

Preheat the oven to 110°C (225°F/gas mark ¼).

Just before *Shabbat*, ensure that all the ingredients are covered by liquid and place the pot in the oven to cook slowly until lunch the next day.

Bolognese
sauce

2 tablespoons light olive oil

1 medium onion, finely chopped

1 large garlic clove, crushed

450g (1lb) minced beef

1 × 500g (1lb 2oz) jar of passata or chopped
  tomatoes

flat-leaf parsley sprig

handful of torn fresh basil leaves

splash of wine (optional)

salt and freshly ground black pepper

1 teaspoon sugar

Serves: 4

Storage: Refrigerate 3 days

Freeze: 2–3 months

M

MEAT

Heat the oil in a pan and fry the onion and the garlic until soft and golden.

Add the minced beef and fry until brown, then add the passata or tomatoes and herbs.
Cook for 1 minute.

If using the wine, add now and cook for a further 2 minutes.

Season and put in the sugar, then simmer for 30 minutes.

Thai-style
burgers

450g (1lb) minced lamb, beef or chicken

1 tablespoon fresh mint, chopped

1 teaspoon lime zest

1 teaspoon fresh lemon grass,
  finely chopped

1 small onion, chopped

1 red chilli, deseeded and chopped

1 garlic clove, chopped

1 tablespoon lime juice

1 tablespoon Thai curry seasoning spice

Serves: 4

Storage: Refrigerate 3 days

Freeze: 2–3 months

M

MEAT

Combine all the ingredients in a large bowl, mix well and shape into patties.

Cook gently on a griddle or grill for 4–5 minutes each side.

Melanzana
ripieno

4 medium-sized aubergines (eggplants)

salt and freshly ground black pepper

150ml (¼ pint) vegetable, olive or corn oil

120g (4oz) mushrooms (optional)

120g (4oz) breadcrumbs

120g (4oz) grated cheese

4 medium eggs

1 tablespoon capers

for the sauce

olive oil

½ large Spanish onion, chopped

1 × 400g (14oz) tin of chopped tomatoes

Serves: 4

Storage: Refrigerate 2 days

Freeze: Not suitable

DAIRY

Preheat the oven to 180°C (350°F/gas mark 4).

Cut the aubergines in half. Scoop out the flesh and chop into cubes. Place the cubes in a bowl of cold, salted water and the empty shells in another bowl of salted water. Leave overnight or for at least 4 hours.

To make the sauce, drizzle some olive oil into a saucepan and heat. Add the chopped onion and fry until transparent, then tip in the tinned tomatoes and a little water and stir until boiling. Season with salt and pepper to taste. Turn down the heat and simmer until the vegetables are soft and the sauce has thickened. Keep to one side until needed. (If sauce becomes too thick, add a little water.)

Oil the bottom of a large, deep baking dish and add the aubergine shells skin-side down, then pour the 150ml (¼ pint) of oil into a large, deep saucepan and heat through.

Squeeze the water from the aubergine flesh, then add to the saucepan and fry until soft. Add the quartered mushrooms if using and drain off any excess oil by pressing the mixture down with a large spoon. Then add the breadcrumbs, stirring all the time, and the grated cheese, reserving some for the top. Stir in the eggs, one at a time, add the capers and season to taste.

Fill each aubergine shell with this mixture, sprinkling grated cheese over the top. Then spoon tomato sauce over each aubergine and into the corners of the dish.

Bake for between 45 minutes and 1 hour. After 30 minutes check to see if the aubergine is becoming soft and baste with sauce, adding a little water if the dish is looking too dry.

desserts

Crème
brûlée

600ml (1 pint) double (heavy) cream

4 medium egg yolks

40g (1½oz) caster sugar

½ teaspoon vanilla essence

for the topping

225g (8oz) granulated sugar

120ml (4fl oz) water

Serves: 6

Storage: Refrigerate 3 days

Freeze: Not suitable

DAIRY

Preheat the oven to 150°C (300°F/gas mark 2).

Pour the cream into a heavy-bottomed saucepan and bring to just below boiling point.

Whisk together the egg yolks, the caster sugar and the vanilla essence. Add the cream to this mixture and stir to combine. Pour into a shallow baking dish and place in a roasting tin half-filled with hot water.

Bake for about 45 minutes until set and chill overnight.

To make the topping, put the granulated sugar and the water into a saucepan and heat slowly without stirring. Let the mixture boil until it is light brown, then quickly put the base of the pan into cold water to stop the cooking process.

Pour over the crème and serve immediately.

Tiramisu

450g (1lb) curd cheese
5 medium eggs, separated
120g (4oz) caster sugar
a pinch of salt
1 large packet sponge fingers
100ml (3½fl oz) strong black coffee
4 tablespoons brandy, rum or other alcohol
   (optional)
unsweetened cocoa powder to cover

Serves: 6–8
Storage: Refrigerate 3 days
Freeze: 3 months

DAIRY

Beat the cheese in a bowl until soft.

In a separate bowl, beat the egg yolks with the sugar until the mixture is pale, yellow and fluffy. Gradually beat in the softened cheese.

In another bowl, beat the egg whites with the salt until they form stiff peaks, then fold into the cheese mixture.

Line either a large or several individual serving dishes with the sponge fingers and sprinkle some of the coffee and the alcohol over until the biscuits are moist but not saturated. Cover with half the cheese mixture. Add another layer of sponge fingers moistened with coffee and alcohol, and cover with the rest of the cheese mixture.

Sprinkle with cocoa powder and leave in the refrigerator for at least 1 hour before serving.

Pineapple
pudding

2 × 400g (14oz) tins of crushed pineapple
120g (4oz) sugar
1 tablespoon each of cornflour and custard
     powder, dissolved in 120ml (4fl oz) water
1 medium egg, separated

Serves: 8
Storage: Refrigerate 3 days
Freeze: Not suitable

PAREV

Put the pineapple in a saucepan and add the sugar and 225ml (8fl oz) water (or make up to this amount with the liquid from the tins). Bring to the boil, stirring occasionally, until all the liquid has gone.

Add the cornflour and custard powder mixture, followed by the egg yolk, and stir for a few minutes so that everything is well combined.

Remove from the heat and transfer to a cold dish so the mixture can cool quickly.

When it is cold, add the whipped egg white and transfer to a medium-sized bowl for serving.

Chocolate
mousse
cake

8 medium eggs, separated

225g (8oz) caster sugar

225g (8oz) dark chocolate, plus extra for decoration

4 tablespoons hot black coffee

4 tablespoons brandy

1 medium parev whip

Serves: 8–10

Storage: Refrigerate 3–5 days

Freeze: 3 months

PAREV

Preheat the oven to 150°C (300°F/gas mark 2).

Start to whisk the egg whites, gradually adding the sugar.

Melt the chocolate in the coffee, then add the brandy and the egg yolks. Mix to combine well.

Continue to whisk the egg whites until they are stiff, then gently fold into the chocolate mixture.

Put three-quarters of the mixture into a 25cm (10in) springform tin and bake for 25 minutes. Allow to cool in the tin for 5–10 minutes.

Whip the parev whip until stiff and fold into the remaining mixture. Spread over the cake. Decorate with grated chocolate and freeze.

Remove from the freezer 1 hour before serving.

Hot
chocolate
cake

225g (8oz) margarine

225g (8oz) granulated sugar

4 medium eggs

175g (6oz) self-raising flour

4 tablespoons cocoa powder

4 tablespoons water

for the sauce

225g (8oz) brown sugar

4 tablespoons cocoa powder

600ml (1 pint) boiling water

Serves: 8

Storage: Refrigerate 7 days

Freeze: Not suitable

PAREV

Preheat the oven to 160°C (325°F/gas mark 3).

In a bowl, cream together the margarine and sugar, beat in the eggs and mix together the remaining cake ingredients, then transfer to a 5cm (2in) deep oven-to-table dish.

Dissolve the brown sugar and the cocoa powder in the boiling water and pour over the raw cake batter.

Bake for 40 minutes. The sauce will appear at the bottom of the cake.

Sticky
toffee
pudding

50g (2oz) softened butter or margarine

175g (6oz) granulated sugar

1 medium egg

1 teaspoon vanilla essence

225g (8oz) self-raising flour

1 teaspoon baking powder

300ml (½ pint) boiling water

175g (6oz) chopped dates, rolled in sugar

1 teaspoon bicarbonate of soda

for the topping

120g (4oz) soft brown sugar

300ml (½ pint) double (heavy) cream

Serves: 8

Storage: Sealed, refrigerate 3–5 days

Freeze: 3 months

DAIRY

Preheat the oven to 180°C (350°F/gas mark 4).

Cream together the butter and the sugar.

Beat in the egg, the vanilla essence, the flour and the baking powder.

Pour the boiling water over the dates, add the bicarbonate of soda and then add to the cake mixture.

Mix well into a batter and turn into a greased 23cm (9in) cake or flan tin. Bake for 30–40 minutes.

For the topping, combine the sugar and the cream, then pour over the warm cake. Return it to the oven until the topping starts to bubble – about 10 minutes.

Bread & butter pudding

50g (2oz) unsalted butter, softened

12 medium slices of white bread with crusts removed

8 egg yolks

175g (6oz) caster sugar, plus a little extra for caramelised topping

300ml (½ pint) double (heavy) cream

300ml (½ pint) milk

a few drops of vanilla essence

25g (1oz) sultanas

25g (1oz) raisins

Serves: 8

Storage: Covered, refrigerate 3–5 days

Freeze: 3 months

DAIRY

Preheat the oven to 180°C (350°F/gas mark 4).

Butter the bread.

Whisk together the egg yolks and the caster sugar.

Bring the cream, the milk and the vanilla essence to the boil, then allow to cool. Pour into the yolk mixture, stirring all the time.

Cut the bread into triangles or halves and arrange in an ovenproof dish in 2 layers, sprinkling the fruit in between.

Pour over the custard sauce and allow the dish to stand for about 20 minutes. (If you are cooking this in advance, it can stand for a few hours now.)

Place the dish in a roasting tray half-filled with hot water and bake for 20–30 minutes until set.

Remove from the tray and sprinkle with caster sugar. Glaze under the grill on a medium heat until golden.

Peaches
cardinal

6 ripe peaches
175g (6oz) caster sugar
1 teaspoon vanilla essence
350g (12oz) raspberries

Serves: 6
Storage: Refrigerate 5 days
Freeze: Not suitable

PESACH   PAREV

Place the peaches in a bowl of boiling water and leave them for 1 minute, after which their skins will peel off easily.

Fill a saucepan with enough water to cover the skinned peaches and add 120g (4oz) of the sugar and the vanilla essence. Bring to the boil, then simmer until the sugar has dissolved. Add the peaches to the syrup mixture and poach gently until soft.

In the meantime, purée the raspberries in a food processor, then put them through a fine sieve to remove the seeds. Add the remaining sugar.

Pour the raspberries over the peaches and chill until ready to serve.

Plum
pudding

250g (9oz) margarine

300g (10oz) caster sugar

1 large tin of plums, drained, halved and
  destoned

4 medium eggs, beaten

175g (6oz) self-raising flour

50g (2oz) ground almonds

1 teaspoon baking powder

Serves: 6–8

Storage: Refrigerate 3–5 days

PAREV

Preheat the oven to 180°C (350°F/gas mark 4) and grease a 20cm (8in) cake tin.

Melt 25g (1oz) of the margarine with 150g (5oz) of the caster sugar for about 6 minutes, until the sugar has dissolved, and pour into the prepared cake tin.

Place the plums skin-side down in the cake tin.

Beat the remaining margarine and sugar until pale and fluffy, then add the eggs, one at a time, and continue to beat until everything is well combined.

Mix together the flour, the ground almonds and the baking powder, then fold into the mixture and spoon over the plums.

Bake for 40–45 minutes until well risen and firm to the touch. Leave to cool in the tin.

When ready, place a serving platter over the tin and turn it gently upside-down.

Orange sorbet

BY DENISE PHILLIPS

10 juicy oranges
225g (8 oz) caster sugar
200ml (7fl oz) water
3 egg whites

Serves: 6
Freeze: 3 months

PESACH   PAREV

Finely pare the zest from the oranges, using a citrus zester, then squeeze the juice.

Place the juice and the zest in a saucepan with the sugar and the water and heat gently to dissolve the sugar. Increase the heat and boil for 1 minute. Remove from the heat.

Strain the syrup into a bowl and chill in the refrigerator for 40 minutes.

In a separate bowl, whisk the egg whites until they are frothy, then whisk them into the orange mixture.

For the best results, use an ice-cream maker. Alternatively, pour the orange mixture into a shallow freezer-proof container and freeze for 1 hour or until the sorbet is almost frozen. Mash well with a fork and refreeze until solid.

Remove the sorbet from the freezer about 10 minutes before serving.

Serving suggestion: If not cooking for Pesach, this sorbet is marvellous accompanied by Chocolate Langues de Chat biscuits, the recipe for which follows. To be really stylish, place 3 scoops of orange sorbet in a glass dish and position 2 biscuits on top.

Chocolate langues de chat

BY DENISE PHILLIPS

100g (3½oz) unsalted butter, or margarine for
a parev option
100g (3½oz) caster sugar
3 egg whites
100g (3½oz) plain flour
75g (3oz) plain chocolate

Makes: 30

Storage: 5 days in airtight container

PAREV

Preheat the oven to 200°C (400°F/gas mark 6).

Cream the butter or margarine and the sugar in a food mixer.

Whisk the egg whites until soft peaks have formed, then carefully fold into the creamed mixture using a metal spoon.

Carefully add the flour.

Line 2 baking trays with baking parchment paper. Put the mixture into a piping bag fitted with a medium-sized plain nozzle. Pipe 5cm (2in) lengths of mixture, leaving a gap between them. As the mixture will be sticky, in order to achieve even-shaped biscuits, break off each one as you are piping by reversing direction at the end and jerking up.

Bake for 5–7 minutes or until the biscuits are a golden colour and brown at the edges. Lift them off the baking sheet and cool on a wire rack.

Melt the chocolate in a microwave or in a small bowl over a pan of boiling water. Dip each cooled biscuit carefully into the melted chocolate so that one-third is evenly coated. Leave to set on baking parchment.

Parev
ice
cream

1 litre (1¾ pints) parev whip
350g (12oz) caster sugar
8 medium eggs
1 teaspoon vanilla essence

Serves: 12–16
Freeze: 3 months

PAREV

Beat the parev whip stiffly, gradually adding the sugar.

Once they are combined, add the eggs, one at a time, while continuing to beat.

Finally, add the vanilla essence and freeze the mixture in a 20cm (8in) loose-bottomed tin.

Serving suggestion: For a variation on vanilla ice cream, try carefully folding in one of the following flavourings before freezing:

- 3 tablespoons cocoa powder

- 1 cup halva and ½ cup pistachio nuts, roughly chopped

- ¼ cup black coffee

- 1 cup raisins and ¼ cup brandy

- 1½ cups crushed chocolate-sandwich biscuits

- 1 cup chopped soft fruit: e.g. strawberries, blueberries, raspberries

cakes
&
breads

Deluxe
cheesecake

450g (1lb) soft cheese

175ml (6fl oz) soured (sour) cream

2 teaspoons vanilla sugar

3 medium eggs, separated

120ml (4fl oz) orange juice

grated rind of 1 lemon

450g (1lb) caster sugar

3 tablespoons plain flour

½ teaspoon baking powder

175g (6oz) rich tea biscuits

25g (1oz) margarine

Serves: 10

Storage: 3 days

Freeze: 3 months

DAIRY

Preheat the oven to 180°C (350°F/gas mark 4).

Combine the cheese, the soured cream, the vanilla sugar, the egg yolks, the orange juice, the lemon rind and half the caster sugar in a bowl by hand. Then add the flour and the baking powder.

Beat the egg whites and the rest of the sugar in a separate bowl, then fold into the cheese mixture.

Crush the biscuits into small pieces and heat them gently on a low heat, adding the margarine. Let it melt for a few minutes until the crumbs are crispy.

Arrange half the crumbs in an even layer at the bottom of an 18cm (7in) pie dish and smooth the cheese mixture over the top. Cover evenly with the remaining crumbs.

Bake for 45 minutes.

Fresh
rhubarb
cake

120g (4oz) softened butter
350g (12oz) brown sugar
2 medium eggs
1 teaspoon vanilla extract
450g (1lb) self-raising flour
1 teaspoon baking powder
1 tablespoon fresh lemon juice
225ml (8fl oz) milk
450g (1lb) fresh pink rhubarb, coarsely
  chopped
120g (4oz) pecans or walnuts, chopped
120g (4oz) granulated sugar
1 teaspoon cinnamon

Serves: 8–10
Storage: Refrigerate 7 days
Freeze: Not suitable

DAIRY

Preheat the oven to 180°C (350°F/gas mark 4).

Cream the butter until light, then add the brown sugar gradually and continue to beat until fluffy. Beat in the eggs and the vanilla.

Sift together the flour and the baking powder.

Combine the lemon juice and the milk, then add to the creamed mixture alternately with the flour. Gently fold in the rhubarb.

Pour the mixture into a greased and floured 23 x 33 x 5cm (9 x 13 x 2in) pan.

Blend together the nuts, the granulated sugar and the cinnamon, then sprinkle them evenly over the batter.

Bake in the oven for 45–50 minutes. Let the cake cool in the tin for at least 30 minutes.

Serving suggestion: Dusted with cinnamon and topped with slightly sweetened whipped cream, this cake is also delicious as a dessert.

Fruit
cake

1 x 400g (14oz) tin of crushed pineapple in juice
450g (1lb) mixed dried fruit
1 teaspoon mixed spice
4 tablespoons oil
2 medium eggs, beaten
225g (8oz) self-raising flour

Serves: 8

Storage: 7 days at room temperature in airtight container

Freeze: 3 months

PAREV

Preheat the oven to 160°C (325°F/gas mark 3).

Pour the contents of the tin of crushed pineapple into a saucepan and add the dried fruit, mixed spice and oil. Bring slowly to the boil and continue to boil for 3 minutes, then leave overnight.

Add the beaten eggs and flour to the fruit mixture.

Grease and line an 18cm (7in) cake tin and bake for 1 hour until a skewer inserted in the centre of the cake comes out clean. Cool on a wire rack.

This recipe is suitable for diabetics. The cake can be frozen in slices and taken out one at a time.

Date, walnut & apple cake

75g (3oz) margarine
175g (6oz) plain flour
75g (3oz) caster sugar
1 teaspoon cinnamon
175g (6oz) dates and walnuts, chopped
120ml (4fl oz) apple sauce
1 teaspoon bicarbonate of soda
2 tablespoons milk

for the topping
1 tablespoon dates and walnuts, chopped
1½–2 teaspoons caster sugar
½ teaspoon cinnamon

Serves: 6–8
Storage: 7 days at room temperature in airtight container
Freeze: 3 months

DAIRY

Preheat the oven to 190°C (375°F/gas mark 5).

In a large bowl, rub the margarine into the flour until the mixture resembles fine breadcrumbs, then add the sugar, the cinnamon and the dates and walnuts.

Make a well in the middle of the mixture and pour in the apple sauce. Dissolve the bicarbonate of soda in the milk and also add to the bowl. Stir everything together, pour into a lined 450g (1lb) loaf tin and smooth the surface.

Combine the topping ingredients and sprinkle over, then bake in the oven for 1 hour. Cool in the tin before cutting into slices.

Irish barm brack

450g (1lb) mixed dried fruit
300ml (½ pint) tea
60–75ml (2–3fl oz) whisky, brandy or wine
450g (1lb) self-raising flour
2 handfuls of wheat or oat bran
1 medium egg

PAREV

Serves: 12

Storage: 14 days foil- or film-wrapped in cool place

Freeze: 6 months

Soak the dried fruit overnight in the tea.

Preheat the oven to 180°C (350°F/gas mark 4).

Put all the ingredients in a bowl and mix thoroughly with a wooden spoon, then turn the mixture into a greased 1kg (2lb 2oz) loaf tin.

Bake for 1 hour until well risen and firm, and a skewer inserted in the centre of the loaf comes out clean and dry. Do not mistake the stickiness of the fruit for uncooked cake mixture.

Eat as it is or toasted with butter.

Joan's
kiddush
biscuits

225g (8oz) hard margarine
450g (1lb) self-raising flour
225g (8oz) caster sugar
1 medium egg
1 teaspoon almond or vanilla essence
almond flakes or glacé cherries for decoration

Serves: 8
Storage: 1 month in airtight container
Freeze: 2 months

PAREV

Preheat the oven to 180°C (350°F/gas mark 4).

Rub the margarine into the flour, then add the sugar.

Fold in the egg and add the flavouring.

Refrigerate the dough for 30 minutes, then roll it out to a thickness of 5mm (¼in) on a floured board. Cut out with shaped cutters and place a flaked almond or a glacé cherry on top of each biscuit.

Bake for 20 minutes and then cool on a wire rack.

Marron log

120g (4oz) margarine, plus a little extra
120g (4oz) icing sugar
375g (13oz) chestnut purée
2 teaspoons strong instant coffee
200g (7oz) rich tea biscuits
150ml (¼ pint) wine
225g (8oz) plain chocolate

Serves: 6–8
Storage: Refrigerate 7 days wrapped in foil
Freeze: Not suitable

PAREV

Cream together the margarine and the sugar, then add the chestnut purée and coffee, mixing until creamy.

Dip each biscuit briefly in the wine and arrange side by side on a well-oiled sheet of greaseproof paper in 3 vertical rows.

Pile the marron mixture on the centre row of biscuits and draw up the outer rows by holding the edges of the greaseproof paper so that the biscuits form a pyramid.

Leave on a flat dish and allow to set for 2 hours in the refrigerator, before removing and peeling the paper sides down.

Melt the chocolate with a small amount of margarine, then coat the sides of the pyramid. Allow to set before serving.

Florentines

450g (1lb) cornflakes
225g (8oz) sultanas
65g (2½oz) condensed milk
200g (7oz) natural (unsalted) peanuts
rice paper, cut into 20 small circles
120g (4oz) plain chocolate

Makes: 20
Storage: Refrigerate 7 days in airtight container
Freeze: 3 months

DAIRY

Preheat the oven to 200°C (400°F/gas mark 6).

Mix the cornflakes, the sultanas, the condensed milk and the peanuts together in a bowl.

Drop a tablespoon of the mixture on to small circles of rice paper on a baking sheet.

Bake in the oven for 15 minutes, then allow to cool on a wire rack.

Melt the chocolate in a bowl over boiling water, then dip the Florentines in and turn them upside-down to set.

Easy
honey
cake

1 teaspoon bicarbonate of soda
225ml (8fl oz) instant black coffee
175g (6oz) caster sugar
175g (6oz) clear honey
1 large egg, beaten
350g (12oz) self-raising flour
¼ teaspoon ground ginger
¼ teaspoon mixed spice
120ml (4fl oz) vegetable or sunflower oil

Serves: 10
Storage: 10 days in airtight container
Freeze: 2 months

PAREV

Preheat the oven to 180°C (350°F/gas mark 4).

Stir the bicarbonate of soda into the coffee.

Blend together the sugar and honey, adding the egg and the coffee.

Add the flour and spices, mixing well, and finally stir in the oil.

Pour the mixture into a tin 30 x 25cm (12 x 10in) lined with greaseproof paper and bake for 40–45 minutes.

Leave the cake to cool before removing it from the tin.

This cake is lovely to serve at *Rosh Hashanah* and to break the fast after *Yom Kippur*.

Apple cake

150g (5oz) margarine
150g (5oz) caster sugar
2 medium eggs
grated rind of ½ lemon
225g (8oz) self-raising flour
1 teaspoon baking powder
¼ teaspoon salt
450g (1lb) cooking apples,
    peeled

for the topping
1 teaspoon cinnamon
juice of ½ lemon
a little apricot jam (optional)
50g (2oz) chopped walnuts
    or almonds
50g (2oz) demerara sugar

Serves: 10
Storage: 3 days in airtight container
Freeze: 1 month

PAREV

Preheat the oven to 180°C (350°F/gas mark 4).

Cream together the margarine and the sugar, then add the eggs and lemon rind, mixing well.

Sift together the flour, baking powder and salt, then fold them in.

Pour two-thirds of the mixture evenly into a greased, lined tin 30 x 20 x 5cm (12 x 8 x 2in).

Cut the cooking apples into slices and lay them overlapping on top of the batter. Sprinkle with the cinnamon and the lemon juice and dot with some apricot jam if using.

Cover with the remaining mixture and place in the oven for 10 minutes.

Remove, quickly smooth the cake mixture over the top and sprinkle with the nuts and the sugar.

Bake for a further 35 minutes until golden brown.

Serving suggestion: As well as being a lovely cake, this can also be served warm with vanilla ice cream as a dessert. For a variation, replace the apples with plums or pears.

Mandarin
cheesecake

50g (2oz) melted butter

120g (4oz) digestive biscuits, crushed

325g (11oz) low-fat soft cheese

1 medium egg

175g (6oz) granulated sugar

1 teaspoon lemon juice

1 teaspoon vanilla essence

for the topping

250ml (8fl oz) double or whipping (heavy)
cream

1 × 200g (7oz) tin of mandarin oranges

Serves: 10

Storage: Refrigerate 3 days

Freeze: 3 months

DAIRY

Preheat the oven to 190°C (375°F/gas mark 5).

Mix together the butter and the biscuits, then flatten them in a 15cm (6in) loose-bottomed tin.

Combine the remainder of the cheesecake ingredients and spread over the base.

Place in the oven for about 10 minutes or until the cheese mixture begins to firm slightly.

Remove from the oven and allow to cool, then push out of the tin on to a serving plate.

Whip the cream and spread on top. Decorate with mandarin oranges.

Poppy seed
cake
with a
mango
sauce

2 medium eggs

225g (8oz) caster sugar

1 teaspoon vanilla extract

175g (6oz) ground poppy seeds

2 teaspoons orange rind, finely grated

120g (4oz) self-raising flour

120ml (4fl oz) milk

120g (4oz) unsalted butter, melted and
   cooled

2 tablespoons sunflower oil

icing sugar

for the sauce

1 large, very ripe mango

40g (1½oz) caster sugar

3 tablespoons lemon juice

Serves: 6–8

Storage: 4 days in airtight container

Freeze: 3 months

DAIRY

Preheat the oven to 180°C (350°F/gas mark 4) and grease a 23cm (9in) ring cake tin.

Beat the eggs, the sugar and the vanilla for 4–5 minutes until light in colour, then fold in the poppy seeds and the orange rind.

Fold in the sifted flour alternately with the milk, followed by the cooled butter and the oil.

Transfer to the prepared tin and bake for 40–45 minutes until the surface is firm to the touch.

Leave the cake in the tin to cool for 10 minutes, then transfer to a serving plate and dust with icing sugar.

To make the sauce, peel the mango over a bowl and cut all the flesh away from the stone. Process or blend with the sugar and the lemon juice until absolutely smooth – about 1 minute – then chill.

To serve, spoon a little of the sauce alongside each slice of cake.

166

Sponge
cake

8 large eggs, separated
300g (10oz) caster sugar
300ml (½ pint) orange or lemon juice
2 teaspoons orange rind, grated
350g (12oz) plain flour or 175g (6oz) matzah
cake meal and 1 tablespoon potato starch

Serves: 6
Storage: 7 days wrapped at room temperature
Freeze: 3 months

PAREV   PESACH

Preheat the oven to 180°C (350°F/gas mark 4).

Beat the egg whites until soft peaks form that curl over when the beaters are lifted. Gradually add 50g (2oz) of the sugar and beat until stiff and glossy.

Beat the egg yolks slightly, then gradually add the remaining sugar and continue beating until thick and creamy.

Stir in the orange or lemon juice and rind, then add the flour or matzah cake meal.

Fold a quarter of the egg whites into the mixture to lighten, then fold in the remaining whites.

Pour into an ungreased 25cm (10in) ring tin, levelling the surface. Tap the pan to release any air bubbles and bake for 1 hour on the lower shelf of the oven until the cake springs back when lightly touched and a skewer inserted in the centre comes out clean.

Invert the tin over the neck of the bottle (this ensures the cake will remain risen until set) and cool completely before removing from the pan.

Fabulous
chocolate fudge
cake with
berry
sauce

350g (12oz) margarine
175g (6oz) caster sugar
250ml (8fl oz) orange juice
350g (12oz) semi-sweet chocolate, roughly
   chopped
6 large eggs

for the sauce
300g (10oz) frozen berries, defrosted
2 tablespoons sugar

for the topping
cocoa powder
fresh berries
orange zest

Serves: 10–12
Storage: Refrigerate 7 days
Freeze: 1 month

PAREV

Preheat the oven to 180°C (350°F/gas mark 4).

Melt the margarine, then add the sugar and the orange juice and stir to blend. Remove from heat and add the chocolate, letting it melt.

When cool, whisk in the eggs until well combined.

Pour into a 23cm (9in) springform lined tin and bake for 35–40 minutes.

Cool in the tin and refrigerate to set for a minimum of 3 hours.

To make the sauce, combine the berries and sugar in a food processor until smooth, adding extra sugar if necessary.

Before serving, dust the cake with cocoa powder and decorate with fresh berries, orange zest and berry sauce on the side.

Dina's
challah

for the dough
1½ tablespoons dried yeast
825ml (28fl oz) warm water
175g (6oz) granulated sugar
1½ tablespoons salt
120ml (4fl oz) oil
3.5kg (7¾lb) strong white flour

for the glaze
1 egg, beaten
sesame seeds

Makes: 4–6 medium loaves
Storage: Refrigerate in sealed plastic bags for 3 days
Freeze: 3 months

PAREV

In a large bowl, dissolve the yeast in the warm water.

Add the sugar, the salt, the oil and half the flour. Mix well with a wooden spoon or plastic spatula.

Add the remaining flour and stir – the dough will become quite thick. When it begins to pull away from the sides of the bowl, turn onto a floured board and knead for about 10 minutes.

Add water if necessary to make the dough more manageable. It should be smooth and elastic, and spring back when pressed lightly with the fingertips.

Let the dough rise in a warm place for 2 hours, punching down twice in that time while keeping the dough covered.

Preheat the oven to 220°C (425°F/gas mark 7).

Separate the *challah* with the blessing (see box), then divide and shape into 4–6 loaves. Place the loaves on well-greased pans or baking sheets and let them rise for about 40 minutes until doubled in size.

Brush with beaten egg and sprinkle with sesame seeds.

Bake for 25–30 minutes until browned. The loaves should sound hollow when tapped.

Taking *Challah*

There is a ceremony to be performed and a special blessing to be made when preparing large quantities of dough. An olive-sized piece of dough must be separated from each batch of dough that weighs 1.2kg (2lb 10oz) or more. This piece is wrapped up and either burned in the oven or disposed of carefully. If the batch of dough weighs more than 1.634kg (slightly over 3lb 10oz), a quantity called a *kezayit* – 15g (½oz) – should be separated and a blessing (which can be found in the *Siddur*) is recited on this separation. The piece of dough should be wrapped and either burned or disposed of, as above. The reason for this is that while the Temple stood in Jerusalem, a portion of bread was set aside for the *Kohen* and, since its destruction, we continue to commemorate this with the symbolic separation of *Challah*.

Breadmaker
challah

for the dough
2 beaten eggs in measuring jug made up to
    250ml (8fl oz) with water
450g (1lb) Canadian challah flour or high-
    gluten bread flour
3 tablespoons caster sugar
1 teaspoon salt
2 tablespoons sunflower oil
1 sachet dried yeast

for the glaze
beaten egg
poppy or sesame seeds

Makes: 3 medium or 2 large loaves
Storage: Refrigerate in sealed plastic bags for 3 days
Freeze: 1 month

PAREV

Put the eggs and water in the bottom of the breadmaker tin, then tip in the flour so that it completely covers the water. Spread out the flour with the back of a spoon, ensuring that no liquid breaks through.

Make two small channels on opposite sides of the tin and add the sugar to one and the salt to the other. Pour in the oil near the salt and away from where you will be putting the yeast (you need to keep the salt separate from the yeast to avoid a chemical reaction). Make a well in the flour that is just large enough to take the contents of the yeast sachet but does not go right down to the water (this will keep the yeast away from the other ingredients until the right time). Pour the yeast into the well.

Set the breadmaker to 'Dough Only', put in the tin and then start the machine. The process will take about 2 hours and the dough should be removed from the tin as soon as it is ready.

Weigh the dough and separate the *Challah* portion with a blessing if required (see box). On a board, cut the remaining dough into two or three pieces, depending on the number of loaves you want. Then divide each piece into three for plaiting. Cover the dough you are not working on with a tea towel to stop it drying out and try to shape all the dough before it starts to rise.

To plait the loaves, roll the three pieces of dough between your palms into long, thin sausages and lay them next to each other on the board with their tops touching. Fold the top ends under, plait the sausages and then fold the bottom ends under carefully. Put the loaves on a solid baking tray lined with baking parchment, allowing space for them to swell. Cover with a clean tea towel and leave in a warm place for between 1½ and 2 hours, during which time they will double in size.

Preheat the oven to 180°C (350°F/gas mark 4). Uncover the loaves and brush with beaten egg (or egg and water, if you prefer) and scatter with either poppy or sesame seeds to taste. Bake medium-sized loaves for 18 minutes and large loaves for approximately 22 minutes. The challah should sound hollow when tapped on the base.

14

Life Cycle Events

Introduction

The Jewish community is one big family, knitted together throughout the generations by relationships and shared experiences. Our closeness leads us to celebrate happy and sad occasions with our extended family and circle of friends and, whatever the reason that brings us together, there is always food! Each life cycle event has its traditional rituals and recipes, which vary from community to community, albeit with common themes.

The fulfilment of a *Torah* obligation (*mitzvah*), such as getting married or circumcising a baby boy, is marked with a *Seudat Mitzvah* – a celebratory meal – to publicise its performance with pride, and to share its *simchah* – its joy – with others.

In the Beginning

The birth of a child is a celebration for the entire Jewish people, because every new life helps to guarantee the continuation of our way of life. As in many cultures, children are regarded as a precious gift and their arrival is greeted with a series of parties.

Shalom Zachor
Welcoming a Son

A baby boy is officially welcomed into the world on his first *Shabbat* with a party in the family home on Friday night. This takes place after Friday night dinner and it is traditional to announce the party in synagogue after the service.

Shalom Zachor means greeting the new-born male, and this custom is rooted in the *Talmudic* dictum '*Ba zachar la-olam, ba shalom ba-olam*' – when a male is born into the world, peace comes unto the world. This applies specifically to males because they bring peace to the world through their study of the *Torah*.

173

There is another idea that a baby in the womb is taught the entire *Torah* by an angel, but forgets it just before birth when the angel touches him just above the mouth (where we all have a small dimple). Thus the *Shalom Zachor* celebration is meant to console the baby for the learning that he has forgotten, and to express the hope that he will 'remember' it again (*zachar*). It also serves as consolation to the child's soul, which mourns the lofty abode it had to leave in order to descend into our physical world.

The idea of mourning alongside celebration explains the custom of serving chickpeas or lentils, traditionally mourners' food, alongside the cakes and biscuits, fruit and (plenty of) alcohol to drink '*L' Chaim*' to the baby.

Menu Suggestions:
Fruit Cake – page 156
Joan's Kiddush Biscuits – page 159
Cooked Chickpeas or Lentils

Brit Milah
Covenantal Circumcision
Source: Leviticus 12:5

A new-born male enters the Jewish community when eight days old through his circumcision, known as *Brit Milah* or *Bris*. On this occasion he will also receive his Jewish name. It is traditionally held after the morning service, in the presence of at least ten men, either at the synagogue or at home, and followed by a festive meal.

New parents will usually consult with a *Mohel* soon after the birth of a boy, and he will visit to check on the health of the baby before confirming the date of the *Brit*. He will also advise on the arrangements to be made beforehand and the care of the baby after the ceremony, which is carried out to the highest standards of medical care and hygiene.

The evening before a boy's *Brit* can be an apprehensive time for the family and there is a custom for the baby's father to say extra prayers and study *Torah* texts in his merit, or to invite children to the house to say the *Shema* and sing psalms to the baby, for which they are rewarded with sweets and raisins.

Because this *mitzvah* is so important it is customary to perform a *Brit* as early in the morning as possible, to show our devotion. It may be followed by a special festive sit-down breakfast, perhaps including croissants, bagels, smoked salmon and other delicacies. However, as a *Seudat Mitzvah*, some people say that the meal following a *Brit*

Milah should include meat and wine. Candles are placed on the table, to add a festive atmosphere and to remind us that when Moses was born the entire house was filled with light. There are special *brachot* for the baby and his parents to be included in the *Birkat HaMazon (bentsching)* at the end of the festive meal.

A qualified *Mohel* can be found through the Initiation Society on 020 8455 2008.

Menu ideas:
Turkey Schnitzels – page 127
Cabbage & Almond Salad – page 88
Cakes and Fruit Platters

Naming a Child

A baby girl is usually named on the first *Shabbat* after her birth by her father, when he is called to the reading of the *Torah* in the synagogue. He will say a prayer for the health of the mother and announce his new daughter's name to the community, who usually respond with singing and congratulatory cries of '*Mazal Tov!*'

Naming a baby boy or girl in the *Ashkenazi* Jewish tradition is often a way of remembering and honouring departed ancestors, by giving the baby the same or similar Hebrew names. It is often possible to find a name which approximates to that of a relative, or to find a modern Hebrew equivalent of a traditional Yiddish name. Not only do we perpetuate their memory, but we also invoke their merit and their positive qualities to give the baby a good start in life. In the *Sephardi* tradition, it is usual to name a child after its living relatives, which is seen as a great honour.

It is customary for a woman to give thanks for a safe delivery from childbirth at the earliest opportunity, and preferably before she visits homes other than her own. She recites the blessing *Birkat HaGomel* in the company of ten men, usually in the synagogue during or just after the reading of the *Torah*, either on *Shabbat* or on a weekday morning.

Simchat Bat
Celebrating a Daughter

A father takes the first opportunity to name his daughter in the synagogue, but the rest of the family may want to celebrate the birth of a daughter in other ways. For example, among *Sephardi* and Italian communities, an elaborate welcoming ceremony called

Zeved HaBat (gift of the daughter) takes place the first time the mother brings the baby to the synagogue.

Other families may choose to celebrate a *Simchat Bat* when the baby girl is thirty days old, which is when she would officially have been counted in the census in ancient times, or on *Rosh Chodesh*, the first day of the new month which is dedicated to women.

This party takes place at home and some mothers take the opportunity to recite the *Birchat* HaGomel if there are ten men present. There are also selected psalms, verses from the *Song of Songs* and *techinot* (prayers often written in Yiddish or Ladino) which are appropriate for this occasion.

Another nice idea is to pass the baby among the guests, who each bestow their own blessings on her and welcome her into the community. Siblings can be included in the celebration, by reciting the *Shema* or a chapter of psalms. Some families mark the occasion by concluding the study of a tractate of the *Talmud* in a ceremony called a *Siyum*, which is followed by a *Seudat Mitzvah* – a celebratory meal.

Menu ideas:
Roast Salmon Fillets with Warm Tomato & Olive Vinaigrette – page 114
Queen Esther's Salad – page 93
Poppy Seed Cake with a Mango Sauce – page 166

Pidyon HaBen
Redemption of the First Born
Source: Numbers *18:15*

Redeeming the male first born is a Biblical *mitzvah*, but it only applies when a boy is the first child born to its mother, and not by Caesarean section, when neither parent is from the tribe of *Kohen* or *Levi*. It is therefore quite a rare privilege to make a *Pidyon HaBen*.

The ceremony takes place on the thirty-first day of the child's life, among a gathering which includes ten men, in the context of a celebratory meal. The ceremony takes place after the guests have washed and eaten bread and are seated for the meal, but before the food is served. The baby is placed on an ornate silver tray and brought to a *Kohen* – someone descended from the priestly *Kohen* tribe. The baby is redeemed by his parents by giving the *Kohen* five special silver coins, and the *Kohen* then blesses the child and hands him back to his parents.

177

In some communities the baby is passed among the guests, who place their gold and silver jewellery around the child to beautify the *mitzvah*, in the same way that we adorn the *Torah* scroll with silver. Some have the custom of placing cloves of garlic and cubes of sugar on the tray, or around the table, and these are later distributed to the guests, who will take them home and use them to flavour large quantities of food and so extend the *mitzvah* of the *Pidyon HaBen* to others.

Menu ideas:
Spanish Lentil Pasties – page 105
Tammy's Pasta Sauce – page 108
Parev Ice Cream – page 152

First Steps

The duty of educating one's children about their Jewish heritage is incumbent upon the parents and is a cornerstone of our faith. References can be found to this priority in the first paragraph of the *Shema* – our most important prayer – and teaching the children is one of the main themes of the *Seder* service on *Pesach*. The Talmud lists the particular obligations of every father as including the duty to teach his children *Torah*, as well as the practical skills they will require to earn a living in later life, and the vital skill of being able to swim.

Even when a child attends a Jewish kindergarten or school, this obligation is not discharged, since it is too important to delegate to teachers! Parents are partners in the process of bringing up a Jewish child and theirs is the delightful challenge of showing them the beauty of the rituals of the Jewish home and answering their early questions. Some parents give their children their own *kiddush* cup from an early age and they can be helped to light their own *Chanukah menorah*, for example.

Opshiren
Hair-cutting

Opshiren (hair-cutting in Yiddish) is a beautiful custom observed mainly by *Chassidim* marking a Jewish boy's third birthday and first haircut. This is based on the custom of not cutting the child's hair before the age of three, as a reminder of the Biblical prohibition against eating fruit from a new tree during its first three years.

This *mitzvah* teaches us not to expect instant gratification and, just as a tree needs time to grow and develop, we spend the first three years of a child's life investing energy, love and affection in our sons before we can begin to enjoy the fruits of our labour. The *Opshiren* is thus the formal introduction to the child's Jewish education and *mitzvot*, such as the wearing of *tzitzit* and a *kippah* or *yarmulke* (skull cap). Friends and family members celebrating this occasion are invited to assist in the *Opshiren* by symbolically snipping a lock of hair. (The haircut is then finished off by a professional!)

As part of the ceremony, the boy may be invited to read the letters of the *Alef-Bet* (Hebrew alphabet) and is rewarded with honey or other sweets. This is done to teach that the study of *Torah* is sweet. In some communities this is done by dipping the letters of the *Alef-Bet* in honey and getting the child to lick the sweetness.

Other milestones in a child's education are marked in ceremonies at home or at school, such as presenting them with their first Siddur when they have learned to read. Throughout the process of education, it is important to imbue children with a love of Judaism and an enthusiasm for learning.

Bat Mitzvah / Bat Chayil
Daughter of the Commandments

When a girl reaches the age of twelve, she reaches maturity and comes of age according to Jewish law. From this day all the responsibilities and privileges of an adult Jewish woman are incumbent upon her. The custom of celebrating this coming of age with a *Bat Mitzvah* event of some kind varies from community to community.

Some families choose to celebrate at home among family and friends, while others prefer a more public acknowledgement on a par with a *Bar Mitzvah*. Some girls choose to deliver a *D'var Torah* speech at the synagogue on *Shabbat* or at a separate ceremony on a Sunday, and a *Kiddush* or party for family and friends may be appropriate. There is a tradition that the *Bat Mitzvah* girl joins in the baking of *challah* and performs the ceremony of taking *Challah* (page 170) for the first time in honour of her *Bat Mitzvah*, as an example of one of the special *mitzvot* which she is now able to fulfil. In some communities *Bat Chayil* ceremonies are carried out during *Havdalah* at the end of *Shabbat*.

Bar Mitzvah
Son of the Commandments

When a boy reaches the age of thirteen, he comes of age according to Jewish law and all the responsibilities and privileges of an adult Jewish male are incumbent upon him. On his thirteenth birthday he becomes a *Bar Mitzvah* and, to mark this event, he is called up for an *Aliyah* to the public reading of the *Torah* in synagogue at the first opportunity, to symbolise his entrance into the community. Once he is *Bar Mitzvah*, he can also begin wearing *Tefillin* (phylacteries – a pair of square cases containing Biblical passages, worn by Jewish men on the left arm and head during weekday morning prayers) and can lead the congregation in prayer and read from the *Torah*.

After the *Bar Mitzvah* has completed his *Aliyah*, it is customary in some congregations to throw sweets at him, as will happen one day when he is called up as a *Chatan* prior to his wedding. The celebration of a *Bar Mitzvah* typically culminates with a festive meal, either on *Shabbat* or on Sunday. A beautiful custom has arisen to visit the *Kotel* – the Western Wall in Jerusalem – either to celebrate the *Bar Mitzvah Aliyah* or soon afterwards, to celebrate a boy's full status among the Jewish people at our holiest site.

Coming Together

Many books have been written about the centrality of marriage and the Jewish home, and many jokes are told about the desperation of Jewish mothers to see their offspring happily married! From the birth of a baby, good wishes given to its parents will include blessings that they should deserve the privilege of bringing the child to a wedding *Chupah* one day, as well as teaching them *Torah* and Jewish traditions – these are inextricably linked as the goals of Jewish parenthood.

Once a couple decides to 'tie the knot', a whole army of *simchah*-planners and dress-makers swing into action. It is often difficult to focus on the true meaning of matrimony and the excitement of setting up a new Jewish household. Surrounded by well-wishers from both families, the young couple may need space and time to make their own important decisions. The advice of married friends and neutral advisors can be very helpful in negotiating the minefield of wedding plans!

Engagement

There are a number of different traditions surrounding becoming engaged. In some communities, it is considered as binding a contract as the marriage ceremony itself if *Tenaim* are signed. This dates back to a time when marriage was a contract between two families, and indeed the wedding *ketubah* is a binding legal document giving details of these financial arrangements.

A less formal ceremony is usually called a *Vort*, Yiddish for 'word', as the partners' families give each other their word that the wedding will take place. At a *Vort* nowadays it is usually a rabbi or family friend who does the talking, giving advice and blessings to the couple, and their mothers will break a china plate together to symbolise the future union of their families to create a new household (and perhaps also the special relationships of mothers-in-law!).

Among the other wedding preparations, it is usual to visit the rabbi who will be performing the marriage ceremony to arrange the details of the *Chupah* and to discuss matters pertaining to married life. In the UK and Israel, both partners will be asked to present their parents' marriage documents to the local rabbinical authority, to obtain permission to marry according to religious as well as civil law. They may also be encouraged to sign a pre-nuptial agreement to avoid later problems.

Aufruf
Calling-Up

It is customary, on the *Shabbat* before his wedding, for a bridegroom to be honoured with an *Aliyah* in his own synagogue. This is an old and beautiful custom dating back to the 16th century at least, and there are several reasons behind it. Firstly, it is believed that the *Shabbat* is the source of energy and blessing for the week to follow, and he is therefore called up to the *Torah* and receives a blessing for the most significant week of his life. Secondly, this *Aliyah* helps the groom, or *Chatan*, to focus on his new responsibilities as a Jewish husband and to resolve to build his home upon the firm foundations of the *Torah*.

The *Chatan* may be called up for *Maftir* (final *Aliyah*) and to read the *Haftarah* portion (see page 21) and it is customary for the women to throw packets of sweets or dried fruit, rice, nuts or sugared almonds at the *Chatan* at the conclusion of the *Aliyah* or *Maftir* blessings. This represents our wish that the young couple should enjoy a sweet life together and also acts as a fertility symbol – the origin of wedding confetti!

The groom's family may host a *Kiddush* (reception) for the community, especially if the wedding is taking place out of town. The bride and her family usually attend the *Aufruf* but there is an over-riding custom that bride and groom do not see each other for some days before the wedding, which may make this impossible, and she may celebrate her *Shabbat Kallah* separately on the same day.

Shabbat Kallah
The Bride's Shabbat

The bride often spends the afternoon of the *Shabbat* before the wedding in the company of her friends and relatives at her home. This *Fahr-Shpiel* (pre-celebration in Yiddish), or

Shabbat Kallah, is a time of singing and rejoicing, often accompanied by an elaborate tea party. Sometimes the bride's friends get a chance to demonstrate their creativity by preparing interesting desserts for the party, prior to *Shabbat*.

Menu ideas:
Deluxe Cheesecake – page 154
Fabulous Chocolate Fudge Cake with Berry Sauce – page 168

Henna Party

This is a *Sephardi* tradition, in which the bride's family hosts a party that culminates with the *Henna* ceremony. The night before the wedding, the women of the family escort the bride to the *Mikveh* (ritual bath) with great pomp and sometimes even with musical accompaniment. After the bride has submerged, the ladies apply *henna* dye to her palms, sometimes in beautifully intricate patterns.

The source of this custom is probably Asian, although it is interesting to note that in *Song of Songs*, written by King Solomon, *henna* is one of the spices growing in the tropical garden to which the 'beloved maiden' is compared. She, in return, compares her groom to 'a cluster of henna in the vineyards of *Ein Gedi*'. These all-female pre-nuptial celebrations continue well into the night, as the guests are treated to special pastries and sweetmeats, which are prepared uniquely for these occasions.

Chupah
Wedding Ceremony

The *Chupah* is actually the name of the canopy under which the wedding ceremony takes place but, as it symbolises the establishment of a new Jewish home, it is synonymous with the wedding ceremony itself. On the day of their wedding, the bride (*Kallah*) and groom (*Chatan*) are required to fast and pray, treating this auspicious occasion as the start of a new life and an opportunity to wipe the slate clean. The wearing of white – the bride's dress and the groom's white robe (*Kittel*) – also alludes to this being their personal *Yom Kippur*.

Before the ceremony there may be a small reception for the male guests and the *Chatan*, while the *Kallah* sits on a beautifully decorated chair and receives her visitors like a queen. The rabbi helps the *Chatan* to sign the *ketubah* wedding contract which will be read under the *Chupah*. The *Chatan* is then brought to the *Kallah* to put on her veil. This *Bedeken* ceremony has various different Biblical sources and symbolises the modesty of the bride, who wishes to dedicate her beauty to her husband alone.

First the *Chatan* and then the *Kallah* is brought to stand under the *Chupah* canopy, where they are surrounded by their immediate family. One of a number of nice customs is for the bride to walk seven times around the groom while the *'Eshet Chayil'* song from Proverbs is sung, symbolising her protection of him. Over a cup of wine various blessings are recited which constitute the betrothal and marriage ceremony itself. In front of two valid witnesses, the *Chatan* gives the *Kallah* a ring and announces that she is now his wife. The *ketubah* contract, written in Aramaic, is read out and given to the bride to keep.

The second part of the ceremony involves the recitation of *Sheva Brachot* over the cup of wine. These seven blessings reflect the seven blessings with which G-d blessed Adam and Eve, because every marriage is a re-enactment of the creation of the world, full of promise and potential. It is customary to end the ceremony by breaking a glass in memory of the destruction of the Temple, to slightly reduce our celebration.

Whether because the couple are now married, or because the *Chatan* manages to stamp on the glass and break it, everyone shouts *'Mazal Tov!'* at this point, and the ceremony is over. The couple must now spend a few uninterrupted moments together in a private room to complete the marriage process before the celebrations begin in earnest. This *yichud* time is also a chance for them to break their fast.

Sheva Brachot
Seven Blessings

Jewish tradition extends the wedding celebration to the seven days following the wedding, as another reminder of the seven days of Creation. Rather than escaping on a honeymoon, the couple can enjoy each other's company for seven days and spend each evening being feted and fed by friends and relatives. During this week they are likened to a king and a queen and receive royal treatment. We greet them with song and rejoice in the establishment of a new family that will contribute to the continuity of our people.

The first of these wedding feasts is on the evening of the wedding day itself. Each is a festive meal and, if a *minyan* of ten men is present, each ends with the recitation of the same seven blessings recited under the *Chupah* – the *Sheva Brachot*. At each meal people who were not present at the wedding are invited, but this is not required on *Shabbat*, since the *Shabbat* itself is deemed a new guest.

Since there are usually at least twenty guests present at a *Sheva Brachot* meal, to make up a *minyan*, the logistics of large-scale catering tend to dictate the menu. According to the dictum, a *Seudat Mitzvah* should include meat and wine, but nowadays fish is as prized as meat and, for the sake of the bride and groom, the seven meals should be as varied as possible!

Birkat HaMazon (Grace after Meals) is recited over a cup of wine. A second cup of wine is then filled and passed around six male relatives or friends, who in turn recite one of the seven blessings. The person who led the *Birkat HaMazon* will read the last of the seven, the blessing over wine, over the first cup, and the wine from the two cups is then mixed and re-divided between two cups, one for the bride and the other for the groom. There is a custom to then share the wine in these cups with unmarried friends, to spread the luck of getting married.

Menu ideas:
Broccoli Soup – page 78
Moroccan Chicken – page 122
Golden Spiced Rice – page 101
Orange Sorbet – page 150
Chocolate Langues de Chat – page 151

Mourning

The Jewish rituals and rules of mourning are sensitively designed to help both the relatives of the deceased and their friends through the difficult process of coming to terms with their loss. Jewish law recognises the need for a suspension of normality in order to cope with intense grief, followed by a gradual return to normal life over the period of a year. At the same time, these formal events, which remain more widely practised than almost any other part of Jewish ritual life, provide a commonly accepted framework for others to offer help and consolation.

Mourning periods are different for a parent than for other relatives, i.e. brother, sister, child or spouse. The mourning period of thirty days applies to all but is extended to one year for a parent.

Levayah
Funeral

It is our custom to bury the dead without delay and to take steps to avoid post-mortem examinations wherever possible. Until the funeral has taken place, mourners are exempt from any *halachic* obligations, including daily prayers, except for *Shabbat*, as it is their primary duty to arrange the funeral. Once notified, the rabbi, synagogue administrator and *Chevra Kadisha* will make arrangements for the funeral and *Shivah*, and help to publicise the details. The *Chevra Kadisha* is a group of volunteers who perform the ritual preparation of the deceased prior to internment. Some members are also involved in bereavement counselling.

Just prior to the funeral service, the ceremony of *Kriah* is performed on the mourners. This is where an item of clothing is torn to symbolise the permanent loss that has taken place in their lives. This torn garment will be worn for the week of *Shivah*.

Levayah is the *mitzvah*, a positive commandment, to accompany the dead to burial. At the funeral it is customary for someone to eulogise the deceased, but this custom is suspended on Fridays and certain festival days. After the funeral, the mourners return to one home and commence the *Shivah* week with a symbolic small meal consisting of a boiled egg and bread roll. Their round shape is symbolic of the circle of life and is a reminder that sometimes there is sadness and sometimes there is joy.

Shivah
Week of Mourning

Judaism provides a beautifully structured approach to the process of mourning, whose psychological benefits are recognised and appreciated. *Shivah* means seven because this period of intense mourning lasts seven days from the date of the funeral, although it stops on the morning of the seventh day and may be curtailed by any festival that occurs during that week.

The *Shivah* period is a time when mourners refrain from their usual activities and receive consoling visits from family and friends. They sit on low chairs, wearing the garment which was torn at the funeral, and non-leather shoes or slippers. They are not permitted to work, bathe, have a haircut, shave or change their external clothes, and must abstain from marital relations.

This period is considered very therapeutic because it enables the bereaved to focus exclusively on their grief while others come to console them and bring cooked food for the mourners' meals, as they are not permitted to prepare their own food. Paying a *Shivah* visit is a great *mitzvah* and visitors should take their cue from the mood in the house and offer appropriate consolation, generally by talking about the good qualities of the deceased person and sharing happy memories.

Because the mourners should not leave the *Shivah* house, prayer services generally take place there, and it is traditional for friends to gather each evening for services in particular, where further eulogies may be given. The mourners lead the services and say the *Kaddish* prayer. *Kaddish* means 'sanctification' and it is about reaffirming our faith in G-d and His promise to rebuild the Temple in Jerusalem and resurrect the dead in The World To Come. It is recited in the presence of a *minyan* by the sons in memory of the departed, at each of the three daily services (four or five on certain days) for eleven months and on the anniversary of their death. If this is not possible, someone else can be asked to take on the obligation to recite *Kaddish*. Women do not traditionally recite *Kaddish* in public, but they may arrange to say it quietly along with the men while standing in the women's section.

We believe that we can improve the status of the deceased in the next world by saying *Kaddish* and learning *Torah* in their memory and merit during this year. One custom is to arrange for the sections of the *Mishnah* to be studied in their memory by various friends, culminating in a *Siyum Mishnayot* – a meal on the first *Yahrzeit*.

On *Shabbat* some of the rules of *avelut* (mourning) are relaxed and the mourners can go to the synagogue. At the end of the *Shivah* period the mourners 'get up' and can resume their work activities and dress normally. It is customary to visit the grave at the end of the *Shivah* week, the end of *Shloshim* and on the *Yahrzeit*, the anniversary of the death of a loved one.

Shloshim
Thirty Days

The period from the end of the *Shivah* to the completion of thirty days after the funeral is a period of second-degree mourning called the *Shloshim*. Rather than returning to normal life, the mourners retain certain restrictions such as not cutting their hair or shaving, to show that they have not yet come to terms with their loss. They should not attend parties or celebrations. In the event of a wedding or another *Seudat Mitzvah*, a festive celebration associated with a *mitzvah*, such as a *Brit*, they should consult with their rabbi as to whether they may attend. They should also abstain from listening to music and going shopping for non-essential items. Again, this *Shloshim* period is curtailed by any major festival that falls within it.

For a bereaved spouse, parent or sibling, the restrictions end with *Shloshim*, but children in mourning for their parents continue to observe certain restrictions for a further eleven months. Some men will retain their beard for this period, and they continue to say *Kaddish* and lead the community in prayer at weekday services. It is usual to sit in a different seat in the synagogue during the year of mourning, provided that this will not lead to a public demonstration of the *avelut* on *Shabbat* and festival days. Attendance at some celebrations is restricted and they should not attend parties or musical events or buy new clothes unnecessarily. These restrictions are lifted after twelve months, usually on the day of the first *Yahrzeit*. In a Jewish leap year the twelve months of *avelut* ends one month before the *Yahrzeit*.

Yahrzeit
Anniversary

Every anniversary of the day that a parent or other relative died is observed by the family as an occasion for remembrance. Although a time of sadness, it may also be possible to recollect special memories and celebrate the positive aspects of the life of a departed loved one. As the years pass, a *Yahrzeit* is a day for recalling the past and reflecting on how we continue to honour the memory of our loved ones.

Having carefully noted the Hebrew date of their death and with which English date it coincides that year, a twenty-five hour *Yahrzeit* candle should be lit at home in the evening of that Jewish day, namely the evening before. It is customary to give charity on a *Yahrzeit* and to learn *Torah* in the memory of the person being mourned and to visit their grave if possible. Some people also have the custom to fast on a parent's *Yahrzeit*.

Kaddish is said in the evening, morning and afternoon prayers of the day by the mourner, who may be asked to lead the prayer services. One should make special effort to attend synagogue on a *Yahrzeit* in order to say *Kaddish* with a *minyan*. On that day, or the closest day on which the *Torah* is read in the synagogue, a man commemorating a *Yahrzeit* (and in some synagogues the husband of a female celebrant) is called up and a memorial prayer, '*El Malei Rachamim*', is said in their name.

Yizkor
Remembrance

Just as happy occasions are celebrated both privately and communally, so the remembrance of the dead has its place in the Jewish calendar in the *Yizkor* memorial prayers. *Yizkor* means 'He [G-d] will remember' and special remembrance prayers for deceased parents and children are said in the synagogue on *Yom Kippur*, the last day of *Pesach* on the second day of *Shavuot* and on *Shemini Atzeret*. The Hebrew names of several people can be included in the individual's memorial prayer, which is different for male and female relatives. During *Yizkor* the community will also say prayers for Jewish martyrs, victims of the Holocaust, and Israel's fallen soldiers. Some people observe the custom that a mourner does not participate in *Yizkor* during the first year after their bereavement because they may have greater difficulty in controlling their feelings. There is also a custom for children and those with living parents to leave the synagogue during the private *Yizkor* prayers.

Every year a *Yahrzeit* candle should also be lit on *Yom Kippur* in the home of someone who has lost a parent or child. Electric memorial candles are sometimes also lit in the synagogue on *Yom Kippur* and on the *Yahrzeit*.

15

Men & Women, Love & Marriage

We find in the story of Creation that men and women were created differently to assist one another. This may not sound politically correct in today's world, where women are as comfortable in the boardroom as they are in the kitchen, but it should be understood as a descriptive rather than a prescriptive principle. Few people today would go so far as to argue that men and women are identical, physically or emotionally. Most people accept that each gender is equipped to perform some tasks better than the other, but across the wide spectrum of Jewish religious life, almost all matters involve men and women equally.

The one area in which Judaism has a quite different approach is our view of public/private priorities. The fact that society in general, and our understanding of Judaism in particular, nowadays focuses on the public domain – the synagogue in particular – has perhaps skewed our view of a woman's role in religious life, ignoring her crucial part in ensuring Jewish observance in the home and guaranteeing Jewish continuity through the education of children. In Judaism the private role is primary and the public ritual role secondary. Women are not discouraged from praying, studying *Torah* and performing all *mitzvot*, including most of the ones from which they are exempt. In fact, some women devote themselves to prayer in particular, travelling to the *Kotel* in Jerusalem for example, every day to recite psalms for the Jewish people.

When a man and a woman get married, their obligations to one another are spelt out in their *ketubah*, which is usually read out at their wedding ceremony in Aramaic. It is well worth looking at the English translation to see what the Jewish marriage contract entails. While this fascinating 2,000-year-old document places the primary obligation on the husband to provide for his wife, under Jewish law the wife is allowed to assume the role of principal breadwinner if she wishes. Thus women can maintain total financial independence within marriage, if they so desire. A Jewish husband is nevertheless always obliged to honour his wife above himself and to satisfy all her emotional and physical needs.

In a secular world, where every television programme and advertising hoarding shouts about society's obsession with sex, the currency of marital intimacy has become seriously devalued. At the other extreme, we find that people's understanding of a 'religious' viewpoint often assumes that physical relationships are frowned upon as the opposite of holiness, and only allowed for the purposes of procreation. In fact, Judaism takes an entirely different approach. We believe that G-d created us with natural physical desires, which we are required not to suppress but to channel and use for higher spiritual purposes. Just as we do not eat like animals, we should not be animalistic in our personal lives. Just as we can elevate the physicality of our possessions by using them for good purposes, we can elevate ourselves through the proper direction of our physical desires within the context of marriage.

The *Torah* tells us that the purpose of marriage is for a man and wife to join together and to become one flesh. This union contains within it the highest possibility for spirituality, not just because of its potential for procreation, but because it creates a new and deep spiritual reality between the couple. Marriage brings together two halves of the same soul, which was split and placed into two unborn babies. When they grow up to find their life partner, this soul is reunited in an explosion of spiritual renewal. All of the wonderful feelings between them culminate in marital intimacy, which is the physical realisation of their spiritual potential.

Having given us the extraordinary power to satisfy each other through our physical relationship, G-d has also given us guidelines to use this power to its maximum potential. The principles of family purity are not only a route to spiritual fulfilment, but are also tried-and-tested ways of strengthening a marriage and sanctifying its physical aspects. In previous generations, Jewish families would not have dreamed of living without these rules, which are as fundamental to our faith as *Shabbat* and *Kashrut*. Today we are seeing a resurgence of the traditions of *Taharat HaMishpachah* (family purity) and widespread use of the *mikveh* (a pool of natural water) in many communities.

Water is the primary source of physical life, which existed before the world was created. It is the closest thing we have to heaven on earth. By immersing ourselves totally within the water, as if to return to the very origins of our own existence, we reunite with our spiritual source and emerge renewed. Just as washing our hands before eating bread is not designed to wash off germs but to sanctify the very physical act of eating, so immersing our whole bodies in the *mikveh* is not about physical cleanliness but spiritual connection and the sanctification of our whole being, particularly our sexuality.

Mikveh also refreshes marriage by creating a space during which physical intimacy is suspended. This encourages a couple to strengthen their emotional relationship and prevents intimacy from becoming routine. Many women appreciate this opportunity, when they may be feeling less than brilliant, to put their sexuality to one side for a short time each month. Men learn to appreciate other qualities in their wives and to exercise self-control within the marriage, as well as outside it. Disagreements simply cannot be solved by kissing and making up, but have to be talked through and resolved properly. The monthly 'honeymoon' reunion after visiting the *mikveh* also helps to keep the relationship fresh and strong.

16

Choosing a Jewish School

Nowadays more Jewish children in the UK go to Jewish day schools than not. It is only in the last fifteen years that Anglo-Jewry has built enough Jewish schools to satisfy this growing demand. In fact, during the last few years, the number and choice of Jewish day schools has increased three-fold in the London area, as well as in many regional communities – a sign of a vibrant community which is investing in its future.

Choosing the right school for your child is a cultural and social decision as well as a religious one. Parents realise that much of their social life will revolve around the friends that they make through their children, and they look for a group of like-minded parents. Schoolfriends form the basis of their social life during childhood and also for the rest of their lives. Being at a Jewish school certainly gives children a head-start in the Jewish continuity stakes.

However, Jewish schools are much more than schools for Jewish children. They provide a warm and caring Jewish environment and give the children a firm grounding in Jewish knowledge and practice, together with a love of Israel. The provision of Jewish Studies in the curriculum aims to give the pupils a knowledge and love for Jewish traditions and an appreciation of morality and citizenship, together with a respect for the moral code on which Judaism is built.

Most Jewish schools also have nationally recognised high standards in secular education and many of them can be seen year after year at the top of the league tables of local schools. Thanks to investment by the community, they often have wonderful modern facilities, providing outstanding surroundings and the best possible opportunities for learning. Parents' organisations are usually very involved in all aspects of school life and particularly active in arranging social and fundraising events to keep the school supplied with extra equipment.

Jewish schools are not only for religious people. The only pre-condition of entry into schools which are under the auspices of the United Synagogue is that the children must be recognised as being Jewish by the Office of the Chief Rabbi, under whose religious authority the schools operate. To verify each child's Jewish status, the schools will ask for a copy of the parents' *ketubah* and the child's full birth certificate.

The schools are intended to serve their local Jewish communities and therefore reflect the nature of those communities. In allocating school places, there is sometimes a preference for families who are affiliated to one of the local synagogues. Families are usually encouraged to share and support the school's objectives – for example, in ensuring that kosher food is always provided at birthday parties. Much of the success of Jewish schools can be attributed to the support that children receive from their parents in reinforcing the values which are taught in the classroom.

Due to the increasing popularity of Jewish day schools, the number of children attending part-time Hebrew classes (*Chadarim*) has inevitably reduced. *Chadarim* for children are run by many communities on Sunday mornings and sometimes in the evenings after school. The teachers go to great lengths to make their lessons enjoyable and to give the children an understanding of what Judaism means in the modern world.

Many communities have youth groups and run holiday schemes for children, which offer them an insight into their Jewish heritage. Interestingly, some non-Jewish secondary schools with a large Jewish intake allow them to hold Jewish assemblies or lunchtime clubs with outside speakers. While none of these facilities can in any way replicate the kind of Jewish education on offer in Jewish day schools, in some circumstances it may be worth looking for environments where children can imbibe something about the religion of their parents.

Some people argue against schools which cater for only one religious group – that they do not prepare children for the real world, or that they give them too narrow a perspective on life. Multi-culturalism is a popular buzzword, but experience in the United States and elsewhere has shown that multi-culturalism requires people to have a strong sense of their own ethnicity, as well as a respect for other cultures, in order to succeed. By following the National Curriculum and imbuing the children with Jewish values of tolerance and concern for the wider world, Jewish schools equip children to wear their Judaism with pride rather than arrogance.

17

Recommended Reading & Websites

Cookbooks

Essential Jewish Festival Cookbook – Evelyn Rose (Robson Books, London 2000).

Modern Jewish Cooking with Style – Denise Phillips (Robson Books, London 2000).

The Book of Jewish Cooking – Denise Phillips (Salamander Books, London 2001).

The New Complete International Jewish Cookbook – Evelyn Rose (Robson Books, London 1998).

LifeCycle Guides

Bris Milah – Circumcision – The Covenant of Abraham – Paysach J. Krohn (Artscroll Mesorah Publications, New York 2001).

Death and Bereavement – A Halachic Guide – Abner Weiss (Ktav Publishing, New Jersey 2001).

Made in Heaven – A Jewish Wedding Guide – Aryeh Kaplan (Moznaim Publishing Corp., New York 1983).

The Jewish Way in Death and Mourning – Maurice Lamm (Jonathan David, New York, 2nd edition 2000).

The Jewish Way in Love and Marriage – Maurice Lamm (Jonathan David, New York 1991).

To Be a Jewish Woman – Lisa Aiken (Jason Aronson, New Jersey 1992).

Waters of Eden – The Mystery of the Mikvah – Aryeh Kaplan (Orthodox Union/Artscroll, New York 1976).

The Jewish Year

Let My People Go: Insights to Passover and the Haggadah – Jeffrey M. Cohen (Jason Aronson, New Jersey 2002).

Menucha V'Simcha: Basic Laws and Themes of Shabbos and Yom Tov – Mordechai Katz (Feldheim, New York 1982).

1,001 Questions and Answers on Rosh Hashanah and Yom Kippur – Jeffrey M. Cohen (Jason Aronson Inc., New Jersey 1997).

1,001 Questions on Pesach – Jeffrey M. Cohen (Jason Aronson Inc., New Jersey 1996).

The Book of our Heritage – Eliyahu KiTov (Feldheim, Jerusalem/New York 1997).

The Chief Rabbi's Haggadah – Jonathan Sacks (HarperCollins, London 2003).

The Shabbos Home – Simcha Bunim Cohen (Artscroll Mesorah 2001).

Understanding the High Holy Day Services – Jeffrey M. Cohen (Hebrew Publishing Co., New York 1983).

Kashrut

The Jewish Travel Guide – ed. Stephen W. Massil (Valentine Mitchell, London 2001) (or subsequent editions as available).

The New Practical Guide to Kashrus – Shaul Wagschal (Feldheim, Jerusalem/New York 1991).

The Really Jewish Food Guide 2002 – United Synagogue publication (available from Jewish bookshops and kosher food outlets in the UK and www.kosher.org.uk) (or subsequent editions as available).

Jewish Philosophy

Celebrating Life: Finding Happiness in Unexpected Places – Jonathan Sacks (HarperCollins, London 2000).

Handbook of Jewish Thought – Aryeh Kaplan (2 volumes, Moznaim Publishing Corp., New York 1993).

Living Inspired – Akiva Tatz (Targum Press, Jerusalem 1993).

Politics of Hope – Jonathan Sacks (Vintage, 2000).

Radical Then, Radical Now: The Legacy of the World's Oldest Religion – Jonathan Sacks (HarperCollins, London 2001).

Will We Have Jewish Grandchildren? Jewish Continuity and How to Achieve it – Jonathan Sacks (Valentine Mitchell, London 1994).

Useful Websites

http://www.unitedsynagogue.org.uk

http://www.chiefrabbi.org.uk

http://www.kosher.org.uk

http://www.artscroll.com

http://www.feldheim.com

http://www.jewishcookery.com – Denise Phillips' Jewish cookery school.

http://www.kosherfinder.com

http://www.totallyjewish.com

Please note: The United Synagogue cannot endorse the *kashrut* of the content of websites which are not under their direct control.

Useful phone numbers

Board of Deputies Enquiry Desk – 020 7543 5400

United Synagogue – 020 8343 8989

Kashrut Division of the London Beth Din – 020 8343 6255

Agency for Jewish Education – 020 8457 9700

18

Synagogue Contacts

London & the Home Counties

Barking & Beacontree
200 Beacontree Avenue
Dagenham
Essex RM8 2TR
Tel: 020 8590 2737

Barnet & District
Eversleigh Road
New Barnet
Hertfordshire EN5 1NE
Tel: 020 8449 0145
Email:
administrator@barnetsynagogue.org.uk

Belmont
101 Vernon Drive
Stanmore
Middlesex HA7 2BW
Tel: 020 8426 0104
Fax: 020 8427 2046
Email: office@belmontshul.fsnet.co.uk

Borehamwood & Elstree
PO Box 47
Croxdale Road
Borehamwood
Hertfordshire WD6 4QF
Tel: 020 8386 5227
Fax: 020 8386 3303
Email: admin@bwoodshul.demon.co.uk

Bushey
177/189 Sparrows Herne
Bushey
Hertfordshire WD23 1AJ
Tel: 020 8950 7340
Fax: 020 8421 8267
Email: administrator@busheyus.org

Catford & Bromley
Crantock Road
London SE6 2QS
Tel: 020 8698 9496

Central

36–40 Hallam Street
London W1N 6NN
Tel: 020 7580 1355
Fax: 020 7636 3831
Email: centralsyn@brijnet.org

Chelsea

Smith Terrace
Smith Street
London SW3 4DL
Tel: 020 7352 6046

Chigwell & Hainault

Limes Avenue
Chigwell
Essex IG7 5NT
Tel: 020 8500 2451
Email: chshul.@breathemail.net

Clayhall

Sinclair House
Woodford Bridge Road
Ilford
Essex IG4 5LN
Tel: 020 8551 6533
Fax: 020 8551 9803
Email: clayhallsynagogue@hotmail.com

Cockfosters & North Southgate

Old Farm Avenue
Southgate
London N14 5QR
Tel: 020 8886 8225
Fax: 020 8886 8234
Email:cns-syn@brijnet.org

Cricklewood

131 Walm Lane
London NW2 3AU
Tel: 020 8452 1739

Dollis Hill

Parkside
Dollis Hill Lane
London NW2 6RJ
Tel: 020 8958 6777

Ealing

15 Grange Road
London W5 5QN
Tel: 020 8579 4894
Email: rabbi@ealingsyn.freeserve.co.uk

Edgware

Parnell Close
Edgware Way
Edgware
Middlesex HA8 8YE
Tel: 020 8958 7508
Fax: 020 8905 4449
Email: edgwareunited@talk21.com

Enfield & Winchmore Hill

53 Wellington Road
Bush Hill Park
Middlesex EN1 2PG
Tel: 020 8363 2697

Finchley

Kinloss Gardens
London N3 3DU
Tel: 020 8346 8551
Fax: 020 8349 1579

Finsbury Park
220 Green Lanes
Finsbury Park
London N4 2NT
Tel: 020 8800 3526

Golders Green
41 Dunstan Road
Golders Green
London NW11 8AE
Tel: 020 8455 2460

Hackney & East London
Brenthouse Road
Mare Street
London E9 6QG
Tel: 020 8985 4600
Fax: 020 8986 9507

Hampstead
Dennington Park Road
West End Lane
London NW6 1AX
Tel: 020 7435 1518
Fax: 020 7431 8369

Hampstead Garden Suburb
Norrice Lea
London N2 0RE
Tel: 020 8455 8126
Fax: 020 8201 9247
Email: office@hgss.org.uk

Harold Hill
Trowbridge Road
Harold Hill
Romford
Essex RM3 8YW
Tel: 01708 348904

Hemel Hempstead
c/o Devreaux Drive
Watford
Hertfordshire WD1 3DD
Tel: 01923 232007

Hendon
18 Raleigh Close
London NW4 2TA
Tel: 020 8202 6924
Fax: 020 8202 1720
Email: benson118@aol.com

Highams Park & Chingford
81a Marlborough Road
Chingford
London E4 9AJ
Tel: 020 8527 0937

Highgate
57 North Road
Highgate
London N6 4BJ
Tel: 020 8340 7655

High Wycombe
c/o 33 Hampden Road
High Wycombe
Buckinghamshire HP13 6SZ
Tel: 01494 529 821

Hounslow, Heathrow & District

100 Staines Road
Hounslow
Middlesex TW3 3LF
Tel: 020 8572 2100

Ilford

22 Beehive Lane
Ilford
Essex IG1 3RT
Tel: 020 8554 5969
Fax: 020 8554 4543

Kenton

Shaftesbury Avenue
Kenton
Middlesex HA3 0RD
Tel: 020 8907 5959
Fax: 020 8909 2677
Email: office@kentonsynagogue.org.uk

Kingsbury

Kingsbury Green
London NW9 8XR
Tel: 020 8204 8089

Kingston & Surbiton

33/35 Uxbridge Road
Kingston-upon-Thames
Surrey KT1 2LL
Tel: 020 8546 9370

Mill Hill

Brockenhurst Gardens
London NW7 2JY
Tel: 020 8959 1137
Fax: 020 8959 6484
Email: shulmail@aol.com

Muswell Hill

31 Tetherdown
London N10 1ND
Tel: 020 8883 5925

Newbury Park

23 Wessex Close
Newbury Park
Ilford
Essex IG3 8JU
Tel: 020 8597 0958

New Synagogue

Victoria Community Centre
Egerton Road
London N16 6UB
Tel: 020 8880 2731

New West End

St Petersburgh Place
Bayswater Road
London W2 4JT
Tel: 020 7229 2631
Email: nwes@newwestend.org.uk

Northwood

21–23 Murray Road
Northwood
Middlesex HA6 2YP
Tel: 01923 820 004
Fax: 01923 820 020
Email: nusbo@hotmail.com

Palmers Green & Southgate

Brownlow Road
London N11 2BN
Tel: 020 8881 0037
Fax: 020 8441 8832

Peterborough

142 Cobden Avenue
Peterborough
Cambridgeshire PE1 2NU
Tel: 01733 264 151

Pinner

1 Cecil Park
Pinner
Middlesex HA5 5HJ
Tel: 020 8868 7204
Fax: 020 8868 7011

Potters Bar

Meadowcroft
Great North Road
Bell Bar
Hatfield
Hertfordshire AL9 6DB
Tel: 01707 656202
Email:office@pottersbarshul.org.uk

Radlett

22 Watling Street
Radlett
Hertfordshire WD7 7PN
Tel: 01923 856 878
Fax: 01923 856 698
Email: radlettus@hotmail.com

Richmond

Lichfield Gardens
Richmond-on-Thames
Surrey TW9 1AP
Tel: 020 8940 3526

Romford

25 Eastern Road
Romford
Essex RM1 3NH
Tel: 01708 741690

Ruislip

9–17 Shenley Avenue
Ruislip Manor
Middlesex HA4 6BP
Tel: 01895 622059

St Albans

Oswald Road
St Albans
Hertfordshire AL1 3AQ
Tel: 01727 854872

St John's Wood

37/41 Grove End Road
St John's Wood
London NW8 9NG
Tel: 020 7286 3838
Fax: 020 7266 2123

Shenley

c/o 3 Wickets End
Shenley
Hertfordshire WD7 9EX
Tel: 01923 857 786

South Hampstead

21/22 Eton Villas
Eton Road
South Hampstead
London NW3 4SP
Tel: 020 7722 1807
Fax: 020 7586 3459

South London

45 Leigham Court Road

London SW16 2NF

Tel: 020 8677 0234

Fax: 020 8677 5107

South Tottenham

111–113 Crowland Road

London N15 6UL

Tel: 020 8880 2731

Staines

Westbrook Road

South Street

Staines

Middlesex TW18 4PR

Tel: 01784 462 557

Email: staines.synagogue@btinternet.com

Stanmore & Canons Park

London Road

Stanmore

Middlesex HA7 4NS

Tel: 020 8954 2210

Fax: 020 8954 4369

Sutton

14 Cedar Road

Sutton

Surrey SM2 5DA

Tel: 020 8642 5419

Wanstead & Woodford

20 Churchfields

South Woodford

London E18 2QZ

Tel: 020 8504 1990

Watford

16 Nascot Road

Watford

Hertfordshire WD17 3RE

Tel: 01923 222755

Welwyn Garden City

Barn Close

Handside Lane

Welwyn Garden City

Hertfordshire AL8 6ST

Tel: 01438 715686

Wembley

8–10 Forty Avenue

Wembley

Middlesex HA9 8JW

Tel: 020 8904 6565

Email: office@wembleysyn.org

Western Marble Arch

32 Great Cumberland Place

London W1 7DJ

Tel: 020 7723 9333

Email:office@wma.synagogue.org.

West Ham & Upton Park

95 Earlham Grove

Forest Gate

London E7 9AN

Tel: 020 8552 1917

Willesden & Brondesbury Park

143–145 Brondesbury Park

London NW2 5JL

Tel: 020 8459 1083

Woodside Park
Woodside Park Road
London N12 8RZ
Tel: 020 8445 4236

Synagogues under the Aegis of the Chief Rabbi
Regions of the United Kingdom

Blackpool United Hebrew Congregation
Leamington Road
Blackpool
Lancashire
Tel: 01253 628164

Bournemouth Hebrew Congregation
Wootton Gardens
Bournemouth
Dorset BH1 1PW
Tel: 01202 557433

Brighton & Hove Hebrew Congregation
66 Middle Street
Brighton
Sussex BN1 1AL
Tel: 01273 601088

Bristol
Park Row
Bristol BS1 5LP
Tel: 0117 942 2610

Bury Hebrew Congregation
Sunnybank Road
Bury BL9 8HE
Tel: 0161 796 5062

Cambridge Hebrew Congregation
3 Thompson's Lane
Cambridge CB5 8AQ
Tel: 01223 515 375

Cardiff United Synagogue
Brandreth Road
Penylan
Cardiff CF23 5LB
Tel: 02920 473728

Cheetham Hebrew Congregation
453 Cheetham Hill Road
Manchester M8 9PA
Tel: 0161 740 7788

Cheltenham
St James's Square
Cheltenham
Gloucestershire GL50 3PU
Tel: 01242 525032

Edinburgh Hebrew Congregation
4 Salisbury Road
Edinburgh EH16 5AB
Tel: 0131 667 3144

Glasgow – Giffnock & Newlands Synagogue
222 Fenwick Road
Giffnock
Glasgow G46 6UE
Tel: 0141 577 8250

Hale & District Hebrew Congregation
Shay Lane
Hale Barns
Cheshire WA15 8PA
Tel: 0161 980 8846

Heaton Park Hebrew Congregation – Manchester
Ashdown
Middleton Road
Manchester M8 4JX
Tel: 0161 740 4766

High Wycombe
c/o 33 Hampden Road
High Wycombe
Buckinghamshire HP13 6SZ
Tel: 01494 529821

Leeds Beth Hamedrash Hagadol Synagogue
399 Street Lane Gardens
Leeds
West Yorkshire LS17 6HQ
Tel: 0113 269 2181

Leicester
Highfield Street
Leicester LE2 1AD
Tel: 0116 2706622

Northampton
Overstone Road
Northampton NN1 3JW
Tel: 01604 633345

Norwich
Earlham Road
Norwich NR2 3RA
Tel: 01603 506482

Nottingham Hebrew Congregation
Shakespeare Villas
Nottingham NG1 4FQ
Tel: 0115 947 2004

Portsmouth & Southsea
The Thicket
Southsea
Hampshire PO5 2AA
Tel: 01705 821494

Sale & District Hebrew Congregation
Hesketh Road
Sale, Cheshire M33 5FB
Tel: 0161 973 3013

Solihull & District Hebrew Congregation
3 Monastery Drive
Solihull
West Midlands B91 1DW
Tel: 0121 707 5199
Fax: 0121 706 8736
Email: rabbipink@aol.com

South Manchester Synagogue
Wilbraham Road
Manchester M14 6JS
Tel: 0161 224 1366

Southend & Westcliff Hebrew Congregation
Finchley Road
Westcliff on Sea
Southend
Essex SS0 8AD
Tel: 01702 344 900
Fax: 01702 391 131

Swansea Hebrew Congregation
Ffynone
Swansea
West Glamorgan SA3 5JR
Tel: 01792 401205

Whitefield Hebrew Congregation
Park Lane
Manchester M45 7PB
Tel: 0161 766 3732

Acknowledgements

A special thanks to the members of the Association of United Synagogue Women, who have been involved in the project from its inception.

Project Co-ordinators:
Tammy Russell
Sarah Manning
Geoff Abrahams
Jane Donovan

Contributors:
Geoff Abrahams
Dayan Ivan Binstock
Rev. Michael Binstock
Dina Brawer
Joy Conway
Ruth Franks
Simon Goulden
Lady Amelie Jakobovits
Alison Leach
Lesley Levene
Leonie Lewis
Sandy Littman
Sheila Mann
Heather Robin
Barbara Ross
Reva Ross
Tammy Russell
Mrs Elaine Sacks
Chief Rabbi Professor Jonathan Sacks
Rabbi Z M Salasnik
Karen Shooter
Howard Shooter
Sue Soloway

Lynne Stock

Diana Wolfin

Recipe Contributors:

Pauline Binstock, Northwood United Synagogue

Anita Bloomberg, Hendon United Synagogue

Dina Brawer, Northwood United Synagogue

Fortuna Davis, Waltham Forest Hebrew Congregation

Gillian Fine, Northwood United Synagogue

Melanie Fishman, Northwood United Synagogue

Sara Franks, Hampstead Garden Suburb United Synagogue

Estelle Freedman, Northwood United Synagogue

Rita Garber, Kenton United Synagogue

Joan Goldberg, Catford & Bromley United Synagogue

Ruth Grabinar, Catford & Bromley United Synagogue

Lillian Graham, Catford & Bromley United Synagogue

Debora Kadish, Dollis Hill United Synagogue

Alan Koch, United Synagogue Head Office

Freda Koppel z"l, Netanya, Israel

Diana LeCore

Irene Leeman, Kenton United Synagogue

Gill Lerner, Cockfosters & N. Southgate United Synagogue

Debbie Lewis, Kenton United Synagogue

Leonie Lewis, United Synagogue Head Office

Judith Lyons, Northwood United Synagogue

Vera Miller, Newbury Park United Synagogue

Bernice Monty, Wanstead & Woodford United Synagogue

Anne Moss, Central Synagogue

Milly Myers, Hendon United Synagogue

Ayala Newmark, Finchley United Synagogue

Doreen Ohayon, Ealing United Synagogue

Sheila Perl, Stanmore & Canons Park United Synagogue

Paula Pitts, Pinner United Synagogue

Tammy Russell, United Synagogue Head Office

Ruth Rutstein, Cockfosters & North Southgate United Synagogue

Mildred Salter, Bushey United Synagogue

Caroline Shapiro, Northwood United Synagogue

Chanie Shochet, Mill Hill United Synagogue

Sue Soloway, United Synagogue Head Office

Josephine Wayne, United Synagogue Visitation Committee

Gail Weinstein, Pinner United Synagogue

Shuli Whitefield, Finchley United Synagogue

With thanks to the Association of United Synagogue Women and to Evelyn Rose and Denise Phillips for contributing several recipes.

General Index

Recipes Index

PAGE ONE

Also in Collaboration with Participant Media:

Food, Inc.
Oceans
Cane Toads
Waiting for "*Superman*"

CONTENTS

MAGNOLIA PICTURES, PARTICIPANT MEDIA, and HISTORY FILMS

present

A FILM BY ANDREW ROSSI

PAGE ONE:
INSIDE THE NEW YORK TIMES

DIRECTED BY
Andrew Rossi

PRODUCED & WRITTEN BY
Kate Novack and Andrew Rossi

PRODUCERS
Josh Braun, David Hand, Alan Oxman,
Adam Schlesinger

EXECUTIVE PRODUCERS
Daniel Stern, Daniel Pine

ASSOCIATE PRODUCERS
Keith Hamlin, Luke Henry

INTRODUCTION

In 2007, The New York Times moved into a soaring modern glass tower sheathed in heat-sensitive ceramic tubes on the west side of midtown Manhattan. The building stands a couple of blocks from the tangle of avenues and streets that was called a square and was named for the paper more than a century before. The paper's old newsroom, despite the elegance of its Gallic facade, was a romanticized warren of cluttered desks, narrow hallways and stained carpets.

At the new headquarters, technological and environmental advances abound—automatically controlling, for example, the level of the window shades shielding cubicles from bright sunlight streaming in from the west.

In the lobby, dozens of small vacuum tube screens project snippets of articles culled from the paper's archives by an algorithm designed by an artist and a statistician. The phrases wash over the screens and then skitter away, to be replaced by a new batch. The exhibit is called Moveable Type, an inventive homage to the paper's traditions.

The airy new headquarters represents the twin concepts of transparency and light. The building was—and is—intended as a statement. The Times was shedding its skin as an old-line

ix

newspaper company and proclaiming itself a confident, even a defining, player on the modern media stage.

Within two years, however, amid shifts in the news industry and a collapsing economy, the Times Company appeared to be listing, not towering. Its parent company's debt was valued as junk by the credit rating agency Standard & Poor's. So the company borrowed $250 million from Mexican billionaire and telecommunications magnate Carlos Slim Helú. The Times Company also entered into a so-called sale-leaseback agreement—it sold its share of the brand-new building for $225 million, paying its new landlord for occupying its floors. It retains the right to buy back the property in 2019 for $250 million.

All of this would have been just one more item of corporate consternation during an economic downturn were The Times itself not a key part of an industry that, on its better days, makes a credible case that it is indispensable to the functioning of democracy in the United States.

In recent years the paper has revealed a massive wiretapping program conducted by the federal government; has documented the unraveling of the subprime mortgage market; and, despite claims by some critics that it fails to hold local or liberal politicians accountable, has doggedly reported scandals involving New York's two most recent governors and its most powerful congressman—all Democrats.

It has also embraced the new forms of journalism allowed by new technologies, adding audio, visual and graphic forms of storytelling that have only enhanced the richness of its online report.

Yet increasingly, news coverage is being treated as a commodity—another information stream that can course through any number of channels. At the same time as fewer people are willing to pay for the print edition of The Times and other papers, online readers have not proved willing to pay significant sums to read general-interest news online. Advertisers refuse to pay more than pennies on the dollar to reach digital readers compared to what they pay for print ad rates.

In March 2011, the Times Company responded by charging frequent readers of articles and features on The Times Web site or on other digital devices, such as the iPad. The cost of journalism has to be borne, publisher Arthur Sulzberger Jr. said.

In so doing, The New York Times was seeking to remain the leading American exemplar of that peculiar hybrid of commercial enterprise and public service. The deep recession notwithstanding, the paper's journalists periodically still risked legal penalties, their readers' goodwill and, at times, their own safety. Times reporter David Rohde was held captive for seven months by the Taliban in Afghanistan and Pakistan. Photographer Joao Silva lost two legs after stepping on a landmine in Kandahar province. Several Times journalists were held for days, beaten and assaulted by Libyan authorities during the uprising there early in 2011.

The Times's problem, shared by battered news organizations serving communities large and small across the country, is the unraveling of the decades-long marriage that knit significant profits to service for the public good.

In early 2009, I undertook a thought experiment: What would happen to a city if its primary news source simply went away? I visited Hartford, Connecticut, on a bitterly cold winter morning amid the depths of the current financial crisis. Hartford made sense because it was a poor city in a rich state, the seat of state government and the home of three of the nation's largest corporations.

The Hartford Courant, the dominant local daily, is America's oldest continuously published newspaper, since its founding as a weekly in 1764. By 2009 it had suffered rounds of debilitating layoffs. The Courant was owned by the bankrupt Tribune Company. Although it was in no immediate threat of shutting down, the thought sent shivers down the collective spine of many people there. "Even a bad review is important to us, frankly," said Julie Stapf, marketing director of the respected Hartford Stage, "because it still brings awareness to the community about what we're doing here at the theater."

Over at the State House, an experienced local television reporter said no other outlet generated as much news as the Courant, even in its diminished state. Mark Pazniokas, the Courant's senior political reporter, warned that the loss of the paper would mean the loss of a sense of shared belonging for people there. "If everybody is looking at dozens or hundreds of different news sources," Pazniokas told me, "you don't have the common point of reference that—not to be corny—[is] an important part of democracy and community."

As I wandered around the press room at the State House, mail was piled high on what was marked as the desk of The New York Times. The Times had abandoned its daily coverage of Connecticut state politics the year before.

* * *

A new generation of national news powers has emerged. Some cover specific niches: ESPN for sports, Politico for horse race politics, Fox News and MSNBC for ideologically driven talk shows leavened with some news coverage, Bloomberg largely for business and finance developments (though its general news coverage is impressive).

Others are either relatively new or newly consequential players on the American media scene, such as the BBC, The Economist, The Guardian, The Huffington Post and The Week.

Under its new controlling owner, Rupert Murdoch, The Wall Street Journal has altered its focus and mix of stories to challenge The Times's title as the nation's leading general-interest paper instead of remaining the nation's preeminent financial publication. NPR News, for all its stumbles, has enjoyed years of growth in the scope and depth of its reporting reach and the size of its audiences.

But The Times has few other national peers that match its aspirations. The audience for the nightly newscasts of national television networks has withered remarkably and enterprise reporting is rare. The Washington Post, The Los Angeles Times and Time, while each capable of illuminating work, have been forced by fiscal strains to make tough choices and scale back elements of coverage. Tens of millions of Americans continue to rely on The New York Times in print and online every month for writing of grace, wit and insight, as well as photography of beauty and haunting pain.

And yet there is no shortage of Times critics, some of whom appear to be rooting openly for its demise. The paper has committed enough missteps to offend readers of just about any creed, faith, hue or ideological stripe. Recent years have seen the fundamentally flawed coverage of claims before the U.S.-led invasion of Iraq that Saddam Hussein had weapons of mass destruction and the credulous and extensive front-page coverage of allegations of rape against Duke University lacrosse players who were later exonerated.

The Times can no longer stand imperiously above the fray, if it ever truly could. The instantaneousness and ubiquity of the flow of information on the Web allow readers, bloggers, sources, competitors and rivals to challenge the paper's work and even fire back.

Some new ventures do so in constructive ways. PolitiFact, an offshoot of the St. Petersburg Times, evaluates the claims of politicians, government officials and, occasionally, media outlets with scrupulous research. MediaBugs advocates on behalf of angered readers seeking corrections, posting an online account of the contested claims and the results. NewsTrust provides people with social media tools to gauge the trustworthiness of specific news outlets and individual stories.

Others, on blogs, cable news and talk radio, take aim at The Times with less genteel intentions. But why wouldn't they? Democracy has always been a boisterous, brawling affair. These days, The Times's executive editor Bill Keller sometimes punches back.

Yet for all its projection of confidence, The Times confronts the future with a hint of fragility.

* * *

A profound appreciation for the role of The Times and an almost equally profound fear for its fate sparked the curiosity of the filmmakers Andrew Rossi and Kate Novack, as they explain on subsequent pages. Times Company executives now say that they expect to pay off that debt to Carlos Slim with a check on the very first day the agreement allows. But as Rossi and Novack set out in 2009, disaster did not seem so remote. Several major newspaper companies had declared bankruptcy. The Newark Star-Ledger had, just a few months earlier, bought out more than 40 percent of its newsroom on a single day.

The filmmakers were guided by the talented, profane and charismatic David Carr, The Times's media columnist and reporter. The resulting film, "Page One: A Year in the Life of The New York Times," explores the viability, mission and achievements of the paper through what Carr calls the "keyhole" of the media desk—the reporters assigned to cover their own ailing industry and, on occasion, their own institution.

Rossi and Novack won extraordinary access and witnessed a singular newspaper struggling with the economy, its finances, and the news itself. Never in recent history had the paper been more threatened. And yet as fewer news organizations sought to match its ambitions, never had The Times been more vital in covering the confusion of war, local corruption, environmental catastrophe and financial fraud.

This book takes the movie as a starting point; among the essays readers will encounter are those written by Carr, by one of The Times's lead reporters on the WikiLeaks cables of 2010, by a former Times reporter who was one of its first bloggers and by a journalism scholar who wrestles with the implications of The Times's arrangement with WikiLeaks. The book also considers other issues confronting journalists more generally, drawing on leading thinkers, practitioners and innovators in the field from all over the country, from the Northeast to D.C. to California to Florida to the Pacific Northwest—and, for that matter, from across the Atlantic. This collection also reflects the eagerness among many journalists to seize the opportunity afforded by technological breakthroughs and to shatter journalistic conventions.

Among the voices in this book are two former top newspaper executives differing over who will pay for journalism; a digital entrepreneur who says The Times should make peace with news aggregators such as The Huffington Post; a journalist and book publisher who argues for the often-ignored importance of public radio; the former top editor at The Chicago Tribune and The Los Angeles Times, who chronicles those newspapers' declines; an innovator who asks whether the news focuses too much on the new; former journalists championing a new movement teaching students to think critically about the news; an editor who contends collaboration is replacing cutthroat competition in the news business; and the nation's leading journalism philanthropist on what he's learned from investing his foundation's money about what lies ahead.

This book capitalizes on the energy of the film "Page One" to offer an inside look into America's newsrooms of today and of the future. It is a tale not just of anxiety but excitement. It is, as one of our contributors writes, one hell of a story.

DAVID FOLKENFLIK
New York, NY

PART I

THE NEW YORK TIMES

ONE

The Back Story to "Page One"

Kate Novack and Andrew Rossi

The husband-and-wife documentary team of Andrew Rossi and Kate Novack are best known for their films about food. "Eat This New York" captures the challenges of two best friends trying to start a restaurant from scratch in Brooklyn, while "Le Cirque: A Table in Heaven" portrays the struggles of an Italian American family seeking to reinvent a famed but fading high-end Manhattan restaurant. Rossi, trained in law at Harvard, came by his interest honestly: his parents owned an Italian restaurant in New York City. A curiosity about the news business might not seem as obvious.

Yet Rossi was an associate producer on the documentary "Control Room," about the Al Jazeera satellite television news service in the wake of the U.S.-led invasion of Iraq. And Novack was previously a reporter covering arts and media for Time magazine. Both were already invested, personally and professionally, in figuring out more about the modern media age. Yet as the two filmmakers explain below, they did not initially set their sights on The New York Times.

On a frigid night in February 2009, more than 10 stories above Park Avenue in the New York City apartment of Strauss Zelnick, a fierce debate about the future of media was in full swing. Zelnick, the media industry investor and occasional host of salon-like dinner parties, had convened a group that included older lions of the content economy like Norm Pearlstine, late of Time Inc. and now chief content officer at Bloomberg News; early-stage financial backers such as Fred Wilson of Union Square Ventures; and young Web entrepreneurs such as Ricky Van Veen of College Humor.

Andrew, in developing a documentary commissioned by HBO about the young guns of Web 2.0, had tagged along with Ben Lerer, the 20-something founder of a digital tip sheet for urban hipsters called Thrillist. Over fried chicken and ice cream sundaes in the wood-paneled dining room, the conversation started with the decimation of the advertising market and wound its way to the challenges to news reporting looming ahead. It was a feisty debate: Can marquee journalists leave their legacy media homes and make it on their own with tumblr and Twitter accounts? Should opinion and news gathering be disaggregated to save money? Does anyone still look to newspapers as the supreme authority? And, finally, on the heels of Carlos Slim Helú's loan to The New York Times Company and its $57.8 million losses in the past year, the question arose, "Will The New York Times survive?"

It was a question that Michael Hirschorn had dared to ask publicly just weeks earlier. "What if The New York Times goes out of business—like this May?" he wrote in a provocative Atlantic magazine piece ominously entitled "End Times." "It's certainly plausible," he posited. After all, financial industry stalwarts Lehman Brothers and Bear Stearns recently had met a similar fate. Why not The New York Times?

It was during this seemingly vulnerable moment for the paper that Andrew met with David Carr, The Times's media columnist who would eventually become the breakout character of "Page One." But the goal that day was to interview Carr for the Web 2.0 project. The idea was that after all the excess and froth of the first Internet boom 10 years earlier, there was a new breed of start-up that was leveraging social media, emerging technologies and stringent budgets, and we wanted to follow them on the path to success as a sort of sequel to the 2001 documentary—and cautionary tale—"Startup.com."

In his trademark gravelly voice, Carr talked about the rise of geo-location services like Foursquare, and the perils of mapping tastes and preferences in a project like Chris Dixon's Hunch.com. But the conversation kept circling back to the appropriate role for the legacy media in this changing universe. Meanwhile, The Times's cavernous newsroom, with its three floors linked by a series of fire-engine red staircases, beckoned as an ideal cinematic backdrop. And as Andrew listened to Carr, he thought, *I want to make a movie about The Times instead.* We imagined chronicling the paper during a time of transition in the way that Gay Talese had in his best-selling book "The Kingdom and the Power" in 1969, a period of record profits for the company, when The Times stood as "necessary proof of the earth's existence."

"Go talk to my bosses," Carr told Andrew. (He has since admitted that it was the most polite way he could think of to make Andrew go away.)

The one question audiences always ask is, Why did The Times let you inside? It took about six months of conversations and meetings with editors and reporters inside the paper before the project was green-lit. In hindsight, though, The Times probably opened its doors because of something executive editor Bill Keller told Andrew during one of those meetings: "I'm proud of my journalists and I'd like the world to see them."

In the newsroom, Andrew worked as a one-man crew. Having a boom operator and a field producer hovering over a video screen would have compromised the intimacy we were trying to achieve. In the first weeks of filming, Andrew often would sit for hours on the low filing cabinets that the writers have next to their cubicles, mainly just watching. The goal was to become part of the furniture and to give the film a naturalistic vérité feel of a movie by, for example, D.A. Pennebaker, the filmmaker behind "Don't Look Back" and "The War Room," and one of our heroes.

We are both regular readers of The Times, but we didn't want this to be an exercise in Times worship. We knew that if Andrew was going to be "embedded" in the newsroom for more than a year, we'd need to step outside its walls throughout the process of filming. So Kate began wading through the countervailing perspectives on the future of news—from Marc Andreessen, the cofounder of Netscape who once called on The Times to stop publishing on paper or perish (and who gently turned us down), to Elizabeth Eisenstein, the academic behind the classic "Printing Press as an Agent of Change." With a cast of cooler talking heads, we would create, we hoped, a counterpoint to the intimate, direct cinema inside the newsroom.

One of our first interviews was with Kurt Andersen, who'd written for Time and The New Yorker and edited New York magazine. He was also a cofounder, in the '80s, of Spy, which had a column devoted entirely to critiquing The New York Times. We'd recently heard Kurt compare The Times to the Vatican, which intrigued us. Did the paper really still hold such sway?

"In the secular church of establishment opinion and press, The New York Times is where the encyclicals come and where life is organized and ruled. You know, it's the great position of authority," Kurt told Kate in an interview. "What The New York Times thinks, says, does, *is*," he continued, "doesn't quite have the power of infallibility of the pope." Then he stopped and caught himself: "Of course, the pope doesn't anymore, does he?"

The notion of The Times as an influential institution during a time of turmoil, somewhat like the Catholic Church itself, stayed with us. This was not a story of continuity of authority but of disruption and transformation.

Perhaps no one had been more outspoken on the disruption occurring in media than Clay Shirky, the New York University new-media professor. Shirky had been a mentor to Dennis Crowley, the student who went on to start Foursquare. He was a folk hero of sorts for the crowd-sourcing camp. He'd been comparing the advent of the Internet to the invention of the printing press in the 15th century, before such talk was stock book party banter. We went to see him just before commencement, when the students in NYU's Interactive Telecommunications Program were exhibiting their thesis projects. As we wound our way through the show to get to Clay's small office in a downtown loft building, we wondered if one of these seemingly quaint projects might be the next Foursquare.

In Shirky's view, the erosion of the mainstream media's authority was less of an explosion than a slow burn. "When they buried Walter Cronkite, it was a funeral for a man, but it was also a funeral for a role, that Platonic ideal of the authority figure, the deliverer of truth," Clay told Kate. "Cable TV, then CNN and the spread of everything from Fox to C-SPAN—every one of those—was a ratcheting up of the amount of discourse available to the public and then suddenly the Web goes mainstream and The Times is now one of many, many, many voices in a marketplace."

Whether the loss of authoritative media figures was a good thing or a bad thing was another question. "I go back and forth," Katrina vanden Heuvel, the editor of The Nation, would later tell us. "Sometimes I think the voice of Walter Cronkite, the three broadcasts bringing you the news every evening, was very important, and sometimes I think it's too nostalgic to think of that as a great thing."

After the interview with Clay, he walked us to the elevator. "So who are the key newcomers to watch?" Kate asked as we stood waiting for the doors to open.

"Julian Assange," he replied immediately.

The name Assange was already creeping onto the mainstream radar. Weeks earlier, Andrew had arrived at The New York Times building to find Brian Stelter, the former collegiate blogger who now covers media for the paper, hunched over his laptop.

"A former hacker with a whistle-blower Web site"—whom we now know as Julian Assange of WikiLeaks—had posted a chilling video of a U.S. Army Apache helicopter shooting down two journalists and several Iraqi civilians. Reuters had been trying for two years to obtain the footage through traditional, legal channels, and somehow Assange had managed to get his hands on the video and post it on YouTube. The talk that day at the Media Desk was about how the leak was a modern-day Pentagon Papers. No one needed to drop off thousands of pages of secret documents to reporters for The New York Times, as Daniel Ellsberg, the leaker of the Pentagon Papers, did decades ago. When we interviewed Bill Keller later that week, he explained. "The bottom line is Daniel Ellsberg needed us. WikiLeaks doesn't."

What struck us most that day wasn't Keller's candor. We'd been impressed with the newsroom's openness ever since the paper's editors agreed to let the camera in months earlier. What really surprised us was how clearly something fundamental was changing—not just in the news business, but also in how we as a culture access and interpret and internalize information. Suddenly, The Times and other institutions like it seemed—to borrow a line from David Carr—"like trains whose cabooses have square wheels." Months later, after The Times had published several stories based on information originally obtained by Wiki-Leaks, we sat down with Susan Chira, the paper's foreign editor, in her office. "I think we're all much more humble about what we think we can control," she told us.

In the last scene of "Page One," the journalists gather in The Times's newsroom like crew in the hub of a luxury cruise ship. But it's not the Titanic. The apocalyptic vision of Michael Hirschorn's "End Times" did not come to pass.

Keller has assembled his staff to announce the paper's Pulitzer Prize winners for the year. Reporters are unusually re-laxed and the paper's publisher, Arthur Sulzberger, Jr., who's rarely in the newsroom, surveys the scene with a smile.

But the questions that prompted the film more than a year earlier linger. Will The New York Times survive? Will newspa-pers? Some industry watchers give newspapers just 10 more years. Even inside The Times, the idea of the single all-powerful arbiter of authority, the Zeus figure throwing thunderbolts from the sky, seems a relic of a pre-digital era.

As Keller ascends one of the red staircases that zigzag be-tween the three stories of the newsroom, David Carr leans back in his chair, looking on. "The Times," he says, "does not need to be a monolith to survive."

Print Is Dead:
Long Live The New York Times

David Carr

When The New York Times's media columnist David Carr writes a piece, moguls pay attention and often pay a price. In the case of the Chicago-based Tribune Company, for example, Carr's reporting toppled the morally bankrupt leadership of a financially bankrupt corporation. But Carr did not take a stereotypical path to his perch. Instead, he paid his own way through college in his home state of Minnesota, taking seven years to graduate. Starting as a writer, Carr ultimately led two alternative weeklies—the Twin Cities Reader and the Washington [D.C.] City Paper—before joining The Times as a reporter in 2002. Wide-ranging in his interests, Carr took on journalism, entertainment and commerce as his brief.

In his memoir "The Night of the Gun," Carr unsparingly turns his reporting skills on himself, relaying the story of his own past addiction to crack, replete with arrests and violent outbursts. The book has become a best-seller.

Below, Carr describes the surreal world of writing about the perils confronting journalism while leading one of its exemplars—and of being tailed by a filmmaker while doing so.

Five years ago, while already a reporter at The New York Times, I was offered the opportunity to write about media in a column for the business page. I had recently escaped to general assignment duties in the culture department, and I could not have been less interested.

There were two problems with the offer. Media reporters often write about the work of other reporters who are often describing the work of other people who actually do actual things. The meta-ness of it can make it seem like a less than serious activity. And in 2005, I was coming up on 10 years straight of the media beat. Every year and every day, people on that beat would tell me that the sky was falling. And it never did.

Then, after some prodding, I took the column. (The Times was the first daily at which I worked, and my colleagues patiently explained the importance of regular, defendable space.) And then, almost immediately, great big pieces of the sky began to give way. Business models tumbled, national media brands that historically took years and tens of millions of dollars to build came out of nowhere. Reporters, previously the lone conductors of the music of fact, were now confronted by an audience that could orchestrate its own version of the news online, and television viewers used DVRs to program their own commercial-free schedules. CraigsList neatly met the local needs of consumers at a cost of precisely zero, and bloggers in all realms began breaking news, often over the keening of hacks like me.

Platforms emerged and gave way. Great magazine franchises sold for a dollar while news Web sites funded on credit cards were valued in the millions. Citizen intellectuals the world over created Wikipedia, its own kind of miracle and a vast storehouse of human knowledge. Well-financed and carefully conceived political campaigns were derailed by a lone individual recording a video on a cell phone. The primacy of mainstream media as the arbiter of what mattered was replaced by algorithms and the wisdom of the crowd. Many looked at these tectonic events and decided that The New York Times was no longer relevant, or at least had lost importance.

Working on the broader story and being inside the one that was taking place at The Times, I reached precisely the opposite conclusion. Convenient, I know, seeing as I have staked my future and that of my family on the continued relevance of the newspaper, but in this case I tell myself that self-interest and the public interest are aligned. (Dirty politicians often reach the same conclusion, so I'm stepping gingerly here.)

Everyone at The Times, including me, spends most of the day trying hard to make stories that reflect the state of play and the facts as we know them, to arrive at something that is really good. I still believe that the front page of The Times can convey authority unlike any other media artifact on the planet. Early in my career at The Times, I had written my first page one story—I am not a frequent visitor there—and was out late in New York City with some pals. I made an announcement, "Let's see what the seven most important stories in Western civilization are today," and went into a bodega and bought a paper.

There it was. My story about how all of the editors of Cosmo from around the world had fanned out throughout Manhattan, shopping for the day. Okay. In retrospect, I'm not that proud of the piece, but it still makes me happy that it made the front.

* * *

When Andrew Rossi first talked about making a movie about the tumult confronting the mainstream media and The Times in particular by following the media desk, I tried not to giggle. "This place looks like an insurance company, with a bunch of doughy middle-aged people sitting in cubes with headsets typing on desktops. There is no way you are going to find a movie in any of that."

I was wrong about that. I admire "Page One" for many reasons, but most acutely because Andrew, the director, took a very prosaic visual environment and an undramatic activity—the accretion of facts by reporters in pursuit of truth, or at least a story that would get their editors off their backs—and made it into a movie.

His movie works because he understands how a newspaper works. For 14 months, he would sit there with his big cow eyes staring at me or other people in the media pod, camera at the ready, endlessly waiting for something to happen. And it did. Amid all the wandering around, the broken plays, the mediocre stories, he found a heroic narrative in the work that we do.

Part of it is darkroom magic. Andrew is a skilled moviemaker and so he was able to craft images, music and a burst of action and meaning into not only a cohesive narrative but a real kind of movie-movie. But he also saw and told a true and even exciting story. Some talking heads really were suggesting that The Times was going out of business. Others argued the culture might be better off without it, and those of us who worked there began to wonder about its future amid all the noise.

I know I did. As I wrote story after story about layoffs and the sudden tumbling of once legendary America media institutions, I worried about how it might end. Would I be pounding away at the computer one day and find myself typing something like "A number of people were laid off at The Times, including David Carr, who often reported on layoffs elsewhere"?

All of those endless fears and huge shifts are visible in "Page One." You might say that Andrew got lucky by showing up when he did. And you'd be wrong. In retrospect, nothing seems accidental about his decision to knock on the front door of The New York Times in 2009 and somehow talk his way in. That year was by far the worst in newspaper history, and the remarkable rise of insurgent media took a huge leap.

By 2010, Andrew was firmly embedded in the media department at a time when the business model seemed to be up for grabs, as well as the apparatus for gathering and disseminating information. He saw the import of WikiLeaks almost before we did. He found talking heads who helped identify that something very real was at stake, and found men and women in the newsroom—including Bill Keller, who runs the place—who were willing to talk frankly about how it felt being in the middle of things.

* * *

Outside the paper, there are as many New York Timeses as there are readers. Some think the paper begins and ends with what Maureen Dowd has to say. Others don't look at the rest of it until they have knocked out the crossword. There is The New York Times of the foodies, the urbanists, the internationalists, the opera buffs, the Beltway wonks, business types, hard-core public policy enthusiasts and fashion freaks. There's the paper that serves as mere grist for the grammar ninnies who, like crows on a wire, come caw-cawing with a vengeance every time they catch us dangling a participle. And there's the paper that inspires the people who visit my inbox every time I write about Fox News. They view my employer as the unholy spawn of the ACLU and some kind of floating international conspiracy I can never quite pin down.

And then there is the one I work at.

The Times is just a newspaper, not a cure for cancer or a cancer on our national consciousness. But it is also a kind of magic trick.

Every day, all kinds of data come hurtling at its reporters, who chase it and bundle it and arrange it into a coherent narrative and then send it on to editors who sort it all into a hierarchy through a formula known only to them. I'm sort of new there—

anybody with less than 20 years inside the place had best not claim to know much about the place, and so I don't.

In a functional sense, it is a lot like watching a powerful locomotive hurtle down rickety old tracks. Somehow, it never derails. The newspaper that lands on doorsteps all over the country is really an artifact of negotiation, between finite space and infinite news, between news that never stops and presses that must always roll, between the desire to make it perfect and the desire to make sure it is produced.

For an immigrant like myself—I arrived there in 2001 with no daily newspapering experience—it is a thing of terrible beauty. All manner of chaos in the world is wrestled into a single daily document on paper and into a constantly shifting one in our various digital incarnations. That newspaper, or at least the part of it that I work in, is visible and remarkably rendered in "Page One" because the film reflects the tools and values of journalism in both its execution and message.

Perhaps some chip gets implanted over time in people who go to work at 620 Eighth Avenue in that island off the coast of America called Manhattan. If the chip takes hold, we come to believe in our own exceptionalism. It may also be why some people hate us so much. Some of our more skeptical readers believe that our leadership meets every day to whip up their version of the world and then gives us our marching orders to portray it in our stories.

Honesty compels me to admit that is true in a sense, but not in the way The Times's most fervent critics think. Many of those readers conflate our editorial page—which is somewhat to the left or reflexively liberal, depending on your perspective—with our news pages, which are neither. The women and men who run The Times are less concerned with political cant, at least from what I can tell, than coming up with some beau ideal of a finite news document that perfectly reflects the previous day's news

The majesty of the place, for all its very human shortcomings, is not always apparent from within. Human prerogative tends to race ahead of even the luckiest life, and you begin not to notice, not to be grateful, that you work at a big newspaper that competes ferociously for every piece of consequential news.

At The Times, there are many smart people doing extraordinary things, but every job becomes a job after a while. There are the same cubicles, bosses, memos and protocols that are a common part of American work life. You end up bitching about the coffee, the hours, the editors, and after a while, your job. The sense of privilege of working in journalism, let alone a place where the news matters so much, begins to wane.

And then you take a trip somewhere and instead of being trapped in the cube, in the quotidian aspects that are part of every job, you actually read the damn thing. Often, under those circumstances, the full wingspan of the enterprise becomes manifest. On certain days, it can take your breath away.

Given its daily glories, it often surprises me that I have survived 10 years at The Times. Since I am a media reporter and will never be asked to put on a parachute to cover the revolution in North Africa, you could reasonably question how critical my mission actually is. As I recall, in the aftermath of Hurricane Katrina, I was sent down to New Orleans, but it was after the newspaper's architecture critic and just before the gossip columnist. So there you go.

Here is what I have learned in my decade at The Times. There are muscles that live in the walls of the place, in the spaces in between people, that lift you up and make you a better person, a better reporter and a better writer. Again and again, you might be up against impossible odds and the physical laws of time and space to get something done, and then those muscles of the institution will pick you up and throw you across the goal line.

The editors will often wave a wand and call for a story that cannot possibly be reported and written within the allowed time, and yet, the next day, there it is, gleaming within its four corners. The wand works all the time, sometimes to glorious ends.

Because "Page One" sought to cover the great collapse of the media by watching over the shoulder of the reporters at The Times who cover the industry, the viewer ends up looking at the place through a keyhole, an interesting one, but a pretty small and confined one. They don't see Chris Chivers putting on a pack in the dead of night to head up some scary, dangerous valley in Afghanistan or Tyler Hicks darting through shooting wars with a camera. The movie doesn't show Gretchen Morgenson working all week to nail down a single fact so she can hold to account a bloated, skeevy Wall Street trading company. There are no cameras around when Willie Rashbaum heads out to the good-bye party of some police sergeant out on Staten Island just so he can make nice with his sources. And when Deborah Sontag returned to Haiti long after appetite had waned from most other news outlets, she was pretty much on her own.

And less dramatically, but no less essentially, there are the men and women who wrestle copy to the ground in a way that ensures readers are getting stories that have the virtue of being true. No one will ever make a movie about Joan O'Neill or Rachel Saltz, both of whom are called copy editors, but whose job description does not begin to describe their daily battle to hunt down and vaporize error or imprecision in my copy and everyone else's. Their labors, and the labors of others they sit next to, are very much what make The Times *The Times*. The same holds for the editors and producers who make the Grey

Lady dance on the Web—people like Julie Bloom, an editor in culture whose name rarely appears in the paper, but is every inch, forgive me, a Timesman. The 40 million people a month who stop by our Web site and those who recently agreed to pay to read what we produce in digital realms unknowingly rely on their work as well.

Every once in a while, someone will win a prize or get captured trying to do her job and the world will take notice. But most of the time, the reader will absorb a good story in The Times without wondering what it took to land it.

And that's the way we like it. Reporters at The Times lead a privileged existence, with an owner who tries to do business in a way that enables good reporting, not the other way around. Whether the question is about travel or more time, when something is important, the answer is always yes. Still.

Most important, the human firepower—the 1,100 people behind The Times newsroom—constitutes one of the biggest journalistic assets on earth. If you can't find somebody smarter than you at The Times, or somebody who can help you think a matter through in an altogether new way, you are not looking very hard.

You don't see much about the crucial role of editors in movies about journalism. In "Page One," it is baked right into the film. It shows reporters wandering toward editors with half-baked, harebrained ideas and the editor responding either by administering journalistic CPR to transform it into something real or by taking out a gun and shooting it graveyard dead.

After all, at a time when news moves at the speed of electrons and all known thought is one click away, what is the real value of The Times? The paper matters precisely because people don't just push a button when they have a random thought or merely give some Twitter-driven topspin to a nice little bit of news they see floating by on the Web.

The page one meeting, an incredibly anachronistic exercise in informational Darwinism, still turns out to be one of the best ways of curating a fire hose of information into something useful and comprehensible that lands on your doorstep with a plop. Yes, The Times plays hard in the Web news space—we like a digital scoop as much as the next newsie—but it is the process of turning things over, of scrutinizing and challenging underlying assumptions, even at the speed of the Web, that gives The Times added value in an age when information is a commodity.

It's not always pretty to watch, but what emerges can be impressive to behold.

* * *

Even, surprisingly, on screen.

It was hardly a no-brainer to let Andrew in the door. I was one of the know-it-alls who suggested it would be a great idea to let "The Daily Show" into our midst and the show's correspondent proceeded to do exactly what the show does to every institution in its crosshairs: make us look ridiculous. When Andrew was doing the asking, we were fresh off that little lesson in media management.

My bosses said yes, I think, because they saw in Andrew a reflection of our paper on its best days. A willingness to do what it takes to get the story, to follow it where it goes, and to work to tell that story in a way that is both meaningful in the moment and a worthy subject of historical inspection. Our executive editor, Bill Keller, has said he's proud of what we all do and saw no reason not to allow someone else to have a look at it.

One of my favorite moments in the film comes right in the middle. Brian Stelter is working very hard on a story about WikiLeaks as a pressing deadline approaches. Bruce Headlam, his editor (and mine), asks if he has sent the story yet and Brian indicates he did, even as we can see he is still typing rapidly into . . . something. Bruce, who is one of the funniest guys in a room that has more than a few of them, immediately pivots to the camera and says, "He's lying."

In that moment, you get a picture of where I work. Brian wants the story to be extraordinary, an objective his editor shares, but Bruce would also like it to be in the next day's paper with all of the facts pinned down. Their objectives are seemingly in conflict, but here's the thing: they were both trying really hard to make it good.

THREE

The Designated Redactor

Scott Shane

Scott Shane is a reporter covering national security issues from the Washington bureau of The New York Times who has long written about the role information plays in public policy and politics. In the late 1980s and early 1990s, Shane was Moscow bureau chief for The Baltimore Sun, where he chronicled the collapse of the communist empire. Shane's insight that Mikhail Gorbachev's effort to loosen restrictions ran away from him formed the basis of his book, "Dismantling Utopia: How Information Ended the Soviet Union." (Among his friends and competitors were Bill Keller of The Times and David Remnick, then of The Washington Post.) Since then, Shane has written extensively about intelligence activities taken by U.S. authorities and foreign powers, including a series on the National Security Agency that helped inspire a highly fictionalized blockbuster film and stories about the CIA's off-the-books actions to interrogate terror suspects outside domestic laws. When The Times gained access to 250,000 U.S. diplomatic cables through the WikiLeaks project, Shane was a natural to help lead the coverage.

It was on October 1, 2010, that I chanced upon the Dagestani wedding.

My colleagues and I at The New York Times had just begun perusing the State Department cables obtained by WikiLeaks, and here was a small masterpiece—an anonymous American diplomat's vivid eyewitness account of wild upper-crust nuptials in Dagestan, a restive republic in the Russian Caucasus. The writer captured with sardonic appreciation the excesses of the oligarch class: the vacation home, "a 40-meter high green airport tower on columns" with "a grotto whose glass floor was the roof of a huge fish tank"; the guests throwing hundred-dollar bills at dancing children; the drunken wedding party heading out for nocturnal jet-skiing on the Caspian Sea; the arrival of the brutal strongman who ran neighboring Chechnya, accompanied by his well-armed entourage, and rumored to be bearing a five-kilogram lump of gold as a wedding gift.

The diplomat's wit and powers of observation elevated the cable miles above the dull norm for government writing. The father of the groom, Gadzhi Machachev, the head of Dagestan's state oil company, he wrote, was well-off enough "to afford luxurious houses in Makhachkala, Kaspiysk, Moscow, Paris and San Diego; and a large collection of luxury automobiles, including the Rolls Royce Silver Phantom in which Dalgat fetched Aida from her parents' reception." Even the parenthetical digressions were delicious: "(Gadzhi gave us a lift in the Rolls once in Moscow, but the legroom was somewhat constricted by the presence of a Kalashnikov carbine at our feet. Gadzhi has survived numerous assassination attempts, as have most of the still-living leaders of Dagestan.)"

Unlike dozens of cables that my colleagues at The Times and I would discover over the next few months, this triumph of storytelling had no momentous implications for American policy. But it was a revelation nonetheless. I had dealt with diplomats for years, and they were uniformly . . . diplomatic. Here, by contrast, were the raw, uncensored observations of an alert, well-prepared mind, rendered in stunning prose.

Searching through a quarter-million secret diplomatic cables is a little like exploring a mammoth, uncharted complex of underground caves. You prowl the tunnels, peering into chambers—here, a human rights crackdown in Egypt; over there, a town in Mexico taken over by a drug cartel; across the way, Israeli assassins dispatched to kill a Hamas official in Dubai. You glance at something that glints from a corner, and hours later, you are following a trail of key words (terrorist, nuclear, plot) receding into 2008, 1997, 1985 . . . You trudge dutifully along a long bare corridor that seems to yield nothing of interest, when suddenly you stumble across a gem.

After reading the Dagestani cable I felt a powerful urge to forward the cable to friends who, like me, had worked in Russia, and who I knew would appreciate it. More to the point, I wanted to get this discovery into the newspaper. But for the moment, I would have to keep my find to myself. (When published, the cable would become a modest Internet hit, showing why the art of cable writing is a celebrated, if secret, competitive skill inside the State Department.)

After WikiLeaks became a household name, and the diplomatic cables it made public reverberated clamorously through world politics and helped fuel the Arab revolutions, it seemed odd to recall how secretive we had been when the project started a few months earlier. But when Dean Baquet, The New York Times Washington bureau chief, gathered a few reporters in his office in September 2010 for a speakerphone chat with Bill Keller, the paper's executive editor in New York, we were all a little paranoid.

We had been given a massive cache of 251,287 cables—years of American diplomats' reports from the field on everything from a tense standoff with Libya over highly enriched uranium to Chinese hacking into Google's networks. The cables were intended for a select audience—usually the diplomats' bosses back at the State Department. The newspaper's lawyers thought it conceivable that the United States government might go to court to try to prevent us from publishing them. More likely, they feared British authorities, armed with far more draconian laws protecting state secrets, would get wind that The Guardian was also at work on the cables and seek an injunction to stop their publication.

We felt especially protective of The Guardian, our partner in earlier stories based on field reports from the wars in Afghanistan and Iraq that had been passed to us by WikiLeaks. Julian Assange, the anti-secrecy group's volatile founder and provocateur-in-chief, had taken offense at The New York Times's coverage of his personal problems, including accusations from two Swedish women of sexual improprieties, and decided to shut The Times out of the group's next big scoop, the diplomatic cables. But The Guardian's top editors, with whom we had cooperated in publishing Afghan and Iraq war reports, wanted to keep us in the mix. They ignored Mr. Assange and passed the collection to New York anyway, opening for us, too, an unprecedented window on American diplomacy.

So in the weeks that followed, those of us sifting through the cables were vague when colleagues asked about what we were up to—a challenge when your colleagues are professional snoops. The editors asked me to assess whether and how the cables should be redacted for publication—whether certain names or programs might warrant protection. I began to consult with colleagues at The Guardian and Der Spiegel, the other two publications then studying the cables. We used Skype to communicate because Internet experts believed—or really just made an educated guess—that the Internet phone service was less susceptible than cell phones or landlines to eavesdropping by the National Security Agency and its British and German counterparts.

Reading through the documents would have been a labor of years, and we had mere weeks to meet the publication schedule we had agreed on with The Guardian and Der Spiegel. We were soon joined by Le Monde in France and El Pais in Spain, when WikiLeaks decided to give those newspapers the cables, too.

The Times's computer geniuses in New York kept improving the searchable cable database they had designed. Soon, we could tailor our searches not just by key word but by date or year, embassy of origin and level of classification.

Nothing in the database was classified above the level "Secret/Noforn," government jargon for information too sensitive to be shared with foreign allies. Since nearly all intelligence reports are classified as top secret or above, that meant some topics I eagerly hunted for were missing. I knew, for instance, that there had been many exchanges between American and Yemeni authorities about the radical, American-born cleric Anwar al-Awlaki. He had been imprisoned in Yemen in 2006 and 2007, questioned by visiting FBI agents and later identified as a crucial influence; allegedly he had participated in terrorist plots. Yet I was disappointed to find Mr. Awlaki barely mentioned in the cables.

My colleagues and I quickly discovered that the most efficient searches began with a shrewd key word, a specific embassy and the most recent cables that were labeled "Secret," "Noforn" or both. In other words, we learned to look first at the cables the government wanted most to protect. Those criteria usually produced a manageable result—dozens of cables, instead of hundreds. We divided up the hunt by countries and themes among a dozen reporters, planning an initial series of articles to run for about two weeks. I worked specifically on Yemen and on Afghan corruption, but I also had the job of preparing an overview story that would introduce the cables and sample some of the highlights we had found.

The cables were fascinating but contained few shocking revelations—a trait that caused me to underestimate their potential impact. Instead, they provided incomparable detail, verbatim quotations from confidential conversations, and diplomats' blunt assessments of foreign officials. They were, as I would write later in a story about the cables from Yemen, like crisp color photographs of what we had previously viewed in fuzzy black and white.

We had previously reported, for instance, that the United States had carried out at least four secret missile strikes against the Al Qaeda affiliate in Yemen. But here was that country's canny 30-year president, Ali Abdullah Saleh, inviting the United States to do anything it chose against terrorists on all of Yemen's territory—as long, he added, as the Americans would not blame him for any terrorist plot cooked up on Yemeni soil. We had suspected that Mr. Saleh had approved the missile strikes and helped to cover up their origin. But here he was in the cables explicitly promising a visiting American commander, Gen. David H. Petraeus, "We'll continue saying the bombs are ours, not yours." His deputy prime minister was inspired to volunteer that he had just "lied" to Yemen's parliament on this very question.

Likewise, Afghan corruption was an old and rather tired topic. But the cables gave it new life. One reported back to officials at Foggy Bottom that Afghanistan's first vice president had been discovered entering Dubai, a favorite hideaway for wealthy Afghans, with $52 million in cash in his luggage—"a significant amount," the cable writer deadpanned, that "he was ultimately allowed to keep without revealing the money's origin or destination." Another droll diplomat, discussing the new cabinet, noted that the agriculture minister "appears to be the only minister that was confirmed about whom no allegations of bribery exist."

We had a deadline looming: WikiLeaks and the five publications had agreed that the first cable stories would appear on our Web sites at precisely 4:30 P.M. Eastern time on November 28. It was the Sunday after Thanksgiving, awkward timing for Americans, but our European collaborators outvoted us. First, we planned to inform the government about the classified material we had and give officials a chance to comment or to express any objections to its publication, standard practices for most reporters who write about national security.

About 10 days before the publication date, Dean Baquet let the White House know we wanted a meeting, and he and Rebecca Corbett, a deputy Washington bureau chief, and I met with two National Security Council officials, Ben Rhodes and Tom Vietor, in an Old Executive Office Building adorned with oil portraits of American secretaries of war.

Because Bradley Manning, the 22-year-old Army private accused of leaking documents to WikiLeaks, had bragged in an online chat about the cables, the NSC officials were not surprised at what we had to say.

I told them I would send over the 100 or so cables we had decided to publish along with our stories—a somewhat odd notion, since I was in effect giving them their own secrets. They agreed to advise us, as we requested, on what they viewed as the dangers of publication. The newspaper reserves the right in such cases to publish what it chooses, but hearing the government's views can help inform a decision on what to print. This kind of interaction between a newspaper and the government can be controversial, suggesting to some an invitation for censorship or at least a cozy relationship between government officials and their ostensible watchdog. In this case, as I will explain, I think the unusually extensive consultation was justified.

Two nights before Thanksgiving, Dean and I arrived at the State Department to meet P.J. Crowley, then the assistant secretary for public affairs and the face of the department. When we were led to an upper-floor conference room deep inside the building, however, we found a murder board. A dozen senior officials from State, the Defense Department and the intelligence agencies awaited us, arrayed around a conference table with another dozen aides sitting and standing behind them, some with laptops prepared for note taking. I felt suddenly like a criminal defendant in the dock before a team of prosecutors.

Our meetings were off the record, but I can say that the government's position then was the same that it later stated publicly: The cables were stolen classified documents and we had no business possessing them, let alone publishing them. Their publication could endanger the freedom or lives of countless foreign individuals in authoritarian countries—activists, dissidents, academics, journalists (!)—who had spoken confidentially and candidly to American diplomats.

We explained that we considered the cables newsworthy, that we intended to publish both a selection of them and stories based on them, but that we also intended to withhold some of the names in the cables if necessary to protect people from harm, and we were eager to hear the government's requests for redactions. Our exchanges were heated. I was struck, as I would be repeatedly in speaking with current and former diplomats about the WikiLeaks cables, by their outrage at having the confidentiality of their discussions and views violated on so gargantuan a scale. I was focused on the relatively low level of the cables' classification and the paucity of truly astonishing disclosures. They considered confidentiality a bedrock necessity of diplomacy. If in retrospect their fears of damage to individuals and international relations would seem hyperbolic, those fears were understandable. Nothing like this had ever happened before.

Over the next two weeks, we held telephone conference calls almost daily with the State Department, each covering another set of cables we planned to publish on a particular topic: Iran, say, or arms trafficking. The government's objections fell into three categories. First were individuals named in the cables who might be at risk; we had usually excised those names on our own, and we almost always agreed with State's requests.

Second were glimpses of sensitive American programs, usually intelligence programs. Despite government objections, we published a cable detailing requests made by intelligence agencies to diplomats to collect information on their foreign counterparts, including credit card and frequent flyer numbers, which the National Security Agency can use to track travel. Since some diplomats considered such requests improper, we thought the practice worth airing. Another intelligence program had resulted from years of delicate negotiations; the government argued that it would be destroyed if made public, with potentially grave damage to international security. We decided the news value of the disclosure was outweighed by the likely harm it would cause. We dropped that cable from our publication plans.

The third category of State Department requests was based on its fear of damage to relations with specific countries. Usually the cables contained candid comments by foreign leaders who never imagined their words would be made public. State argued that crucial American relationships would be severely undermined, with uncertain consequences. In nearly all such cases, we rejected the request and chose to publish. We were guided by the belief that, as Defense Secretary Robert Gates would say later, countries cooperate with the United States not because they like Americans or believe Americans can keep secrets, but because they believe it is in their own interest.

As The Times's designated redactor, I found the process nerve-wracking. Excising a name required inserting a code into a hard-to-read computer database, and it was easy to miss, say, the 10th mention in a single cable of the two-letter family name of a Chinese professor who had shared his views on domestic politics. If I missed just one such instance, the poor professor might lose his job or go to prison. And as our State Department contacts pointed out, publishing even the date of an embassy meeting might effectively identify the speaker, since Chinese security officers closely monitor who comes and goes.

These ongoing consultations with government officials about what to publish made us all uneasy, and were later pilloried by such press critics as the Salon blogger Glenn Greenwald. I find such criticism worthwhile but unpersuasive. In one case, I had not redacted the name of a Libyan official quoted in a cable about Muammar el-Qaddafi's travel requirements. The State Department's Libyan specialists shocked us by advising that if he was named, he might well be killed. Their explanation seemed credible; we took the name out. I would argue that such exchanges were not craven subservience to the government, but an exercise of plain decency and common sense. Had we chosen not to remove names, and a diplomatic source was imprisoned or killed as a result, it is easy to imagine the resulting uproar. In such an instance, aside from the catastrophe for the individual named, we believed Congress might well change American law to explicitly criminalize the publication of classified information—a disaster for press freedom.

On the balance between openness and discretion, it is worth noting the conduct of WikiLeaks itself. Though founded in 2006 with an absolute commitment to outing government secrets, WikiLeaks clearly took to heart the broad criticism it drew from human rights groups earlier in 2010 when it published Afghan war reports that identified some confidential informants of the American military. The group proceeded with great care and caution in publishing the diplomatic cables a few months later— I know, because I was supplying it with our redacted cables. It had the power to publish all quarter-million cables verbatim. It chose instead to move slowly, usually reproducing redactions that The Times, The Guardian and other news organizations had made to protect diplomats' sources. Eight months after WikiLeaks got the cables, it had published fewer than 5,500, or about 2 percent. Not every government secret, the group had discovered, is intended to cover up government misdeeds.

In the overheated climate immediately before and after the cables began to appear in print, members of Congress pressed the Obama Justice Department to prosecute Julian Assange, WikiLeaks's founder. Attorney General Eric H. Holder Jr. announced an investigation. If it resulted in criminal charges against Mr. Assange or others at WikiLeaks for publishing classified information, that would be a dangerous break with American precedent. The Bush administration once attempted such a prosecution, charging two officials of AIPAC, the pro-Israel lobby; the case ran into numerous legal challenges and was dropped. Mr. Assange may be anti-American in his views, flamboyant in his public statements and less than impeccable in his personal life. But there is no essential legal difference between what he did and what my colleagues at The Times and I do regularly: publish classified information that we judge to be newsworthy.

In the first four months after publication of the cables began, the anti-WikiLeaks hysteria calmed. Diplomats remained shell-shocked and angry about the leaks. But no American government official had yet identified anyone harmed as a result of the disclosures, except for a handful of officials who lost their jobs. The German foreign minister's chief of staff was fired after cables portrayed him as a mole inside the government feeding American diplomats choice tidbits. The American ambassador to Mexico resigned after the Mexican president made known his anger about the ambassador's remarks in cables questioning Mexico's capability and dedication in fighting drug cartels.

It had become clear that publishing the cables had mixed and sometimes quite profound effects on world affairs. In some Arab countries surprised by pro-democracy uprisings, revelations from the WikiLeaks cables helped feed, or at least explain, the anger that drew demonstrators to the streets. In Tunisia, a site called TuniLeaks featured the comments of appalled American diplomats about the flagrant corruption and conspicuous consumption of President Zine el-Abidine Ben Ali and his family. In Egypt, cables exposed the ferment in the officer corps against President Hosni Mubarak. In Libya, cables exposed "Qaddafi Inc.," the nepotism that put Muammar Qaddafi's children in charge of security agencies and business enterprises alike. Arab activists said it would be a distortion to say the cables caused the uprisings. But some said they were encouraged to learn that American diplomats privately agreed with their own dark views of their leaders.

For every new country that appeared in the news, a plunge back into the cave of cables retrieved an inside story—the bitter rivalry among Muammar el-Qaddafi's sons, concerns about inadequate safety measures at Japanese nuclear reactors, a scandal over political bribery in India. It was true that the cables added mostly what journalists dismiss as mere color. But what I had underestimated was the political power of mere color to expose the foibles of the powerful, and thereby embolden a growing movement to oust oppressive regimes.

And fewer than 6,000 of the cables had been published, which meant there were still 245,000 to go.

FOUR

What Is WikiLeaks?
That's the Wrong Question.

Kelly McBride

Kelly McBride once wrote, "I spent my formative years as a reporter in the Idaho Panhandle, where Nazis and racist skinheads routinely burned crosses and hosted marches through the middle of beautiful Coeur d'Alene, Idaho, at the height of tourist season." She later became a nationally recognized reporter on religion and has also written extensively on sex, violence and sexuality.

Along the way, McBride has become known for her thoughtfulness in sorting through the implications of the choices made by reporters, editors, photographers and producers. She is currently a senior faculty member at the Poynter Institute in St. Petersburg, Florida, where she specializes in ethics, writing and storytelling. She leads its Sense-Making Project, backed by the Ford Foundation, to help citizens choose among the dizzying array of sources of news and information. Most recently, she's led Poynter's newest project as the ombudsman for sports cable giant ESPN.

Now, McBride writes, the emergence of the WikiLeaks project is forcing all journalists to confront fundamental questions about how they define their profession.

———————

To tell the truth, I've been all over the map when it comes to WikiLeaks. Since the site was first founded, I've told Time magazine that the Web site devoted to leaking confidential government documents was a good thing for journalists. I warned Mother Jones that WikiLeaks suffers from a "distorted sense of transparency," which I noted was bad for journalism. To the Associated Press, on the other hand, I characterized the collaboration between The New York Times and WikiLeaks as good for democracy. I told the public radio show "Marketplace," by contrast, that WikiLeaks was being a bit manipulative, just like a big corporation.

The very nature of WikiLeaks is hard to pin down for someone like me who came up through a conventional newsroom.

When the concept of Julian Assange's super-secret, document-leaking Web site initially bounced around the media world, most of us living through or studying the evolution of journalism dismissed it as a well-intentioned but overly trusting idea. If anyone can anonymously post supposedly secret documents, we reasoned, then corporations and governments will create fake documents in an attempt to create a fake reality. In response to that criticism, WikiLeaks created a vetting system by which its founder Julian Assange and a small staff would authenticate the documents.

But then Assange revealed an ulterior motive for creating WikiLeaks. He sought to build great public pressure on the U.S. government to end the wars in Iraq and Afghanistan, and politically damage the British and American politicians responsible for those wars. With that, WikiLeaks became a sticky topic for those of us who analyze the current and future health of journalism and media. Suddenly it wasn't just a site for posting documents. It was a site with an agenda.

At the Poynter Institute, we are charged with providing leadership for journalists as their practice and industry evolve. Part of my professional duty is to gauge how journalism—and by extension, democracy—is faring amid this information revolution. Stronger? Weaker? Holding steady? So when the reporters and producers call, we weigh in on the conversation.

Since WikiLeaks came on the scene, the public has been fascinated with the site's proper place in the journalistic constellation. But here, I believe, the public is actually wrestling with a bigger issue: What exactly constitutes journalism these days?

The curiosity makes sense. We live in a world where fewer than half of American households subscribe to a daily newspaper or watch the evening news, yet thanks to technology, citizens are more informed and engaged than ever.

Discerning mere information from real journalism is harder than it seems. Most citizens are comfortable with the idea that good journalism is critical to democracy, though they may argue vociferously over what constitutes good journalism. But the debate gets very confusing when we as a society can't agree on what journalism is.

To that end, WikiLeaks has become the icon both for all that's holy and all that's profane. To some, WikiLeaks is the organization that undermines national security and endangers the lives of hardworking soldiers and diplomats by indiscriminately publishing sensitive information. To others, it's the ultimate journalistic—and therefore democratic—tool, redistributing power by stealing secrets from those in control and sharing them with the world.

Even Bill Keller, the executive editor of The New York Times, got caught up in the unprecedented, larger-than-life nature of WikiLeaks in a January 2011 essay in The New York Times Magazine. "By the end of the year, the story of this wholesale security breach had outgrown the story of the actual contents of the secret documents and generated much breathless speculation that something—journalism, diplomacy, life as we know it—had profoundly changed forever."

Exactly what has changed is still unclear.

WikiLeaks and other quasi- and even pseudo-journalistic endeavors force those of us who tackle the meta-issues of the news business to confront the most fundamental question of all:

What is journalism?

In their book, "The Elements of Journalism," Bill Kovach and Tom Rosenstiel offer up what is, to my mind, the best working definition: "*The primary purpose of journalism is to provide citizens with the information they need to be free and self-governing.*"

Viewing WikiLeaks through that filter, it would be hard to argue that Assange's creation isn't journalism. Assange himself describes the purpose of his site as achieving the democratic good by revealing information that governments would keep secret.

Yet Assange has been both vague and inconsistent when explaining what he hopes to achieve. He speaks of journalism and democracy. But he also talks about his opposition to the U.S. wars in Iraq and Afghanistan. In a July 2010 interview before a TED audience, he came as close as he ever has to describing true democratic goals.

"What sort of information can achieve reform?" he responded when asked about the kind of information he's looking for. "And there's a lot of information. So, information that organizations are spending economic effort into concealing, that's a really good signal that when the information gets out, there's a hope of it doing some good. Because the organizations that know it best from the inside out are spending work to conceal it. That's what we've found in practice and that's what the history of journalism is."

That's a naive, overly simplistic analysis of how journalism works. Yet it is the foundation for much of the early journalistic success on the Internet. Give me a lever long enough, and a fulcrum on which to place it, the Greek physicist Archimedes is quoted as saying, and I will move the world. Give people the right kind of information about how the world around them works, and a place to voice their own thoughts about it, and power will shift to accommodate them.

Many of the sites that work like journalism post previously unavailable information so that consumers can make use of it. Take the Bed Bug Registry, a wildly successful database of user-generated information where renters and hotel guests can share their experiences with bedbugs. The site was created in 2007 as a side project by the computer programmer Maciej Ceglowski, after the unenviable inspiration of an encounter with the bedbugs in a San Francisco hotel. In 2010, as bedbugs became an epidemic in many U.S. cities, his site's traffic peaked at 50,000 unique visitors a day.

Another power-shifting site is LookBook, a social network for the fashion-conscious. Rather than waiting for fashion magazines to declare the next trends, LookBook members post their own photos, tagging their clothing and accessories with information that indicates their source. Members from all over the world "fan" each other and "hype" certain looks, adding a democratic layer to fashion trends.

WikiLeaks aspires to do the same thing, with loftier goals—to connect an audience directly with raw information, to enable people to take action. While the Bed Bug Registry inspires folks to find another hotel and the LookBook helps its users look cool, WikiLeaks in its most successful incarnation inspires citizens to hold corrupt (or morally corrupt) governments accountable.

In their simplest forms, however, such sites can be manipulated and provide content that is sometimes scattershot or unhelpful. LookBook is now overrun by fashion companies touting their own products. The Bed Bug Registry can be distorted by dishonest users, while a single industry dominates its advertising: pesticide products.

To avoid becoming an unwitting agent for corporate or government interests, WikiLeaks selectively posts documents, rather than allowing anyone to upload anything. When Assange & Co. made their decision to vet the information rather than simply allow a free exchange of information, they took the first step in moving WikiLeaks from social network to journalistic enterprise.

Once vetted and selected, as it turned out, that raw information was still problematic. Most of the time, the audience has to work too hard to make sense of it. Assange himself discovered this in 2007. The public and the press greeted his release of thousands of documents detailing Army purchases in Iraq and Afghanistan with silence. He had built a searchable database and verified the authenticity of the material, but hardly anyone used it. Too much work for too little payoff.

After that, Assange took additional steps away from posting mere information and moved toward the world of professional journalism, strategically partnering with professional newsrooms. He was further embracing the role of editor or curator, rather than information middleman. He even assumed the title editor in chief. In the spring of 2010, Assange and a core group of staff and supporters spent weeks editing a video of U.S. soldiers in an Apache helicopter gunning down 18 people, including children, innocent civilians and two journalists. (Reasonable critics later questioned his editing choices, claiming he distorted the facts in the name of furthering his own agenda, making the work more political spin than journalistic truth.) He debuted the video in front of a group of journalists gathered at the National Press Club in Washington, D.C., seeking maximum impact.

That same year he teamed up with journalists from The New York Times, The Guardian and Der Spiegel, granting them access to thousands of war documents and diplomatic communiqués. The partnerships resulted in two waves of stories, in July and November. (As The Times's Scott Shane writes previously in this book, Assange tried to expel The Times from the partnership, but The Guardian fully shared its materials with its colleagues in New York.)

But 2010 would also prove to be the year that Assange admitted, at least by his actions, that WikiLeaks could never produce true journalism on its own. Instead, as he demonstrated in his treatment of both the Apache helicopter video and the larger cache of classified documents, Assange appropriated some techniques from professional journalism but ultimately relied heavily on his journalistic partners to achieve the impact he desired.

Assange released the secret documents in order to "*provide citizens with the information they need to be free and self-governing,*" just as Rosenstiel and Kovach described. But he learned that information alone cannot get the job done. The key phrase in that definition is "information they need."

In order to become journalism, information must be organized into a coherent system for the intended recipient. Assange did that when he edited the video of the helicopter attack (and found himself judged by journalistic standards for editing out images that supported the notion that at least one of the intended targets was an insurgent with a rocket-propelled grenade launcher). Even after editing the video, however, he urged the mainstream press to distribute it more widely.

When it came to sifting through the 250,000 classified documents, however, the journalists at The Times, Der Spiegel and

The Guardian did the heavy lifting, selecting a fraction of the cables on which to focus and each publishing its own analysis.

What are the qualities and characteristics that elevate mere information to the vaunted status of journalism? How has Assange transformed his information portal into a journalistic outlet?

First by *editing* or *curation*. Journalists help the audience understand why certain information is important, by selectively delivering only the most meaningful stuff. Then by *amplification*. The Internet is often described as an echo chamber where statements and ideas simply bounce around in perpetual motion, propelled by repetition. Unless the information involves a celebrity, it is hard to gain enough momentum to rise above the din. When Assange tapped the three major mainstream news outlets for advance access to the documents, he did so to maximize volume and attention. It doesn't matter how great your information is, you either have a megaphone or you don't. Large mainstream newsrooms are trusted sources for a critical mass. That doesn't happen by accident. Assange needed to borrow their credibility as well as their distribution.

Many digital start-ups have become trusted sources for certain audiences—Perez Hilton on celebrity news, DeadSpin on sports. The same has happened on a smaller geographic level. Look at the Ann Arbor Chronicle, the West Seattle Blog or DallasSouth News, all sites that have gained credibility and critical mass for consumers with a hunger for news about specific areas.

The ability to amplify information is a result of doing journalism consistently over a period of time. It is perhaps the building block of "*information they need.*"

Of course there is a difference between Perez Hilton and the Ann Arbor Chronicle that further delineates a journalistic threshold. If it's journalism, the information provided must enable the recipient "*to be free and self-governing.*" As compelling as the latest celebrity affair may be, a report on it helps few people uphold their civic duties.

There are two additional critical qualities that characterize journalism in service of democracy, which Assange has yet to embrace. The most successful journalism transforms raw information into an *authoritative narrative*. That transformation can only occur when the individual crafting the narrative has *an independent loyalty to the truth*.

The stated primary purpose of WikiLeaks is to expose secrets and hold corrupt authorities accountable. Assange rightly determined in 2010 that his organization didn't possess the staff or the expertise to edit or amplify the vast quantity of documents they had received. But Der Spiegel, The Guardian and The New York Times demonstrated true skill and proficiency as they selected the actual stories they would tell from the trove of information.

Take The Guardian's interactive graphic detailing a single day (October 17, 2006) of civilian deaths, American deaths, car bombs, arrests and kidnappings in Iraq. Or consider The Times's tight narrative of the birth and death of the remote Combat Outpost Keating in Afghanistan. The professionals had the skill, competence and expertise to craft the narrative. And that narrative stood on its own because, regardless of newsroom politics, explicit (in the case of The Guardian) or perceived (The Times), the practitioners were independently loyal to their goal: telling the truth.

Assange and WikiLeaks are not capable of that level of independence. In his public statements, backed up by his actions, Assange has made it clear that his primary targets are political leaders in the United States and other Western nations involved in the wars in the Middle East. His singular focus creates a bias that undermines his stated mission.

Many observers believe that the WikiLeaks founders mostly care about pressuring the United States to end the wars by undermining covert efforts and exposing incompetence and abuse of power. It is a single-mindedness that blinds Assange to the truth, George Grant, of the Henry Jackson Foundation, a London-based foreign policy think tank, wrote in the London-based Daily Telegraph.

"In likening Western governments to Soviet ones, and comparing Western 'War Crimes' in Iraq and Afghanistan to those committed by al-Qaeda and the Taliban, Assange demonstrates a dangerous moral relativism that is shared by a worrying number of people, particularly on the anti-establishment Left," Grant wrote in December 2010.

Could Assange and his colleagues have done it any other way? Sure. They could have hired their own journalists. They did just that as they researched the Apache video, tracking down witnesses and the families of the children who were injured. If that became a standard operating procedure rather than an exception, WikiLeaks might grow into a journalistic endeavor. But it's not there yet.

The Times's Keller, who has insisted all along that Assange is a complicated source, not a journalistic partner, wrote, "Whether the arrival of WikiLeaks has fundamentally changed the way journalism is made, I will leave to others and to history. . . . Long before WikiLeaks was born, the Internet transformed the landscape of journalism, creating a wide-open and global market with easier access to audiences and sources, a quicker metabolism, a new infrastructure for sharing and vetting information and a diminished respect for notions of privacy and secrecy."

There is a contradiction at the heart of Assange's dilemma— and the question of how we categorize WikiLeaks. In order to achieve the true democratic impact Assange espouses, Wiki-

Leaks would have to move further away from its original vision of a social network for agenda-driven document dumpers and closer toward the journalistic roles of editing, amplifying and narrating with an independent loyalty to the truth. Like millions of Arabs and North Africans who protested against autocrats in early 2011, he might find that people gain power as they secure credible, verified information about those who rule. The new technology helped make that happen. But the old values endure.

How The New York Times Learned to Stop Worrying and Love the Blog

Jennifer 8. Lee

Jennifer 8. Lee distinguished herself at The New York Times in many ways—and not merely because her byline carries a numeric element in the middle. (The number 8 is associated with good luck in China.) She became known for her "conceptual scoop," a story that others didn't even recognize, such as the "man date," a dinner outing between platonic male friends. That one got her invited by the CIA to give a talk to analysts about recognizing patterns. She also wrote the book "Fortune Cookie Chronicles."

In her early 30s, after covering the Washington scene, tech issues and New York City politics, Lee took a buyout and explored the news business with a more entrepreneurial bent. After leaving The Times, she did work for the Knight Foundation and even advised WikiLeaks on the release of a controversial combat video from Iraq (though she had not seen the video).

During her years at The Times, Lee sought to help the paper reinvent itself, sometimes against its own traditions and instincts.

For years, the third-floor waiting area of the old New York Times building at 229 West 43rd featured a massive replica of the first page of the first edition of the newspaper. Dated Thursday, September 18, 1851, the newspaper back then was known as The New-York Daily Times. (I love the hyphen.) It was priced at one cent.

I must have walked by that replica thousands of times before I finally paused for a closer look. It was made up mostly of blurbs, many of them just a few sentences long. None was more than five paragraphs. The international news consisted of dispatches from Turkey, Bremen, Bavaria and Prussia, in most cases summarizing local publications rather than offering original reporting. The local New York City reporting was quite chatty, with headlines like "Disturbance by Rival Blacksmiths," "Run over by an Ice Cart," and "Women Poisoned."

Even non-news was news back then. A short dispatch titled "False Alarm" read: "Item gatherer failed to discover the first spark of the fire." And I was taken with a brief from another edition: "Not Dead.—Mr. John Overho, of Prince street, who was reported to be beyond all medical skill on Saturday, from the effect of coup de soleil, we are glad to learn is likely to recover."

But what struck me most that day, as I studied that front page, was a single thought.

This looks like a blog.

The New-York Daily Times was aggregated and chatty. It had flexible means of gathering information, and did not take an arm's-length relationship to its audience.

It reminded me that newspapers have evolved—and evolved again. The stentorian style and not-reported-here syndrome were not always the way.

My first Times job was as a college intern Web producer. I arrived just a few months after the article "The New York Times Introduces a Web Site" ran on January 22, 1996. So my first perspective on The Times came through a digital lens. The best perk was staking out jenny@nytimes.com as my e-mail address.

Back then, the front page of the site was a massive, image-mapped gif file, which could take an excruciating five minutes to load if you were overseas. But The Times was keen on maintaining its visual style. Since the Web was not mature enough to offer online publishers that kind of control, the paper's solution was to turn fonts into images. Web producers had to undertake painfully repetitive hand coding, almost like a high-tech assembly line. So I, like others, taught myself some basic perl script to automate some of the processes.

Four years later, in 2000, I started my full-time reporting career at The New York Times as a technology writer. I still recall having to define the term "blog" to the readers as "short for web log," which, we hastened to explain, "often compiles entries chronologically." By the end of the 2004 election, the need for that shorthand was largely over. Within another three years, The Times was rolling out blogs in earnest. That idea would once have made many in the newsroom wince: most blogs were initially considered more driven by opinion than by reporting.

City Room, the new metro blog where I worked, felt like a little start-up within The Times. The agility of blogs really landed on the managers' radar when the City Room post on the death of the actor Heath Ledger in 2008 racked up 1.78 million page views. It was the most viewed article ever in the history of The Times Web site at that point—in large part because The Times blog was the first news outlet to report his death (thanks to the speed of my then colleague Sewell Chan), giving us a head start on the story and a destination for worldwide interest.

Since stepping back from the daily newspaper churn, I've devoted a good deal of my energy personally and professionally to thinking about the infrastructure needed to create accountability journalism in the new media world.

Newspaper culture most resembles that of the military or hospitals. Papers are designed for a systematized rapid response, optimized for crisis situations. The structure is command and control, even though on the reporter level it doesn't always feel that way.

The most vivid example of this occurred on September 11, 2001. I had been at The Times just nine months, and apparently looked so youthful that my coworkers still often asked where I was going to college. On that day of tragedy, the machinery of The New York Times snapped into place to respond to an event that unfolded before the vast majority of us had even set foot in the office. The choreography spanned the metro, business, foreign, national, Washington, photo and graphics desks. Even our culture reporters were recruited to do on-the-ground reporting. In the chaos, we found order. After all, journalists—like firefighters and police officers—are people who run toward a crisis. That crisis triggered a miraculous, months-long marathon.

But that kind of synchronicity came with a trade-off: a dependency on established process and culture. And like any body with a hardy immune system, it often rejects new presences as foreign.

For The Times, adapting its processes to the new realities of an interconnected information ecosystem requires shedding or altering the outdated parts of an organization's sensibility while keeping its essential principles. And that Herculean task involves qualities on which few newsroom leaders were evaluated as they ascended the editorial and managerial ranks.

As one programmer in a news start-up described the challenge to me: it's not the technology, it's the people. It's a trick to find people who have enough gravitas to have credibility in the world of legacy media, but are fluent in the dynamics of technological reality.

After leaving The Times, I downloaded and read Clayton M. Christiansen's classic book, "The Innovator's Dilemma." I paused when I realized the scenarios he was describing in the hardware industry mirrored what was happening to legacy media outlets.

The dominant players were structurally unable to transition in the face of disruptive technology because their strengths—brand, processes, quality—became their weaknesses.

In our case, news blogs were upstarts. They took smaller profit margins and embraced flexible standards on how to gather the news—and what and when to publish. Those choices—unburdened by weighty tradition—gave them a foothold that allowed them to move upmarket into the mainstream. They eagerly experimented, took risks and forgave failure.

The established brands, because of their cost structures and their focus on brand and reliability, were slow to enter new markets. Once they did, they struggled to be nimble enough to catch up.

For the legacy media organizations, the very things that created their record of credibility—like not publishing something until they are confident it is true—run counter to a world where speed becomes a competitive advantage. The caution about posting an item about a developing event, sometimes just as rumor, on The Times Web site until it had been independently confirmed ensured the paper's standards are secure. It largely prevented The Times from circulating uncertain facts, but it also meant sometimes readers had learned about breaking news somewhere else.

That fierce devotion to the newspaper's brand pervaded all departments, across the organization. I wrote a Sunday Style piece about the "man date," the way in which many straight men socialize, one on one, without the crutch of professional sports or business. When the story generated interest from Hollywood screenwriters, a lawyer for The Times helped me sell the movie option based on the idea of the "man date," which I appreciated. But she told me her highest concern was "protecting the brand" of the institution. I tried to puzzle out how you would even calculate the impact of the insecurity of heterosexual men on The Times's brand.

Inevitably, questions and even tensions arose when the ingrained Times culture rubbed against emerging digital sensibilities. For years, getting a story published on page A1 of The New York Times—the holy grail for most reporters—was a protracted ritual that involved two meetings with a large cast involving increasingly senior editors. The process by which the stories were pitched and debated took hours over numerous meetings across all the different departments.

In comparison, the process of getting a story onto the home page of The New York Times Web site often involved lobbying a 20-something gatekeeper, generally via instant message. The editors of blogs, who had no guarantee their content would even appear in the paper, were strategic about what we would lobby for—and when to do it. The right home page "refer" could send page views soaring.

When I started working on the City Room blog, I asked to see the traffic numbers, a standard metric for any Web site. I was told reporters weren't allowed to see traffic numbers because we didn't want to become too much like television, too ratings-obsessed. Indeed, it made us wince when Gawker tied compensation to page views. But those figures can provide a real-time evaluation of how useful our readers found what we posted. (A little reporting paid off: I found someone on the business side to give me an account for the Web stats, through a lead I met on the elevator.)

Now and then, The Times also struggles with meshing its standards and those widely accepted elsewhere. I was told more than once never to link to Wikipedia within New York Times blog posts, even though Wikipedia is sometimes the best (and indeed sometimes the only) resource on a topic. Some Wikipedia entries are flawed, but many are very good and there is a reason why they generally rank so highly on Google searches. Rather than having a reporter or an editor assess our links on a case-by-case basis, a blanket edict was put into effect.

A friend who works as a copy editor there has tried for years to launch a collaborative wiki version of "The New York Times Manual of Style and Usage," which could allow for much more agility and knowledge sharing on continuing, breaking news stories. The software was built and the entries were ready, but the wiki has been stymied within The Times bureaucracy.

Yet elsewhere, the culture was shifting. Talking Points Memo helped change the tone in its persistent coverage of the U.S. attorneys' firing scandal with its willingness to say: This is what we know. This is what we don't know. Can you, the audience, help us? The pieces came together in large part because of audience expertise and examination of legal documents. And the story kept being propelled forward, ultimately leading to the resignation of U.S. Attorney General Alberto Gonzales.

Slowly, reporting practices reinvented and rethought outside The Times started to reverberate meaningfully within the institution. The vitality and prominence of the Lede blog, by Robert Mackey, with a focus on breaking global news stories—documenting in real time developments concerning an earthquake in Haiti or protests throughout the Middle East—show The Times's willingness to draw upon and promote high-quality information from elsewhere on the Internet.

The Times has sought to maintain its dedication to quality while encouraging a more dynamic metabolism by creating a five-editor rapid response copy desk under Patrick LaForge that swoops in to handle blog posts and other content across the Web site for the various sections. Often they clean up each piece to meet The Times's more stringent standards after it's been posted.

But journalists' competitive sensibilities do help drive change. The metro desk broke the Eliot Spitzer prostitution scandal in 2008 with a Web-first mentality; despite the lamentation of at least one veteran editor who said scoops should be saved for the print edition, the paper stayed with a Web-first mentality, breaking one development after another online. The Times's coverage—both online and print—was cited by the judges who awarded the paper a Pulitzer Prize.

The twin imperatives of news on the Web have long been immediacy and intimacy. News organizations know how to break news, so immediacy has been the easier of the two to adopt. But the quality of intimacy has proved harder for these organizations, as established titles—as brands—to grapple with. Too chatty and there isn't enough gravitas. Too stiff and users aren't engaged.

For a long time, it felt somewhat gauche for Times journalists to create their own Web sites because it was seen as self-promotional, unless they had a book coming out. In 2003, a friend bought me jennifer8lee.com and jenny8lee.com for my birthday but I sat on them for years, uncomfortable doing anything with them. When I created a blog for my book in 2007, I purposely chose to put it at fortunecookiechronicles.com.

Twitter, a platform both intimate and immediate, ultimately released journalists' individual voices from the constriction of their host institutions. Its emergence made Times management focus on the potential gains to be enjoyed through social media.

The original @nytimes Twitter feed was set up by a newsroom engineer named Jake Harris, who wanted a way to get the RSS feeds on his cell phone. He ran the automated feed out of a computer under his desk, until it lost power one weekend and he got an e-mail informing him that a consumer had complained. From then on, it became an official feed. (Times folks will often reserve digital rights on behalf of the institution. In fact, nyt.com was registered by technology reporter John Markoff around 1991, before the World Wide Web came into being and nytimes.com was registered.)

Journalists are ideal Twitter users. They generally have something interesting to say, often original or newsy. And they are recognizable both as individuals and personalities.

Many of us signed up for Twitter out of curiosity in mid-2007. It felt like stepping into a cocktail party where you didn't know anyone, so it took a while for many of us to return.

Once we did, we discovered we had a way to constantly update our own voices on the Internet. The 140-character length focused our thinking to a far more specific point than our lengthier bylined articles, but the links back to our own articles gave it a professionally justifiable purpose.

And in this case, activity bubbling up organically from the newsroom merged with top-down strategy in The Times newsroom.

In early 2009, the top leadership of The Times newsroom sent invitations to newsroom staff to submit new ideas to generate revenue. That alone was a sign that crisis had opened management up to new processes. In response, I wrote a memo about Twitter, which was circulated among editors. Jonathan Landman, then deputy managing editor, announced the creation of a social media editor, a role filled by Jennifer Preston, a significant statement about these new communications tools. But the early Twitter feeds created by Jake Harris and a young marketing employee, Soraya Darabi, had set the stage for a strong Times social presence. The Times now maintains over 100 Twitter accounts, not including those of the journalists themselves, for its blogs, sections and key topics of interest.

If you think of legacy newspapers as department stores—with all kinds of news available behind a single storefront—the future of news is looking more and more like a mall. A single complex aggregates a lot of niche products sold under separate brands—some favoring quality, others volume. That targeted branding is useful in a world where our content is disaggregated and reassembled via Twitter and Facebook feeds. The micro-brands can have their own Twitter accounts, Facebook pages and YouTube channels. This aggregated mall model is already peeking out (some more successfully executed than others), and not only thanks to AOL's acquisition of the Huffington Post and TechCrunch. In the two years since I left, The Times has accelerated its drive to showcase micro-brands in blogs such as the City Room (about New York City), the Caucus (politics), Well (personal health) and the revamped DealBook (on the financial markets).

Few readers would click to "like" The Times's national section on Facebook. But they do become Facebook fans of the Caucus or DealBook. And in the process, The Times has served up evidence it recognizes the strength and value of treating individual reporters and features as micro-brands.

This is a noticeable change from my early days at The Times, when the reporters reflexively deferred to the institution. It was considered unsavory to appear on television too much, or otherwise be perceived as self-promotional. But a few years ago The New York Times communications department started calling reporters to book them for television and radio interviews, and the marketing department started to create Twitter accounts and Facebook pages for many of its reporters.

A lot has happened since The New-York Daily Times first reported on Mr. Overho's "coup de soleil." The newspaper's dedication to quality, and the talented people exemplifying that dedication, persist. But the news has changed. The people reporting, editing and presenting that news have changed. The way readers receive the news has changed.

And so, too, has The Times.

PART II

THE TECTONIC PLATES SHIFT

The Deal from Hell

James O'Shea

James O'Shea was a reporter's reporter, first at The Des Moines Register and then at The Chicago Tribune, where he rose through the ranks to become managing editor. In 2006 he surprised many of his colleagues by agreeing to head west to lead their larger sister paper, The Los Angeles Times, as editor in chief. His tenure there was brief: the Tribune Company's new owners forced out O'Shea because he resisted additional cuts to the newsroom budgets.

He is now editor in chief of the Chicago News Cooperative, a small not-for-profit outfit focusing on local and regional affairs that he helped to create.

This chapter is excerpted from his forthcoming book about the Tribune Company, "The Deal from Hell." "In many respects," O'Shea writes, "the Tribune Company's plight is unique and far more complex than the dire situation that faces other newspapers and media organizations around the country and world. But in many ways, it also represents the stark reality of the battle facing those interested in the future of the news."

The conventional wisdom is that newspapers—and by that I mean the credible, edited information they deliver, not just the paper and ink—fell into a death spiral because of forces unleashed by declining circulations and the migration of readers to the Internet.

But the Internet and declining circulations didn't kill newspapers, any more than long stories, skimpy attention spans or arrogant journalists did. What is killing a system that brings reliably edited news and information to readers' doorsteps every morning for less than the cost of a cup of coffee is the way that the people who run the industry have *reacted* to those forces. The lack of investment, the greed, incompetence, corruption, hypocrisy and downright arrogance of people who put their interests ahead of the public's, are responsible for the state of the newspaper industry today.

I had a front-row seat to the drama, both as a longtime reporter and as an editor at The Chicago Tribune and The Los Angeles Times. In the fall of 2006, Tribune Company executives asked me to leave my job as managing editor running The Chicago Tribune newsroom to become editor of The Los Angeles Times. In normal circumstances, being named editor of a storied paper would have been a capstone to a successful career. But these were not normal times. The Los Angeles Times newsroom had become ground zero in a saga that pitted editors of newspapers against their owners and Wall Street patrons.

Of course, I had doubts about entering such a poisonous atmosphere charged with raw emotions, wounded pride and barely concealed contempt for anyone from Chicago. But my grandfather, a born storyteller nicknamed "Sawdust," had taught me early on the power of a good narrative to overcome adversity. I had a good story. I was first and foremost a journalist, someone who had represented other journalists well and was not afraid to challenge authority. I was a newsman who would try to solve the huge problems facing The Times without diminishing the quality or integrity of a great newspaper. I could not pass up the honor and challenge of being editor of The Los Angeles Times. So I took the job, hopelessly entwining my story and my fate with the narrative of a mega-merger that would go bad, one that would play a signature role in the collapse of an entire industry. For better or worse, I became eyewitness and participant in "the deal from hell."

* * *

Several years before making "the deal from hell," the Tribune Company of Chicago had made a stop in purgatory by acquiring the Times Mirror Company of Los Angeles. The largest newspaper merger in history started with a meeting of two single-minded executives in 1999. John Madigan, the CEO of the Tribune Company, had set up a private meeting at a San Diego hotel with Mark Hinckley Willes, his counterpart at Times Mirror, during a media industry conference.

On the surface the two men could not have been more different. Tall, imposing and impeccably dressed, Madigan walked through the lobby of the Hotel Del Coronado as he always enters a room, like an astronaut approaching a space shuttle. Viewed by Wall Street and company insiders as a master technician, he had risen from the company's chief financial officer to its top executive.

Sitting upstairs in his room, above the din of the industry chatter, Willes had naively suspected nothing of Madigan's call. With neatly groomed silver hair, an easy smile and a melodious voice, Willes, a devout Mormon, brought to Times Mirror a mixture of William Randolph Hearst and Gordon Hinckley, Willes' uncle and the president and prophet who led the Mormon Church through a period of global expansion. Willes had a Ph.D. in economics from Columbia and, at 35, had become the youngest person ever named to head a district bank of the Federal Reserve, later spending 15 years at General Mills before becoming head of Times Mirror.

Yet the two men had something in common: they had driven their respective companies' earnings into the stratosphere. But the sky-high stock prices and fat returns they delivered for Wall Street obscured an alarming trend. Newspaper classified advertising was sinking in quicksand as publishers across the nation struggled to gain and retain readers. For their part, the journalists turned a blind eye to problems in their own industry, thanks at least in part to the time-honored wall between newsrooms and the business side of newspapers erected to maintain the integrity of the news.

In the early 1990s, Madigan's predecessor, Charles Brumback, had tried to interest big publishers in the New Century Network, a consortium of America's nine top newspaper companies that would create a national digital news and information network, for which customers would pay. In return, they would have access to a full range of national newspaper content and services online. But industry leaders preferred to ignore the Internet, fearing it would damage their existing business. Eventually their internecine squabbles destroyed the initiative.

By 1999, Madigan wanted to take a bold step of his own. By merging the two companies, Madigan envisioned a media powerhouse with a print and broadcast advertising scale and breadth that could reach 18 of the nation's top 30 markets, including TV stations, newspapers and budding Internet sites in Los Angeles, New York and Chicago. The combined entity would be the nation's third largest media company; it would own America's best collection of quality newspapers, boasting a combined daily circulation of 3.6 million with television stations that reached an additional 38.4 million U.S. households. Madigan and others suggested that the new company would offer "national footprint, local reach," a showcase for the kind of *convergence* that media executives held out as their salvation.

As much as the prospect of acquisition by the bottom line–driven Tribune Company scared journalists at The Los Angeles Times, the idea intrigued those of us at The Tribune, where I was a senior news editor. The largest newspaper between the coasts, The Tribune never enjoyed the respect afforded papers like The New York Times or The Los Angeles Times, even though the paper routinely delivered superb enterprise journalism to its readers, with two dozen foreign bureaus and a sterling Washington report. There were various reasons for the media cold shoulder, including the challenge of living down the reputation of someone like "the Colonel"—the legendary late Tribune publisher Robert McCormick, whose use of the paper to promote his personal and political agendas stained The Tribune for decades.

But the main reasons for the dismissive treatment of The Tribune had to do with geography, status and power. I hoped that The Tribune, by acquiring The Los Angeles Times, would gain the power and stature necessary to give voice to the Midwest and create a platform to showcase our outstanding journalism.

* * *

Tribune executives and the Chandler family, which controlled Times Mirror, were so eager to ink a deal with Tribune that they pushed out Willes to make it happen. Yet the deal proved a tremendous overreach. Los Angeles resisted Chicago. The company's foothold in New York proved less robust than promised. And the company had not grappled with fundamental changes transforming the industry.

As the larger Tribune Company's stock value flagged, another larger-than-life character—if small in physical stature—stepped in to take control. Sam Zell was a diminutive, balding, elfish-looking, 65-year-old man with gray hair and a beard. I saw him first when he stepped off his large personal jet. By this time I was the editor in Los Angeles. He ranked number 52 on the Forbes list of the 400 richest Americans and had a personal fortune estimated at $4.5 billion, but you never would have guessed it from his appearance. He wore his signature jeans, an open-collared striped shirt and a rumpled blue jacket.

The essence of the deal Zell used to take over Tribune required it to borrow enough money to buy all of the stock owned by the Chandlers, the McCormick Trust, employees and other shareholders and take the company private—that is, remove its stock from public markets. It would become a nonprofit company technically owned by Tribune employees and would be exempt from federal income taxes. The idea would saddle the company with about $12 billion to $13 billion in debt, a staggering sum to mortals but not such a big deal to a real estate tycoon who loved to operate with other people's money.

Zell didn't seem too concerned that the debt would break the company. He had planned a major role at the company for Randy Michaels, a former shock jock he had met when he took over a Cincinnati radio company in the 1990s.

A trusted Zell financial adviser, William Pate, had devised a blueprint for the company. Pate had urged Zell to remove not just Tribune CEO Dennis FitzSimons but numerous other members of his executive team whom he criticized for rushing to close the deal, concerned only about the seven-figure bonuses they'd receive. He recommended meeting with former Chicago Tribune editor Jack Fuller about the idea of recruiting him to a new board, a move that would signal journalism's place in the pie. He suggested sharply downsizing the centralized corporate staff at the Tribune Tower. He also suggested meeting with California billionaires Ron Burkle and David Geffen, who had made noise about trying to buy The Los Angeles Times in the past, to assess the seriousness of their interest.

Michaels drafted a plan, too. In nine pages of bullet points, he reflected a purge mentality: "Identify change leaders and resisters within Tribune, promote and eliminate as appropriate" and seek out people who would "drink the Kool-aid." Michaels sought a culture change: "Begin the process of creating products focused on consumer interest and demand as opposed to some idea of what the citizens ought to know. It's not what they need; it's what they'll read, what they'll watch, what they'll click on, and what they want delivered to the deck of their cell phone."

In his plan, Michaels disparaged Tribune newspapers as "staid, grandfatherly and dated" publications holding the company back, although he gave no hint of how he'd engineer change. Finally, he suggested they conduct a road show. Meet, shake hands with and answer the questions of as many team members as possible. Journalists and The Tribune took themselves too seriously for Michaels' money. In his report, he said they should "have fun."

Zell sided with Michaels.

Although I didn't know about plans for a road show, a preview came to Los Angeles after Pate called and said Zell had been asked to meet with a prominent group of Los Angeles citizens worried about what was going on at the paper, including the late Warren Christopher, the former secretary of state and probably the only high-level member of the Los Angeles community who could rally the disparate political, commercial and cultural factions of Los Angeles.

Christopher and his group had been quite supportive, urging me to stand by my public statements that I would not let the paper deteriorate. They believed that a first-class city needed a first-class newspaper. "We view you as someone who we hope will hold the line and maintain the paper's stature," Christopher told me. So I worked with L.A. Times publisher David Hiller on a plan to stage a lunch at a large room that was once Dorothy Chandler's personal apartment at the newspaper's offices.

A few weeks later, Zell showed up at The Times for the lunch, casually dressed as ever. "I was going to wear a suit and tie," he told the guests, "but I decided not to because I wanted you to see me the way I am." About two dozen women and men sitting around the large U-shaped table seemed charmed at his folksy manner. His questioners came from the world of politics, business, culture and film, men and women of accomplishment who cared about their community and its newspaper.

Over dessert, when Christopher, the gray eminence, spoke, he diplomatically told Zell of the group's concerns about cuts at the newspaper, particularly rumors of cuts in The Los Angeles Times foreign bureaus. "You know, Sam, we view our community as the gateway to the Pacific and we think foreign coverage is quite important."

Without missing a beat Zell shot back, "You know, Warren, I don't give a fuck what you think. What I give a fuck about is what David Hiller here thinks, because from now on he's in charge of this newspaper, not some bureaucrat in Chicago."

The room fell silent and all eyes turned to Christopher in his tailored blue suit, French cuff shirt and tasteful tie, exactly the kind of wardrobe that Zell and his team disparaged. "Well, Sam," Christopher replied, "we appreciate your frankness."

As Zell and I later walked to the Globe Lobby in The Times where his driver was to pick him up, Zell grabbed my tie and said, "What's with this?" I replied that I wanted him to see me the way I came to work every day and that I was sure he would not want me to dress down just for him. He smiled, pulled out a cigarette and left for the airport.

At The Los Angeles Times, Zell, Michaels and their team imposed harsh newsroom cutbacks. They slashed the amount of space devoted to news and eliminated at least 300 newsroom jobs, taking the staff down to fewer than 600 journalists. Times editors masked some of the cuts with a relatively smart redesign of the paper and continued to invest what resources they could in their Web site.

The debt Zell loaded on Tribune proved untenable as the economy tightened. Ironically, thanks to the temporary respite of bankruptcy court, The Times no longer had to cough up much of the cash Tribune needed to repay the crushing debt Zell had piled onto the company. But the markets served by The Los Angeles Times had been hit particularly hard by the subprime mortgage mess, and ad revenues plunged.

Before long, The Chicago Tribune began to resemble a splashy tabloid. The paper still contained serious news, but it was usually relegated to stripped-down wire reports on inside pages. When one Tribune editor pitched a story on the city's troubled public housing program for page one, Jane Hirt, the managing editor, re-jected it for not being in the paper's demographic, an editor at the meeting recounted. Representatives from the newspaper's mar-keting department started "helping" editors select news coverage, and a far more repressive atmosphere took root in the newsroom.

Many decent, committed and talented journalists remain on the staff of The Chicago Tribune, and they continue to pursue great journalism, particularly investigative series on local issues. As a reader, I felt the paper's news judgment became sophomoric, parochial and superficial. In January 2011, when Chicago's own President Obama gave a moving speech in Phoenix, Arizona, af-ter Congresswoman Gabrielle Giffords had been shot in the head by a disturbed young man, The Chicago Tribune barely men-tioned the story on its front page.

Under Zell and Michaels, the company tolerated a fraternity house atmosphere for more than two years until David Carr, a media reporter for The New York Times, exposed the lurid conduct and cronyism in a front-page story that shamed the board into seeking Michaels' resignation. He resigned on October 22, 2010. But many of the people he had placed in charge of the newspaper remain in their jobs; Michaels' team collectively has pocketed more than $50 million in management bonuses.

Tribune editor Gerould Kern and the board publicly expressed dismay at the conduct exposed by Carr and ordered his reporters to cover the situation aggressively. But as the Chicago media columnist Robert Feder pointed out, "Not one of them spoke up about what was going on inside their own company until The New York Times slapped it on its front page 12 days ago."

* * *

When I speak to citizens in Chicago and elsewhere, people ask me, Will we still have newspapers? Of course, we will have newspapers. Newspapers today continue to create great journalism, too. But what great journalism surfaces tends to be episodic, not a systematic examination of significant issues.

Let's not kid ourselves, either. Newspapers and broadcast outlets will find it progressively harder to finance the delivery of high-quality news. We are moving into a world where someone wealthy enough to pay $2 a day and $6 on Sunday for The New York Times or $18,000 to $20,000 per year for a dedicated terminal from Bloomberg News will get high-quality news, as good as or perhaps better than ever.

But gone will be the days when everyone can get the same quality of news delivered to his or her doorstep every day for a fraction of what it actually costs. And that is a fundamental change in our society, the implications of which we've not yet absorbed. Someone has to find a new model based on new economics.

The real question is, Will we still have journalism—not aggregated content gathered to foster ad sales—but hard-hitting, time-consuming investigative and analytical reporting about the major issues of the day?

I helped found the Chicago News Cooperative because I believe we must have that kind of journalism. Throughout my career, I have seen a world without dogged reporting. Time and again, I've seen the press seized and silenced by soldiers marching in the clouds of dust stirred by the despot's boot. We cannot allow apathy and indifference to become the soldiers of silence in America. The answer is out there, perhaps in a fledgling not-for-profit operation like the CNC or one of dozens like it springing up across the land, or perhaps in the head of some entrepreneur. An audience for serious news is out there. It is small, discerning and willing to pay if the information is good and the reporting is solid.

It is out there. And when someone finds it, it will be one hell of a story.

SEVEN

Panel Discussion: Who Should Pay for Journalism?

David Folkenflik, Chana Joffe-Walt, Emily Bell, and Gordon Crovitz

On March 28, 2011, The New York Times installed a new fee structure charging people who read more than 20 articles online each month. On the same day, a discussion took place focused on the question, Who should pay for the news?

Participants included Emily Bell, director of the Tow Center for Digital Journalism at Columbia Graduate School of Journalism, and Gordon Crovitz, cofounder and CEO of Press+, which helps set pricing models that publishers can use to charge online readers.

Each has thought hard about such questions. Bell was formerly director of digital content for Guardian News & Media in the U.K., which offers the news digitally for free, while Crovitz was president of Dow Jones Online and then publisher of The Wall Street Journal; he oversaw his paper's Web site and the creation of its paywall.

David Folkenflik conducted the conversation with his colleague Chana Joffe-Walt of NPR's "Planet Money." An edited transcript follows.

Folkenflik: In some ways, the modern Web started [for] media consumers in '96. What was the thinking [about pricing] at the time?

Crovitz: There was really never any doubt but that there would be some charge for access to The Wall Street Journal in an electronic form. At that time, the challenge was, what medium would work to distribute [the paper] electronically to a massive number of consumers. The Wall Street Journal opted for a paywall—that was the technology that was available. A paywall means you really had to pay to get access to anything from The Wall Street Journal.

[Then] in the early 2000s, 2003–2004, I suppose, we had begun to doubt the wisdom of the harsh paywall. Some casual readers might become more loyal and engaged readers at some point, and so, since the technology didn't allow us to change the paywall, we had to do it almost manually.

Joffe-Walt: What was the way that you were thinking about who your [reader] was and what you were providing them in 1996?

Crovitz: I think in a way it was driven primarily by traditional journalistic ideas and the most core journalistic idea is, How do you know that something that you are doing is being done well unless readers tell you so? And the traditional way, at least in print, was you charge them something.

Joffe-Walt: And if they pay, then you are doing something right?

Crovitz: Correct. And if you are not charging them anything, by what metric do you measure the quality of the journalism? So the idea always was to charge something, even to a print subscriber—to charge much less than a print subscription. Consumers know that digital delivery is much less expensive.

I think there was also a sense, certainly at the beginning and really throughout, that advertising alone was a very weak reed on which to depend for quality journalism. The ad revenues over time, I am confident, will continue to decline and will not support quality journalism. There will have to be other revenue streams. And the most typical one has always been letting the most loyal, avid readers help cover the expense.

Folkenflik: So Emily Bell, I see in front of me the nation's leading news organization, which is of course The Onion, which today put out a story headlined "NYTimes.com plan to charge people money for consuming goods, services called 'bold business move.'"

The key quote is: "The whole idea of an American business trying to make a profit off a product it's hired professionals to create on a daily basis is truly a brave and intrepid strategy. It is almost as if The New York Times is equating itself with a business trying to function in a capitalistic society."

Why was Gordon Crovitz's and The Wall Street Journal's approach to the idea of both measuring what readers value and also obtaining money to fund the journalism and the cost of what they do, why was that not the right approach for The Guardian and for other news organizations?

Bell: At the time when I was at The Guardian we were looking at how to monetize and support online content. We actually had our own paywalls for a short time in 2002–2003, around things like crosswords.

We noticed several things, one of which was they were incredibly difficult and expensive to operate. Second, your audience tended to dwindle to 1 percent of what it would be if it was free content. And thirdly it was, in my mind also, this real imperative to make use of the leverage that the Web gave you and what the Web gives you is an unlimited reach. It gives you international audience.

The Guardian is a very small niche newspaper, even by the U.K. standards. And we were in a very different position to Gordon because we were a [not-for-profit] trust, which means that it doesn't have shareholders, it didn't have share of profit in the same way. But what it did need to do is maintain relevance to an audience.

We felt advertising revenues and allied revenue streams which came from having a bigger presence in the world were a much more sensible way for us to proceed. It is much easier to monetize around high-quality monopoly content of the type that The Journal has and the Financial Times has [as publications with a business and finance emphasis]—particularly when the audience that you are pointing at is a rich audience, which either tends to have expense accounts or credit cards. That is not true of all places.

Folkenflik: Your former colleagues are able to present the journalism to a much broader audience, but at the same time it doesn't sound as if they have solved the nut of how to come up with a profitable budget plan.

Bell: What I would say in our defense is that I think we built digital revenues in a much more effective way than many people did. Towards 30 percent of all revenue at The Guardian were digital at the time that I left.

But it is not a panacea and it is something that we are all discovering now is that there have been long periods where news provision has not been profitable.

In the end The Onion kind of nailed it in a way, which is that it's not a rational business and it performs a function in society, which is not always monetizable.

Joffe-Walt: When you made that shift online, how did that change your relationship with your readers?

Bell: The huge shock for anybody who has come from, if you like, a legacy media business is to realize that you don't really have a relationship with your readers. You just think you do.

And suddenly you had a one-to-one relationship with your audience who could participate and talk back to you. And that was I think an astonishing moment, the first time you truly realized that the genie is not going back in the bottle.

Joffe-Walt: Except they are not paying you any more in that model. That is somebody who is talking back and forth with you, but might not be paying you.

Bell: No, but the traditional model for broadsheet papers in the U.K. was that 70 percent of your revenue really came from advertising, 30 percent came from subscriptions, or circulation as we would call it. And that 30 percent was not nearly enough to pay for the physical product, the actual paper.

Joffe-Walt: But they are your customers, right? It is like they shift from being your customers to being something else.

Bell: You are not selling something to them, but you have a more direct relationship to them and they are proselytizing and spreading your content and your journalism [online] and sometimes participating in it in a way that they weren't before. Now obviously that means that you are not making money from them, but you are getting value from them in a completely different way.

Folkenflik: It leads us to "should versus will." I interviewed [Times publisher] Arthur Sulzberger Jr. a couple of weeks ago, and he says people should pay The New York Times for journalism that is dangerous and expensive to perform. And the question is, Will people pay for this?

Crovitz: I don't think that "should versus will" is the right split. I think the right split is religious beliefs versus data.

Folkenflik: Say what you mean by that.

Crovitz: I think that from the beginning of the Web people focused on Stewart Brand's comment that "information wants to be free." They forgot the second half of his observation, which is "it also wants to be expensive." In other words, in an information age, information is really important to people, whether it is what is going on in the local schools or politics or whatever it might be.

So we now have [data] from several dozen news organizations that Press Plus is supporting with their metered model. And we will soon have from The New York Times data on what works and what does not work. A metered model [means] people can get a certain number of articles free, after which they are asked to pay for unlimited access.

[Papers with meters] have the same experience, which is, they don't lose any online advertising revenue; they don't lose any readers month to month; and they are on a path to converting between 5 and 10 percent of their Web users to pay for unlimited access. The reason they don't lose advertising is they are only withdrawing a certain, quite small percentage of page views through this metered model.

People will come back the next month. If they get to the meter, they decide not to subscribe that much that month, they are happy to come back the next month. Publishers don't lose traffic.

Folkenflik: People aren't turned off?

Crovitz: People are not turned off.

Folkenflik: So you had some thoughts on what this would mean for The Times and its metered structure—$15 a month for straight Web access, all the way up to $35 every four weeks for the Web and iPad.

Crovitz: On a sort of back of the envelope [calculation], I think it is highly likely that The New York Times will earn about $100 million in incremental new revenue without losing any online revenue and without losing the size of the audience.

So the journalistic concern of being out of the debate, which is a quite legitimate issue, that won't happen. They won't lose ad revenue.

Let's say $20 is the average [monthly cost]. At about 400,000 subscribers that would be $100 million in revenue. And 400,000 is a very small percentage of their visitors. They would say that they have about 40 million unique visitors a month.

Folkenflik: Emily, I've got to say: I follow your Twitter feed. That is not where you are coming down on this.

Bell: No. I hear the figures and as Gordon quite rightly says, it is all down to data now. We'll actually see who is right in this. The broader experience from the point of view of the U.K. market, Rupert Murdoch's The Times of London has already put up a paywall. Now, it is not as porous as The New York

Times's paywall, but it saw a very dramatic drop-off in readership and subscription rates to much lower than 1 percent.

Crovitz: I think that on the traditional paywall, which is sort of the old-fashioned approach, in which you really do cut people off, you will find very significant drops in visitors and ad revenue.

This is to me the beauty of the "freemium" approach with the metered approach, where publishers can use the technology to identify just those people that are willing to pay for unlimited access, but then let everybody else in to a considerably large degree.

Folkenflik: But [Emily], you are not feeling the love for freemium either?

Bell: No, not really, because I think that unfortunately few are very hardheaded about this. I think that The New York Times does great journalism. It does some of the best journalism in the world. But it also does a lot of journalism that other people are doing and putting out there for free, and I don't see that the BBC is going to change its charging structure. I don't see that NPR is necessarily going to change its charging structure. Or CNN, or any one of the numbers of other organizations doing this.

It might not be New York Times journalism, but there is a lot of high-quality journalism out there at the moment, which is freely available on the Web—and which I simply don't see going away.

Crovitz: I think first of all the freemium model has been fairly well proven in some other industries. NPR member stations have been pursuing freemium for many years where about 10 percent of active listeners to NPR stations become supporting members. They get the coffee mug and all the good feelings about supporting NPR. So there is nothing really new in the concept of freemium.

In a technologically driven world where spreading of content is so easy and inexpensive, it's great to have large numbers of visitors. The only way really to monetize that audience most effectively, though, is to find the people who might be willing to pay for a more premium experience, such as unlimited access.

And the freemium model acknowledges this. It acknowledges that different consumers have different feelings about each brand and very few people will subscribe to more than a very small handful of news sites that they rely on the most. But they'll continue to access a lot of others.

Folkenflik: You talk about people being willing to pay in the freemium model, you point to NPR as an example. It strikes me that it took decades of educating people that was necessary and a very gradual growth so that NPR and the [public radio] system could be sustained on those contributions, which at one time were a lot lower than they are now.

Crovitz: I think you may have recalled, there was a time where people said people will never pay for TV and yet our cable bills, Emily, as you say, are quite considerable. People are happy to pay for it.

I think this is really marketing 301. It is not marketing 101 or 201, it is a little bit more sophisticated than that and it will take time to get, say, 10 percent of the readers of any particular news site to become paying subscribers, but getting 1, 2, 3, 4, 5 percent, even at that low number it changes the economics of news publishing quite a lot and the only way a publisher would get to 10 percent, would get to considerable revenue, is to start.

Folkenflik: Emily, take a whack at that same question.

Bell: Well, I think that one of the things that we are ignoring here is that news is not like other content. It is ephemeral, it is environmental, it is kind of everywhere. Nobody owns the news. I know that news organizations like to think that they do, but actually they don't. These are things that happen in the outside world. Exclusivity now lasts a nanosecond and I think that comparing it to any other, even to television programs, yes, we'll all gladly pay for a season of "Mad Men," or this high-value reusable content; this is not what news is.

People really never paid for the news in that sense. They have never paid at the point of access. It has always been a broadcast expectation that news that is important will find you.

It will be interesting to see actually whether people can make that sell in a more motivational way, which I think is something that the news business hasn't done particularly well outside public broadcasters.

Joffe-Walt: Do you guys feel that you made a mistake in 1996 when you decided to charge everybody or to make it all free?

Crovitz: The paid model is clearly the right model. The Wall Street Journal has got a decade's head start on almost everybody. It covers an extraordinarily high percentage of the expense and The Wall Street Journal has got a lot of brand loyalty from its fans, but it is a brand loyalty that other brands also have. The New York Times has its fans. The Guardian has its fans. NPR certainly has its fans. And it's that group of people, who are loyal to the brand and want their version of the news, or their version of the content, who I think the data will continue to show are quite happy to pay.

Bell: I think that the very fact that we can discuss The Guardian without explaining what it means, means that it definitely wasn't a mistake not to charge for it because it has a 250,000 daily [print] circulation. In the U.K. it has 37 million monthly unique users [online]. It is a well-known brand now and it has traction and influence as a news brand.

Folkenflik: What do you think of the assessment that that is more of a religious than financial calculation?

Bell: Well, I think that there are some aspects of philosophical adherence rather than religiosity to it. There is a function that news performs in society, which is to keep people informed and to help the will of democracy. I am troubled by a world where you take the logical conclusion of this that people should be allowed the information that they can pay for. I don't see why some people should have better access to information about how their pensions perform than other people.

Crovitz: There are many of us, I think, around the world that are very anxious about a world in which news is funded by government or news is funded only by nonprofits. They have a place in the world, but so too does commercial journalism, where readers get to decide by whether they are paying or not paying.

EIGHT

Does Journalism Exist?

Alan Rusbridger

There are few bigger adherents to the notion that information wants to be free on the Internet in the U.K. than Alan Rusbridger, editor in chief of The Guardian newspaper and executive editor of its sister Sunday paper, The Observer. He has fought for openness and transparency in government but also in news coverage, and his journalists generously link online to original sources of information along with related stories from other news outlets.

In this chapter, adapted from his 2010 Hugh Cudlipp lecture at the London College of Communication, Rusbridger questions the idea of sequestering news in two ways. First, he examines the idea that newspapers can derive meaningful revenues from paywalls that charge people to read on digital platforms. His former colleague Emily Bell makes the same case in detail in the previous chapter. Second, Rusbridger contends that journalists cannot wall off their reporting process from their readers and consumers, who often have much insight to offer. That audience, Rusbridger argues, will find other news sources if it feels shut out.

Ask British journalists to identify their editor heroes over the past 30 or 40 years and two names keep recurring. One is Harry Evans. The other is Hugh Cudlipp.

Why are they so admired? Because they seem to represent the best of journalistic virtues—courage, campaigning, toughness, compassion, humor, irreverence; a serious engagement with serious things; a sense of fairness; an eye for injustice; a passion for explaining; knowing how to achieve impact; a connection with readers. Even if you missed their editorships—as I did with Hugh Cudlipp—both men wrote inspiring books about journalism: about how to do it, but, more importantly, about why it matters.

The one thing Cudlipp and Evans hardly ever wrote about was business models. For one thing, they didn't have to. They lived in an age when, if you got the editorial product right, money was usually not the burning issue.

Lucky them. Insecurity is the condition of our journalistic age. We are living at a time when—as New York University scholar Clay Shirky puts it—"the old models are breaking faster than the new models can be put into place."

There is one business model that would affect all the journalism that follows, and that is the one that says we must charge for all content online. It's the argument that says the age of free is over: we must now extract direct monetary return from the content we create in all digital forms.

Why I find it such an intriguing proposition—one we have to ask, and which, typically, that great newspaper radical Rupert Murdoch is forcing us to ask—is that it leads on to two further questions.

The first is about "open versus closed." This is partly, but only partly, the same issue. If you universally make people pay for your content it follows that you are no longer open to the rest of the world, except at a cost. That might be the right direction in *business terms*, while simultaneously reducing access and influence in *editorial terms*. It removes you from the way people the world over now connect with each other. You cannot control distribution or create scarcity without becoming isolated from this new networked world.

The second issue it raises is "authority versus involvement." Or, more crudely, "us versus them." Here the tension is between a world in which journalists considered themselves—and were perhaps considered by others—special figures of authority. We had the information and the access; you didn't. You trusted us to filter news and information and to prioritize it—and to pass it on accurately, fairly, readably and quickly. That state of affairs is now in tension with a world in which many (but not all) readers want to make their own judgments, express their own priorities, create their own content, articulate their own views, learn from peers as much as from traditional sources of authority. Does our journalism carry sufficient authority for people to pay—both online (where it competes in an open market of information) and print?

Not so long ago, I was at a government seminar on the future of local newspapers when one of the participants suddenly interjected, "I don't believe in journalism." He was William Perrin, a former Cabinet Office civil servant who threw it all in to run a hyperlocal Web site reporting on the area of London where The Guardian now lives—King's Cross.

Perrin absolutely believes in the moral power and importance of what many of us might think of as journalism. But he isn't a journalist, he doesn't call it journalism and he is completely uninterested in the monetary value of what he does. He finds other ways to pay his mortgage. This is what he said:

> I set up a very simple Web site in 2006 . . . to my surprise this
> thing took off and has been very successful. In three or four

years we have written 800 articles on King's Cross, an area a mile long by half a mile wide. . . . We've run big campaigns against Network Rail, where we secured a million pounds for community improvements. We used the Web site again to take on Cemex, a multi-billion-pound company . . . we took them on and we won. We have about four people who write for the site, on average, there's up to six, but normally there's about four of us writing. We all do it as a volunteer effort. It costs us about £11 a month in cash, which is about three or four pints of beer . . . we have a very strong community of people around here who send us stuff. None of the people who work with me are journalists. I'm not a journalist by any stretch of the imagination; it's an entirely volunteer effort. . . . What I do in my community, some people label journalism. It's a label I actually resist.

Depending on your point of view, you may find that vision of new ways of connecting and informing communities inspiring or terrifying. I think it is both—but it is good to be forced to think about what journalism is and who can do it.

So, let's begin by thinking about this question of what the direct value of content is. There is very little agreement on this subject. Rupert Murdoch, who has in his time ruthlessly cut the price of his papers to below cost in order to win audiences and drive out competition, is now being very vocal in asserting that the reader must pay a proper sum for content—whether in print or digitally. The New York Times announced recently that it would be reinstating a form of paywall around its content. Casual online readers will get The Times for free. Repeat, or loyal, digital readers will be expected to pay.

At the other end of the spectrum we have millions of William Perrins, plugging away for free, not to mention a Russian oligarch and former KGB man, Alexander Lebedev, who is conducting an experiment in giving away away everything for free at his titles—in print and digital.

Now, I happen to believe that Murdoch is a brave, radical proprietor who has been a good owner of The Times of London and that he has often proved to be right when he has challenged conventional thinking. But many people who similarly admire him have nagging doubts about whether he's right this time. There is probably general agreement that we may all want to charge for specialist, highly targeted, hard-to-replicate content. It's the "universal" bit that is uncertain.

Murdoch, being smart, knows better than most that a printed newspaper—a tightly edited basket of subjects and articles—becomes a very different thing in digital form. He will know the argument that in future you may be able to charge for mobile, but not for desktops. That specialist information may have value, general information little or none. We all know the Wal-mart-Baghdad subsidy theory—that it is retail display advertising that pays for The New York Times Iraq operation, not the readers.

For universal charging to work, the argument goes, every news organization would have to put all content behind a paywall. One of the favorite Murdoch arguments against the BBC is that so long as it exists and is "free" then that makes it harder for commercial news organizations to charge. James Murdoch describes what the BBC does as "dumping free, state-sponsored news on the market." The Murdochs would like the BBC to be drastically curtailed in order for their business model to have a better chance of success.

I find it difficult to join that particular chorus. As a citizen rather than competitor, I'm afraid to admit that I really like, admire and respect the BBC—including, even, its Web site. Now, of course, there is plenty to criticize—the BBC can be arrogant, hard to work with, complacent, needlessly expansionist and insensitive to the plight of their colleagues in the commercial sector. But the BBC is almost certainly the best news organization in the world—the most serious, comprehensive, ethical, accurate, international, wide-ranging, fair and impartial.

Isn't there, in any case, more to be learned at this stage of the revolution, by different people trying different models—maybe different models within their own businesses—than all stampeding to one model?

My commercial colleagues at The Guardian—the ones who do think about business models—want to grow a large audience for our content and for advertisers, and can't presently see the benefits of choking off growth in return for the relatively modest sums we think we would get from universal charging for digital content.

As an editor, I worry about how a universal paywall would change the way we do our journalism. We have taken 10 or more years to learn how to tell stories in different media—not simply through text and still pictures.

Journalists have never before been able to tell stories so effectively, bouncing off each other, linking to each other (as the most generous and open-minded do), linking out, citing sources, allowing response—harnessing the best qualities of text, print, data, sound and visual media. If ever there was a route to building audience, trust and relevance, it is by embracing all the capabilities of this new world, not walling yourself away from them.

Many readers like this ability to follow conversations, compare multiple sources and links. The result is journalistically better—a collaborative as well as competitive approach that is usually likely to get to the truth of things faster.

The distance between impulse and action is shorter than ever before. Millions of people are realizing they can be publishers, that they don't need intermediaries. The British Museum or the

Tate or the Royal Society or Imperial College doesn't have to wait any longer for the BBC or Channel 4 to ring and suggest a program or series; they can make their own. The same is true of any writer, scientist, politician, photographer or activist.

Governments are freeing up their data, records and information; museums and galleries are throwing open their doors; NGOs and charities are becoming publishers; universities are opening their lecture halls; scientists and corporations are sharing knowledge in ways that would have been unimaginable even 10 years ago. And then there is Google, with its ambition to digitize and organize all human knowledge since time began.

Mention Google, and we think of China: the spread of disorganized information is balanced by organized disinformation and censorship. We can't know yet who will win, but we know what side we must be fighting on.

Where do news organizations think they fit into all this? Are we in, out—or in only if we can make it pay in the immediate future?

Today, in print, The Guardian is, even now, the ninth or tenth biggest paper in Britain. On the Web it is, by most measurements, the second best-read English-language newspaper in the world. With The New York Times charging for access, The Guardian may become the newspaper with the largest Web English-speaking readership in the world. In March 2011 the journalism we're producing was read by 39 million people each month around the world—very roughly a third in the U.K., a third in North America and a third in the rest of the world.

I think back to an essay that C.P. Scott, for 57 years editor of The Guardian, wrote in 1921, in the preface to the American edition of the centenary history of The Manchester Guardian:

The world is shrinking. Space is every day being bridged. Already we can telegraph through the air or the ether, from

Penzance to Melbourne and tomorrow we shall be able to talk by the same mechanism. Physical boundaries are disappearing. . . . What a change for the world! What a chance for the newspaper!

Scott would, I think, have been intensely intrigued to know that the paper he edited for so long—and in whose name a family trust was established to continue the spirit of The Guardian—was so openly available and read around the world. That it was becoming as influential in Beijing and Washington as in Paris or Delhi. That its reporting could change the minds of governments, inspire thinking, defy censorship, give a voice to the powerless and previously voiceless.

In an industry that has grown used to seeing every trend line point to the floor, the growth of newspapers' digital audience should be a beacon of hope. More Americans are now reading The Guardian than read The Los Angeles Times. This readership has found us, rather than the other way round. Our total marketing spending in America in the past 10 years has been $34,000.

Nor is all this being bought by tricks or by setting chain gangs of reporters early in the morning to rewrite stories about Lady Gaga. Our biggest growth areas were environment, technology, and art and design. Science, politics and opinion are up too. My instincts at the moment are to celebrate this trend and seek to accelerate it rather than cut it off.

And that leads to the contest pitting authority against involvement, or "us versus them." Many of The Guardian's most interesting experiments at the moment lie in this area of combining what we know, or believe, or think, or have found out with the experience, range, opinions, expertise and passions of the people who read us or visit us or want to participate rather than passively receive.

Take a scandal that started as a piece of conventional reporting by The Guardian's David Leigh, as well as by the BBC and colleagues in Norway and the Netherlands. After dumping toxic waste in the Ivory Coast, the Trafigura company was hit with a class action by 30,000 Africans who claimed to have been injured as a result. The company employed the Carter-Ruck PR firm to chivvy journalists into obedient silence and then, having secured the mother of all super-injunctions, made the mistake of warning journalists that they could not even report mentions of Trafigura in Parliament.

Fewer than 140 characters later, that legal edifice crumbled.

Within 12 hours of my tweeting a suitably gnomic post saying we had been gagged, Trafigura became the most popular subject on Twitter in Europe. People beavered away trying to find out what it was they were banned from knowing. One erudite tweeter uncovered something called the 1840 Parliamentary Papers Act, which no media lawyers seemed to know about. Others pointed to where a suppressed document was available. Others found and published the parliamentary question we were warned not to report.

Within hours Trafigura had thrown in the towel. The mass collaboration of strangers had achieved something it would have taken huge amounts of time and money to achieve through conventional journalism or law.

It's an example of how a mainstream news organization can harness something of the Web's power. It is not about replacing the skills and knowledge of journalists with (that ugly phrase) user-generated content. It is about experimenting with the balance of what we know, what we can do, with what they know, what they can do.

We feel as if we are edging toward a new world in which we bring important things to the table—editing, reporting, areas of expertise, access, a title or brand that people trust, ethical professional standards and an extremely large community of readers. The members of that community could not hope to aspire to anything like that audience or reach on their own; they bring us a rich diversity, specialist expertise and on-the-ground reporting that we couldn't possibly hope to achieve without including them in what we do.

We are reaching toward the idea of a mutualized news organization.

It's a trend about how people are expressing themselves, about how societies will choose to organize themselves, about a new democracy of ideas and information, about changing notions of authority, about the releasing of individual creativity, about an ability to hear previously unheard voices; about respecting, including and harnessing the views of others. About resisting the people who want to close down free speech.

As The Guardian's Scott said 90 years ago, "What a chance for the newspaper!" If we turn our back on all this and conclude that there is nothing to learn from it because what "they" do is different—we are journalists, they aren't; we do journalism, they don't—then never mind business models. We will be sleepwalking into oblivion.

NINE

Why The New York Times Should Stop Complaining about The Huffington Post

Jim Bankoff

Jim Bankoff has held a series of lofty perches that allowed him to watch the evolution of digital content. In the late 1990s he was president of a leading browser company, Netscape, and he rose within AOL to become executive vice president for programming. Bankoff left the company when he believed it was not focusing sufficiently on content and later briefly served as a consultant to Arianna Huffington and Ken Lerer as they developed The Huffington Post.

More recently, Bankoff led the expansion of a new online network of sports blogs called SB Nation. It casts aside traditional notions of journalistic objectivity to build instead on the passion of fans for each major sports team. More than 20 million people visit its 300 sites every month. Bankoff is CEO for the network, which is moving into new areas such as gadgets and technology.

For all that, Bankoff hails the worthiness of such publications as The New York Times; in this chapter, he challenges news executives to recognize the value that aggregators create as well.

The newspaper industry is reeling, for a lot of reasons. There has been no shortage of debate and recrimination. But no one seems to disagree that there is a business model problem. Just about any newspaper executive will fess up to squandering the industry's historic profit engines—classifieds and local advertising. CraigsList, eBay, AutoTrader, Groupon and Living Social are just a few of the Web commerce companies that came in and built big businesses that once belonged to those with printing presses and delivery trucks to support.

However, many journalists and media watchers seem less inclined to focus on these economic realities and choose to shift the conversation to just how *awful* Internet-only media outlets are for the "future of journalism" and the citizens who consume it. Those who come at it from a traditional media perspective generally frame the questions at stake like this: Do online news outlets depend on editorial methods that undermine the value of the vaunted traditional brands? What do new media outlets and the decline of "real" journalism mean for the future of an informed and open society?

These are important and weighty questions, no doubt, but I am not sure they are the relevant ones. Perhaps the real discussion should focus on whether the success of online news media outlets has anything whatsoever to do with the decline of traditional news media outlets.

Arianna Huffington made her opinion on this topic very clear when she presented the following motto as her five-word acceptance speech at the 2009 Webby Awards: "I didn't kill newspapers,

OK?" No single online news site currently sparks more buzz or vitriol than her creation, The Huffington Post. She, along with partners Ken Lerer and Jonah Peretti, launched the site in May 2005, originally as a left-leaning antidote to the Drudge Report.

But it grew well beyond its roots as a collection of progressive blog commentaries to become one of the best-trafficked news Web sites in the United States. In March 2011, AOL purchased The Huffington Post for $315 million, as the cornerstone of AOL CEO Tim Armstrong's strategy to build the company into a digital content empire. Despite its runaway success with audiences, The Huffington Post became—inside the legacy news industry—a symbol of how the Internet was ruining journalism.

Among the alleged sins: aggressively summarizing the work of other news-gathering sources and linking to their online articles; showcasing the unpaid contributions (blog posts) of guest writers; including too many empty calorie posts and featuring slide shows of scantily clad celebrities (or even accidentally nude ones!); emphasizing liberal opinion and analysis over original reporting; and in perhaps the most reviled act, blatantly pandering to the Google algorithm, all in the name of a few page views.

In one celebrated case in February 2011, on the day before the Super Bowl, The Huffington Post posted a story headlined "What Time Does the Super Bowl Start?" It initially started: "Are you wondering, what time does the Super Bowl Start? It's a common search query, as in, 'what time is the super bowl 2011,' 'superbowl time' and 'superbowl kickoff time 2011,' according to Google Trends." It was like a Google Mobius strip—common search terms strung together in an endless loop for search engines to trip across. After much online derision, that one was revised.

But the implication from critics was that *real* journalistic entities do not do any of these things. As it happens, most of those critics work for organizations they consider to be real journalistic entities. Camps developed and hardened on both sides, dividing those cheering on The Huffington Post from its vocal detractors.

The debate became more rancorous a few days after AOL announced that it would be acquiring The Huffington Post. Bill Keller, executive editor of The New York Times, assumed the role of media critic to bash The Huffington Post and other entities he considered to be news "aggregators." To quote (or aggregate?) Keller, writing in The New York Times Sunday Magazine:

> The queen of aggregation is, of course, Arianna Huffington, who has discovered that if you take celebrity gossip, adorable kitten videos, posts from unpaid bloggers and news reports from other publications, array them on your Web site and add a left-wing soundtrack, millions of people will come.

Keller went on to declare that the AOL merger

> was portrayed as a sign that AOL is moving into the business of creating stuff—what we used to call writing or reporting or journalism but we now call "content." Buying an aggregator and calling it a content play is a little like a company's announcing plans to improve its cash position by hiring a counterfeiter.

Keller's messages were clear. First off, our stuff is important; your stuff is fluff. Second, you are ripping us off—along with other original sources that, like ours, foot the bill for journalism. This slam coincided with the announcement that The New York Times would charge frequent online readers to access articles on its Web site and other digital platforms. As such, it was in Keller's interest to create a debate among media pundits, and ultimately among the public at large. He depicted parasitic aggregators acting against their host journalists.

Let's examine the counterfeiting assertion first. Huffington herself later responded in an interview in Keller's own publication:

> What is amazing is that he did not provide a single piece of evidence. I mean, accusing us of theft and piracy is a pretty strong accusation. So if you're going to accuse the Huffington Post Media Group of theft and piracy and you're following Journalism 101 ground rules, you provide some evidence.

To buy into Keller's argument, you have to believe that The Huffington Post's aggregation of the diligent work carried out by other outlets somehow constitutes counterfeiting. The Huffington Post certainly links to other people's content. It often excerpts a few sentences or even a couple of paragraphs from those articles. And in the process, it drives traffic to the originating outlet. The aggregators have become an important source of traffic and therefore online advertising revenue to the primary sources, which can always opt out of the links.

More importantly, though, when The Huffington Post writers opine on the stories of the moment and create conversations around them, are they not validating those sources as the agenda setters? The largest of all the curators seems to have a big role in conferring relevance on those to whom it links. There is no real evidence that value is destroyed by the news aggregators.

Remember, it is the actors on the business side—eBay, CraigsList and Groupon—that are the real destroyers of newspaper industry economics (assuming you are not counting the newspapers themselves). Moreover, "aggregation" or curation is an essential service in our new media landscape. Let's back up to understand the context here. What does it mean for consumers of news when just about anyone can become his or her own media company?

Big printing presses and delivery trucks are now increasingly irrelevant, replaced by high-speed Internet connections and low-cost blogging software. When the written word won't suffice, you no longer need a spectrum license or a broadcast tower to express yourself via video or audio. You can just set up a free YouTube account or start your own podcast.

The days of local market media monopolies are over. Consumers have more than a choice; in fact they have near-infinite choices. There are so many options, as it happens, that they need filters.

Those filters take on different forms. You can bookmark a whole bunch of "primary source" Web sites or put them into a personalized digital news reader like MyYahoo and bounce from one to the other all day long. But there are drawbacks: it's time-consuming and you wouldn't know if you were missing something on a site outside your favorites.

Next, you have search. Google, more than any company, has created value from media fragmentation. Searching is great when you know what you want. But there's not much serendipity in directed behavior. You usually find precisely what you're looking for—and precious little else.

Also, with big news you often need someone to tip you off, someone you trust. Well, you trust a lot of your Facebook friends who collectively can act as an alternative filter to a Google search. Many of them even have similar tastes to you. But are they experts? They probably don't spend their days filtering out the most salient topics of the day and uncovering some news themselves.

Enter the final method of filtering, the trusted aggregator. If one didn't exist, you'd probably have to invent one in order to figure out what was relevant in a world with so much coverage and so much news. However, if you did invent one, it would probably stink. It would not grow to become one of the largest sites on the Web, as The Huffington Post did. It would not grow enough to afford to pay experienced writers and reporters to act as those aggregators, to contribute their own original reporting, and to enhance amateur blog posts with their own analyses.

In fact, few Web news outlets (or aggregators) without old media revenue streams have survived, let alone create an entity that could rise to be worth hundreds of millions of dollars. Only one has done it so far and that's because millions of people like it and need it.

That leads us to Keller's second claim, one that he shares with many of his fellow newspaper journalists—that The Huffington Post lacks quality. Among the elements likely attracting his ire are the accidental celebrity nude shots (or "nip slips" in common Web parlance), the abundance of photo galleries, guest posts by unpaid contributors and a new section entirely dedicated to the topic of divorce.

The site unquestionably contains a ton of empty calories that form a sort of dessert for the rest of the meal of serious international, domestic, business and sports coverage. Perhaps the dessert has become outsized. How different are newspapers, though? The Times features its own version of cultural candy. Who gets to judge whether the Sunday Style and Men's Fashion sections are any more or less culturally and intellectually relevant than The Huffington Post's short blurbs? Hey, as far as celebrity nudity in newspapers is concerned, The Huffington Post likely learned everything it knows from a newspaper legend: Rupert Murdoch and the page 3 girls in his British tabloid, The Sun. It helps to subsidize his more prestigious—and money-losing—broadsheet daily, The Times of London.

As for those unpaid contributors? Well, first of all, guest blog posts generate very little of The Huffington Post's content and even less of its revenue. The guest blog is a strikingly similar concept to the op-ed page of any newspaper, except that it is not nearly as limited by space and therefore can accommodate many more and diverse voices. In this sense, The Huffington Post provides a great service to those looking to express themselves to a large audience. Newspapers like The Times may provide two slots per day for outside voices, while The Huffington Post's platform is far more expansive. As far as exposure goes, whether you are Bill Clinton or Alec Baldwin, you are not going to have an opportunity to address as large a Web audience in your own words anywhere else.

The unpaid part is probably the most exaggerated of the myths surrounding The Huffington Post for a reason. Obviously, journalists, writers or any professionals do not like to see their trade undercut. At this writing, a minority of those uncompensated writers are suing Huffington at this writing to seek a share of the proceeds from the sale to AOL. It is not gaining widespread sympathy, however. Good journalists know that occasional opinion pieces are not a replacement for the essential work they perform.

But what is the relevance of comparing two excellent services that perform two very different functions? Why compare The New York Times to The Huffington Post? Both are very successful with their audiences.

Other models exist too. The Atlantic has prospered by focusing on high-quality journalism aimed at thought leaders in government, industry and academia. Not only does it command premium ad rates, but it has built a profitable marketing service business featuring conferences and other revenue generators. Premium models will succeed too, but only for journalistic products that deliver true premium value. That said, The Atlantic achieved profitability as a magazine only after sharpening its emphasis on national politics; it too has built up its daily Web presence and network of blogs significantly.

Let's distinguish what makes for a good online news site, as opposed to a traditional newspaper. The Huffington Post and similar, newer media sites understand these principles of the online world well, and they deliver. Here are a few keys:

1. *Be really fast.* Traditional print newsrooms were built around the concept of a daily news cycle. Those days are long gone. In the digital realm, trending topics emerge and are cast aside moment by moment in real time. Yet that fluid sensibility is very hard for most newspaper companies to adopt. They still, after all, have a top priority to package the best of yesterday's news on a daily basis.

2. *Be open.* No news organization has ever held a monopoly on breaking news. Journalists, like scientists and engineers, have a long history of crediting other people's work and then advancing it. In the online world, this is sometimes called curation. Media pundit Jeff Jarvis' oft-quoted mantra "Do what you do best and link to the rest" is a way of life for The Huffington Post. Nico Pitney demonstrated the art of live-blogging a crisis during the Iranian uprising in June 2009. His curation of sources both on the ground and in the media into a coherent and informative narrative proved to be an invaluable resource to consumers and reporters alike. When Pitney solicited questions from Iranians for a White House press conference, President Obama took pains to call on the blogger—no small recognition.

3. *Be conversational.* This may be the least understood part of the new media craft. It's not just about how articles are written, but how sites engage with their audience. Readers often have invaluable responses that advance insight and

occasionally provide information that advances stories. Comment threads can be as valuable as the stories that spark them, if moderated properly in a contextual community. However, when done improperly, audience participation can come off as a poorly planned stunt or a cacophony of dribble from Internet "trolls."

4. Use data intelligently. Too many Web publishers have attempted to build business around pandering to the Google algorithm, simply creating content that has little worth other than to be indexed highly by the search robots. This game will hopefully end soon as Google and other search engines take steps to eradicate "content farms" that provide no insight or value. However, at the other end of the extreme, some organizations are blind to the data that reflect what their audiences respond to. There is a fine line between the desire to provide your audience news about which they're unaware and the arrogance of refusing to listen to their desires through the feedback of search and social data.

So, really, NYT versus HuffPo is apples versus oranges. They are simply different media platforms, attracting many of the same people in different modes of consumption. Both outlets know their audiences and their distinct craft well, and both deliver admirably. Just as the best TV reporters don't often translate into Pulitzer Prize–winning print journalists and those print journalists don't often make for great TV talent, it's also true that the traditional talents that serve print journalism well don't usually translate online. The written word is one important tool in the online storytelling kit, but far from the only one.

Seemingly, the only real question—the resentment, really— underlying all the false-choice comparisons is how arduous, expensive, advertising-unfriendly reporting such as investigative reporting or war zone coverage will be conducted and will be paid for. After all, Keller isn't explicitly arguing that The Times should be charging for restaurant reviews, wedding announcements or sports box scores.

Such insecurity is understandable. The business of journalism is going through a fundamental restructuring right now, and that change includes pain for many talented journalists whose skills may no longer have a home. However, there is every reason in the world to have faith that hard journalism will not only survive but prosper, albeit perhaps not permanently in print form.

Why? Because there is consumer demand for original reporting of substantive topics. The economic models probably won't change much either. Fluffier news with high ad rates supports more substantive news with higher cost and lower ad rates. A product like The Huffington Post, which bundles lifestyle sections with big traffic and high ad rates, can often use those gains to subsidize less profitable news gathering, especially since they don't have to pay for physical distribution. In fact, since the merger with AOL, Arianna Huffington has hired several highly acclaimed journalists and editors from Keller's newsroom and others (perhaps another reason for his attacks on her).

At least one of the journalists who defected from The Times to The Huffington Post, Peter Goodman, expresses few regrets. Goodman told the American Journalism Review shortly after his hiring that the online medium allowed him to do better, more in-depth reporting than print journalism because of the lack of space restrictions and the subsequent editorial judgments. Goodman told AJR he was sometimes inhibited by The Times's lack of appetite for him to return to stories to cover further developments:

My editors said, and I'm not criticizing them, "Well, we already hit the subject." Arianna's whole thing is, "This is the

Web, let's hit it again and again. If we've got another one, let's hit it again."

The reality is that there is no hiding or pretending in today's media environment. Consumers don't really care if you use your bully pulpit to whine about what others are doing or to crow about your most recent successes. They just want to know—edition after edition, post after post—that they can rely on you to serve up the news, in all its glorious forms.

TEN

"We Can All Hang Separately or Survive Together."

Evan Smith

In 2009, Evan Smith, the editor and president of Texas Monthly, told his staff that he would be leaving the magazine after 17 years. The award-winning publication holds barbecue and colorful politicians dear, but under Smith was also known to turn an occasionally gimlet eye on those exercising power in the Lone Star State.

In leaving, Smith wrote that he was joining his friend, Austin venture capitalist John Thornton, to create "a nonprofit, nonpartisan public media organization whose mission is to promote civic engagement and discourse on public policy, politics, government, and other matters of statewide interest." That idea became The Texas Tribune, a multi-platform news outlet. Its staff is small, but The Tribune's offices sit just a few blocks away from the state capitol, and it crackles with an energy missing from many traditional newsrooms.

It's already a must-read for most people in Texas political circles, though The Tribune's survival is not assured. Smith argues it can only succeed by discarding many long-held journalistic truisms.

I spoke those words nearly every day in the run-up to the launch of The Texas Tribune in the fall of 2009, and I hear them trip off my tongue still. In Ben Franklin–flavored shorthand, they convey my feeling about collaboration between media of all kinds these days. At a moment of perhaps the most roiling change that our industry has ever seen, we no longer have the luxury of clinging to a competitive mind-set. It is a kind of professional xenophobia. Instead, we have to throw in with both our enemies and our friends and work together because the future of the communities we serve, as well as our own future, depends on it.

The mission of the nonprofit Tribune is to increase the level of engagement among Texans about issues of statewide concern (higher education, public education, energy, criminal justice, health and human services, immigration and the like) and to facilitate a civil and informed discourse. If the for-profit press had to articulate why they're in business—beyond making a buck—they'd probably come up with something similar. We're all in this to give our readers and viewers food for thought on a range of topics, some serious and some not, and we all want to be forward-thinking in terms of both content and presentation. But we're also resource-poor, collectively and as individual institutions, and that hampers our ability to do as much as we'd like, to do as much as we did only a few years ago. By necessity we have to make choices. We can do some things but not others. And so the question becomes, How do we plug the holes?

That is the coldly practical argument for collaboration in the many forms it takes: by availing yourself of the work of others and allowing them to avail themselves of your work—by joining forces in some form or fashion—everyone wins. Everyone gets to publish more without spending more.

The only hitch is the psychological hurdle that runs counter to the survival instinct. Our board chair, Austin venture capitalist John Thornton, and I discovered that early on as we attempted to make nice with the editors and publishers of the state's biggest newspapers. It didn't matter how often or how slowly we said that we were starting The Tribune to augment and supplement rather than supplant existing statewide coverage, that we recognized how, in challenging economic times, they were doing the best they could, and that we were pure of heart and came in peace. These legacy media vets, many of them longtime friends, viewed us simplemindedly as a threat to their near-monopolistic control over their markets.

In fairness, we could hardly blame them. For as long as there has been a media business, outlets like theirs and ours have locked horns over a finite number of readers and advertisers. Often the battleground has been in the coverage of precisely these subjects—public policy and politics—and you don't have to be a repeat viewer of "All the President's Men" to know why: all of us in this profession of ours want to break the big story first and want to tell it best. That makes us fiercely protective of our turf.

If only they had played the competition card in holding us at arm's length. Instead, in meeting after meeting, we heard excuses for not working with us that amounted to variations on a theme. No one cares about politics and public policy, which explains why they cut way back on covering it or stopped entirely. (Our response, naturally, was that the reverse was true: no one cares about this stuff *because* you stopped covering it.) The Trib couldn't provide anything at the high quality we were promising in the absence of a massive bureaucracy laden with levels of editors and copy editors. Our business model didn't have legs, and so we weren't going to be around long enough to bother partnering with.

In retrospect, one of the funniest push-backs had to do with the price of collaboration—literally, the cost of doing business with us. The Associated Press charges papers more than two bucks per circulation head; one editor of a big-city paper confided to me that his company had written a check to the AP for $1.4 million in 2008. Our initial thought was to charge papers in Texas a fraction of that, perhaps five cents a head, but that trial balloon was popped by an editor who told me that if he sent his bosses a bill for a nickel, they'd ask him for a plan to make back a quarter; there was just no money to be had. And in medium and especially small cities, forget it.

Quickly we pivoted. Ubiquity, we decided and then asserted, was worth more to us than the change the hard-luck media companies might shake loose from their couch cushions. That's how we'd prove our case to foundations and other large donors—by getting as much good journalism before as many people in as many places as possible. Our content would be offered for free.

We delivered the news to the editors of the big five papers in Texas—Dallas, Houston, San Antonio, Austin, Fort Worth— over lunch in mid-September of '09, less than two months before The Trib's launch. Contrary to what they might have heard, we were going to give them everything we generated at no charge. At the time our staff of reporters numbered 12—a mix of young stars and fast risers with more enthusiasm than experience—and they had come, in many cases, from the very papers we were pitching. The conversation, punctuated by long periods of uncomfortable silence, went something like this:

You mean we can run it for free?
Yes, for free.
You're not asking us to pay?
No, free is free.
And we don't have to run all of it? We can run one story today and two tomorrow—or none tomorrow? We can cherry-pick? A la carte?
Yes, that's fine. As much or as little as you want.

At which point one of the friendlier editors leaned back in his chair and folded his arms (or so I remember, anyway) and said, through narrowed eyes:

Well, it's not really free for us to publish your stories.
What do you mean?
We have to buy the newsprint.
No, we said, *we're not going to buy your newsprint.*

Clearly some hurdles were going to be harder to scale than others.

* * *

At The Tribune, we are enthusiastically attempting to ignite at least three different kinds of collaboration. The most passive is the act of republication. From the first, as I just explained, we have offered everything we produce to newspapers, broadcast outlets and Web sites all across Texas at no charge. This free syndication scheme has put the best of our best content in the pages, printed and virtual, and on the airwaves of media outlets in big markets, small markets and everything in between. What we get out of the deal are exposure and branding. What they get out of it is robust, imaginative, multi-platform journalism that they may not have the resources, human or financial, to produce themselves.

It seems elemental—a no-brainer. The people who read newspapers, especially, but also the people who watch TV news or listen to the news on the radio have long been accustomed to encountering work not produced by that paper or that TV or radio station. Whether it's the AP, Kaiser Health News, the New York Times Syndicate, CNN or any other news service, the byline has always been less important to these readers, viewers and listeners than the story. Good content is good content and adds real value to the consumer's experience.

Taking a page from one of our nonprofit brothers-in-arms, we have gone to great lengths to make the act of republication easy. Not only do we send out a mid-afternoon e-mail to editors up and down the masthead at print and broadcast outlets in Texas telling them what we have coming up tomorrow and what's available right now, but we make all of our content maximally accessible through a "republish" button. This minor technological innovation, developed by ProPublica and aped with the permission of the good folks there, allows a syndication partner, with one click, to copy a story, any HTML coding, photos or charts and all other conceivable elements to a clipboard. It truly could not be easier to collaborate with us in this way.

Yes, it's a pretty passive from of collaboration—just as retweeting is a pretty passive form of tweeting. But every little bit helps, and both sides of the equation absolutely benefit.

* * *

A second kind of collaboration is sort of like a premium version of the first. It hinges on republication but requires more muscular advance planning. There's discussion between the collaborators before a story is written, shot or recorded, so it's not just one entity sending its work upstream in hopes that someone has a line in the water. It's a two-way exercise, which means it's bound to be more successful.

Our earliest experience with a collaboration of this sort was our partnership with KUT, Austin's public radio station. We agreed to pay half the salary of one of its reporters, who would work at our offices. He would produce stories to air on the station, cobranded as coming from KUT and The Tribune, and labeled similarly on our Web site. But the decision of what stories to run would route through both the station's news director and our managing editor. We would both have a say in what the reporter was working on. In addition, the station would use our reporters on air to talk about the happenings of the day and broadcast selections from our weekly podcast, in which our editors and reporters, including the reporter we share, analyze the news.

Again, seems like a no-brainer. The station gets more exposure for its content and its brand. We get robust audio journalism and credibility by way of a close association with a venerable, venerated public media organization. And yet what we heard, from the station's general manager all the way up to NPR's recently departed CEO, is that the drama-free, stress-free working relationship between KUT and The Trib was a rarity in the public media world. Elsewhere, would-be partners simply couldn't lay down their competitive arms and check their egos at the door, and so collaboration never came together. For us, there were no obstacles to overcome. We wanted to make it work, so it did.

A better-known example of this kind of collaboration is our partnership with The New York Times, which for 18 months has been publishing the best work of regional nonprofit news organizations on pages that are printed only in those local markets. First the Chicago pages came to be, thanks to the hard work of the Chicago News Cooperative. San Francisco was next, with the nascent Bay Citizen as the providing partner. We were third. It took more than nine months from the initial inquiry by The Times to the execution of our first pages for them.

Unlike our free syndication partners in Texas, The Times pays us for our content; the iconic paper properly views the relationship as work for hire. As such, we work closely with the editors and photo editors there to coordinate our plans in advance—to give them ample heads-up about what we're intending to send their way, story-wise and art-wise, and to ensure that we're not chasing the same news as the bureau chief in Texas, as there would be no point in duplicating our efforts.

From our perspective, The Times relationship could not be more of a win-win. The exposure and validation we've enjoyed cannot be replicated in any other situation. And for The Times, great journalism via The Tribune isn't the only upside. At a time of dwindling circulation in the newspaper business, locally grown content provides Texas readers with a greater incentive to renew their subscriptions or to subscribe for the first time. That's the hope, anyway.

* * *

The third kind of collaboration is the most fulfilling. It occurs when two media organizations pool their resources and jointly tackle a story or launch an investigation—and then both publish the journalism that results, with both organizations credited. This is trickier to pull off because it only happens in the presence of mutual trust and respect. Those competitive impulses have to be completely submerged; those big egos need to be nearly obliterated. The greater good is the goal. You're working in service to the notion that one plus one—your reporter plus their reporter—equals more than two, more than what each of you might have produced on your own.

We at The Trib are indebted to Houston Chronicle editor Jeff Cohen, a skeptic turned supporter, for making this kind of collaboration possible. After several months of keeping us at arm's length, unwilling even to republish our stories passively (including, maybe especially, those by a reporter he previously employed), he reached out to us one day last spring to say that he'd had a change of heart. We should work together after all, ideally by putting one of his reporters and one of our reporters on a story. The result was a scoop of sorts, about the mistreatment of disabled girls at a state-licensed residential treatment center, that ran on the Sunday front page of The Chron, on The Tribune's home page that same day and in the pages of many other papers in Texas. It was made possible by the combined efforts of two terrific reporters working in unison—and it was such great journalism that we entered it, and a few jointly produced follow-ups, for a public service Pulitzer Prize.

After the first Chron-Trib story ran, the floodgates opened up. A multipart series with the El Paso Times followed, and then two big stories with the San Antonio Express-News (like The Chron, a Hearst paper) that ran not only in their pages and on our site but also in The New York Times as part of The Trib's pages—a Tinkers-to-Evers-to-Chance maneuver that, to my knowledge, had never been attempted in the brave new world of collaboration.

As this was becoming a way of life for us, we began partnering with so-called NJOs—nonjournalism organizations that nonetheless have reporters on staff to produce reports, studies, analysis and the like. Early on we did a few stories with the Hechinger Institute, an education organization out of Columbia University in New York, as well as a couple with Kaiser Health News, an outgrowth of the health-oriented, West Coast–based Kaiser Foundation. Our Hechinger and Kaiser collaborations, likewise co-bylined, also ran on our Times pages. Of course, such alliances require careful screening in each instance to make sure that our values, goals and expectations match up. But we're proud of the journalism that emerged. One plus one most definitely equaled more than two.

* * *

The hard work of collaboration is never finished. What we've learned and achieved in the first year and a half of The Trib's existence will surely be dwarfed by whatever occurs in the next. We hope, by then, we'll still be in a richly rewarding relationship with The Times and KUT and who knows who else. We hope the newspapers across Texas that have kindly published our work will still eagerly do so, and the outliers currently drowning in their own competitive juices, that refuse to run our stories, will realize how much more can be accomplished with an open mind to new ways of working together.

Success is never assured, but it's made more likely by a willingness to accept change as it comes, even if that conclusion is driven by a selfish motivation. If the choice posed is hanging separately or surviving together—well, it's not really much of a choice at all.

ELEVEN

Beyond the Tyranny of the Recent

Matt Thompson

In 2004, just two years out of Harvard, Matt Thompson joined with a colleague, Robin Sloan, to create a video that became famous throughout media circles. They foresaw the technological promise that would allow people to sort through and even produce the news on their own, and warned that even The New York Times was in danger of being passed by in the digital age.

At the Poynter Institute and elsewhere, Thompson has worked hard to prevent that very irrelevance from happening. He was an early online reporter at the Fresno Bee and later led the creation of a social-media-driven arts and entertainment site at the Minneapolis Star Tribune. Thompson currently works at NPR to coordinate the development of a dozen local news Web sites as part of a collaboration between the network and its member stations. In this chapter he takes another look at where the news might lead, with another warning, this time about putting too much emphasis on the "new" in news.

L et's start by repeating a cliché: our media landscape has changed dramatically in the past several decades. We walk around with devices in our pockets that hold more information than denizens of centuries past might encounter in their entire lives. This shift toward a world completely awash in information is very new: a time traveler from a century ago would probably find she has more in common with the media habits of the ancient Romans than with our obsessive scrolling on our iPhones.

But amid all this change in our information environment, the basic journalistic formula has long remained the same—the latest news, emphasized according to its importance. If you showed our time traveler the home page of the average American news Web site and gave her some time to get over the shock of the Internet's existence, she'd probably more or less recognize the journalistic vernacular. And if she brought along a stowaway from her ancient Roman vacation, he, too, would probably be able to draw similarities to the Acta Diurna posted daily in public spots around Rome.

In short, the news has been around for a very long time. And so, having begun with a cliché, let me proceed with a heresy: What if the most important role for journalism is no longer to deliver the news?

To give you some sense of how the world—and journalism's role in it—might have fundamentally changed in just the past 40 years, consider two scandals, three decades apart: Watergate and Enron.

The uncovering of the Watergate scandal remains unchallenged as the most legendary moment in the history of American journalism. It inspired thousands of journalism careers, and four decades later still appears in many testimonials to the importance of news. To many, Watergate revealed journalism at its best, with Bob Woodward and Carl Bernstein doggedly uncovering hidden facts in the face of legal threats from powerful men. It required finding information that was not previously on the record and making that knowledge public, actions still considered by many to be the essence of journalism.

Thirty years later, in the months after the downfall of Enron, journalists were not drawing such accolades. Indeed, the company had perpetrated a massive accounting fraud scheme right under the noses of the nation's leading financial reporters.

"It's fair to say the press did not do a great job in covering Enron," the then-editor-in-chief of Business Week told The Washington Post. Yet the journalistic act credited with starting the domino effect that toppled Enron involved no secret documents or anonymous leaks. It was merely a confession by Fortune's Bethany MacLean that she didn't understand how Enron made its money. She aired this confession after combing through the company's 10-K forms—documents that were perfectly public.

Many factors contributed to the failure of journalists (and regulators and analysts and others) to recognize Enron's financial Potemkin Village until it was too late. But it's hard to ignore the symbolism embodied by these two scandals: Exposing Watergate required digging up new information. Exposing Enron required swimming through an ocean of publicly available data.

We've flipped from a world long plagued by a scarcity of information into one massively afflicted with information overload. And what this new world demands of its journalists isn't the revelation of new information. More and more, we need journalists to analyze, synthesize and filter.

Increasingly, we're not looking for news. We're looking for understanding.

The Tyranny of the Recent

The prevailing bias in journalism today is toward novelty. As newsrooms everywhere consider where to direct their coverage, they begin by asking what's new. In an age of time-bounded media—newspapers and broadcast media that had to supply new material day after day—this approach made perfect sense. The advent of 24-hour cable news networks further compressed the news cycle, to the point where each new fact in a developing micro-story, no matter how minor, can be seized on to justify the "breaking news" bug that seems permanently affixed next to each channel's logo.

The press' short attention span means important stories get buried in the avalanche of news. In 2001, a relatively routine story appeared in my old newspaper, the Minneapolis Star Tribune, with the headline, "A bridge too far gone? Repairs overdue on many spans." The story went on to warn that "a bubble of structures built after World War II are wearing out and requiring major renovation or replacement during the next 20 years," and that the state of Minnesota had failed to keep up with the needed repairs.

Six years later, on August 1, 2007, the I-35W bridge in Minneapolis collapsed into the Mississippi River at the height of rush hour, killing 13 people and seriously injuring many others. Built in 1967, the bridge had first been rated as "structurally deficient" in 1990. Subsequent annual inspections through 2006 reiterated this finding. One might argue that the press did its job in this case. The city was warned that bridge repairs were overdue. But the city, the state and Minnesotans did not heed the warning.

But one of the imperatives of the relentless, time-bound news cycle is to warn us every day of new disasters lurking on the horizon. Even as I write, the Star Tribune's Web site conveys fresh concerns: "Deep cuts for health, welfare programs pass Senate." That story, "updated six minutes ago" as of this writing, sits atop a column of other recent headlines involving bomb scares, sex offenders, homicides and bank robbers. Tomorrow, no doubt, will yield a crowd of different dangers. This happens daily, with every day's worries weighted the same as the last. On each Sunday we're served up a few longer stories warning us of graver problems, and then the cycle starts again for another week. Amid this endless stream of troubles, what sort of impact are warnings of structurally deficient bridges intended to have?

Journalism's penchant for breaking news is often couched as a consequence of the public's desire for it. And by many measures, it's true: users can't seem to get enough news. The flood of minute-to-minute headlines about bomb scares and bank robbers generate a steady flow of clicks. That ubiquitous "breaking news" bug arrests viewers who happen by while flipping channels, and seems to keep them watching.

But other data tell a more complicated story of our needs and the long-term patterns of our attention. In 2008, the AP released an in-depth ethnographic study of a group of young news consumers from around the world. "Overall," the study found, "participants . . . constantly checked for news and therefore technically consumed news on a very frequent basis. However, the news they most frequently accessed largely consisted of headlines and updates. . . . We observed consumers click and re-click news updates and headlines and continue to do so, seemingly regardless of the outcome. Unknowingly, they often clicked through a link for more 'depth' and in reality just got the same content from a different 'news brand,' or on a different platform."

The AP study described its participants as having fallen into a state of "learned helplessness"—so overwhelmed and unsatisfied with a flood of meaningless, mostly negative news updates that they merely clicked on headlines without intention, out of sheer boredom. The researchers depicted the participants as hungering for depth and background in their news diet, but finding instead a steady, shallow stream of updates.

As the study suggests, the Web plays a role in exacerbating the worst tendencies of both the press and the public to focus on the latest at the expense of the important. When news is jetting around in 140 characters, there's not much room for depth, context and proportion. But the Internet has a tendency to amplify all our characteristics—the good just as well as the bad. Our adventures on the Web can make us both more solipsistic and more empathetic, more narrowly informed and more broadly so. If we take advantage of the best capacities of digital media, we have the opportunity to invent models of journalism uniquely capable of keeping the latest stories in balance with the larger ones.

The Timeless Web

"Evergreen" journalism—which retains its value beyond any particular news cycle—has long played second fiddle to scoops that keep their sizzle for a day or a week before dying out. An evergreen story used to be one that editors could slot into a broadcast or a paper on slow news days. But with the advent of the Web, where material can continue to accrue audiences long after it's published, news organizations and other media companies are beginning to make real investments in long-lived journalism.

Explanatory journalism—what used to comprise the sidebars to breaking news stories—is quickly gaining prestige as some of the most valuable and necessary work journalists can do. The most downloaded segment in the history of NPR.org is an hour-long, magisterial explanation of the factors that led to the late 2000s financial crisis, an episode of the show "This American Life" entitled "The Giant Pool of Money."

Mother Jones drew widespread praise in 2010 for its dogged coverage of the Deepwater Horizon oil spill. But as the Nieman Journalism Lab's Megan Garber reported, the magazine reached record highs in online attention in February 2011, thanks in part to a series of in-depth but readable guides to the uprisings in Tunisia, Egypt, Bahrain and Libya, and its background piece on labor protests in Wisconsin. These explanatory stories, Garber said, helped fuel a 420 percent increase in unique users for MotherJones.com from February 2010 to February 2011.

Journalism built atop databases has long struggled for recognition within newsrooms; for decades, classic "shoe leather" reporting of the Woodward and Bernstein variety has been prized above scouring through complex data sets on computers. But in a post-Enron era, newsrooms are increasingly seeking journalists with strong programming skills and designers who can vividly render data. These data visualizations, interactive maps, and searchable records can be among the most long-lived material a news organization can create, drawing user interest well after related stories have left the headlines. And they typically allow users to engage with a broader view of a story than a drumbeat of episodic headlines could depict.

Few projects demonstrate the power of these ascendant forms of evergreen journalism more than the St. Petersburg Times's PolitiFact. The site fuses dogged, straightforward fact-checking of political assertions with a database that allows these claims to be tracked, sorted and searched systematically in a variety of ways. It routinely responds to questions or even factual objections raised by readers. This allows for powerful accountability journalism such as the Obameter, a PolitiFact initiative to track progress on each of the promises made by Barack Obama when he was a candidate for president.

In his book "Breaking the News," the thoughtful journalist James Fallows had harsh words for the tendency common among political reporters to focus obsessively on how politicians "handle" the game of politics, rather than reporting on what politicians actually accomplish and how it helps or hurts the country. The Obameter represents an opposite approach to political coverage, giving us a clear, engaging framework for answering the question of what the president has done. It points toward a model of journalism in which stories are routinely followed up on and are weighted not by their importance in a news cycle, but by their importance to a community overall. In 2009, PolitiFact became the first online journalism project to win the Pulitzer Prize.

Long narrative books and articles have been the traditional home for journalism intended not to break news but to convey the bigger picture. Conventional wisdom has suggested that the digital revolution was endangering this work. But a cluster of recent developments has led to a resurgence of long-form journalism. Millions of users have used such online tools as Read It Later and Instapaper to compose daily and weekly digests of leisure reading. Large communities have sprung up around these tools to recommend in-depth works of journalism to consume. Mobile devices such as the Kindle, the iPad and smartphones have enabled pleasurable digital reading experiences that don't require long hours staring at a vertical screen. A nascent market for long-form journalism is now beginning to take off, as Amazon allows authors to charge small sums for sub-book-length works.

As all these types of journalism come into their own, we may well be on the way to ousting news as the default objective of journalistic work. But I still won't be quite satisfied. Even if its role is diminished, news will still be with us, well into the future. And while we're retooling journalism, we ought to take a whack at the shortcomings of news itself.

Reinventing News

In the future, whenever you encounter a news story, you should be presented with a straightforward pathway for acquiring the background information and context you need to process that story. You should also have the wherewithal to figure out how the facts of the story were acquired and verified. The story should tell you what it's missing, what we don't yet know. It should invite you to take part in following up and making it better. And it should give you the option of signing up for any updates or corrections to it.

In short, the future news story might look a lot like a Wikipedia entry.

Wikipedia is a strange beast. As we'd expect of a reference work, the site is often the single best resource for catching up on a story after it's fallen out of the headlines, to get a comprehensive overview of the salient events and how they unfolded. But "increasingly," noted Jonathan Dee in The New York Times in 2007, "it has become a go-to source not just for reference material but for real-time breaking news," as Web users look for a canonical distillation of fast-moving facts. Unlike most journalism that aims to tell us what just happened, the hive effect of Wikipedia tells us what's happening, situating the latest news elegantly within the context of what's come before, and what's most important for us to know.

Furthermore, the talk pages of prominent Wikipedia articles often bear an eerie kinship to the thoughtful conversations that happen in newsrooms when we discuss journalistic decisions. The citations attached to every claim presented in an article make it easy for users to find source material. If an entry lacks key information, editors can attach a note to it saying as much, and ask users to help improve it. Any reader logged in to the site can click a star on any entry to be notified whenever it's changed. What if every news story had these features?

One essential characteristic of a wiki is that it's iterative. Unlike a news story today, a Wikipedia entry is explicitly not a finished product, but instead is constantly in flux, always aiming for a greater articulation of the truth. Wikis share this characteristic with blogs, which allow their authors to pursue a story bit by bit, often with the public's help. Those who followed Ezra Klein's blogging on the recent U.S. health care overhaul at The Washington Post Web site felt like they were party to a classic long-form journalistic quest in the making. The blog rarely broke news, but proved invaluable to a significant audience of people struggling to understand the fate of the U.S. health care system. In late 2009, NYU's Arthur L. Carter Journalism Institute included Klein's blogging on health care among a list of 80 works nominated as the best journalism of the decade.

We often think of journalism as a product—a story or series of stories delivered to the public in their final form. But as Nieman's Megan Garber recently reminded me, journalism at its best is a process—a continual effort to paint a truer picture of our world. There may be many ominous portents on the horizon for news. But if we can imagine a future beyond news as we know it, and dispense with the tyranny of the recent, journalism may yet have its golden age.

PART III

HOW CITIZENS AND CONSUMERS CAN THINK ABOUT MEDIA

TWELVE

Investing in the Future of News

Alberto Ibargüen

In journalism philanthropy, all roads converge in Miami. There, Alberto Ibargüen heads the John S. and James L. Knight Foundation, the nation's largest charity devoted to innovation in news and the arts. Knight focuses in particular on journalism in the digital age as it seeks ways to create more engaged communities. Ibargüen also serves as chairman of the board of the World Wide Web Foundation.

Ibargüen is a graduate of Wesleyan University and the University of Pennsylvania School of Law. Between earning degrees he served in the Peace Corps in the Amazon region of Venezuela and in Colombia. After practicing law in Hartford, Connecticut, he joined the Hartford Courant and then left for a post at Newsday in Long Island, New York. He later became the publisher of the Miami Herald and El Nuevo Herald. At Knight, Ibargüen has been a constant cheerleader as well as funder, exhorting other foundations to devote more of their largess to local news ventures. At any moment, journalism's next big thing may be arriving in his inbox.

A couple of years ago at MIT's Media Lab, a student asked a professor how far he thought our society had evolved in developing communications media, where "10" represented a mature technology. "Two," he responded without hesitation. Then he quickly qualified his answer: he wasn't sure we had even reached *that* level of technological maturity.

Given the speed of technological change and the rate of innovation, constant change is the new normal. If you are not comfortable with that, then this is a very bad time to be in the news business. But if you are able to stomach the disruption, excitement and opportunity await. To manage this threshold moment, we have to shift into an experimental mode that avoids hard-and-fast rules.

Conditions in the news industry changed violently. New owners of legacy media outlets milked a mature industry, demanding increasing profit levels. Nimbler competitors leveraged technological advances to divert audiences and revenues previously taken for granted by established news organizations. The weight of a proud journalistic tradition stood in the way of innovating from within.

As newspaper publishers for many years in Miami, I felt we were playing defense. I saw the opportunity to join the Knight Foundation as a chance to go on the offensive and look for ways to be relevant on the Web, where I thought the world was headed.

Over the course of its first 50 years, the Knight Foundation had become a leading advocate of journalistic excellence, sponsored almost two dozen endowed chairs at as many campuses and supported countless scholarships, mid-career and fellowship programs. By the time I became its president, the endowment had grown to nearly $2 billion and its commitment to excellence in journalism had only grown. What a base to build on!

Jack Knight's brand of journalism sought "to bestir the people into an awareness of their own condition, provide inspiration for their thoughts and rouse them to pursue their true interests." He was a bold innovator; indeed, the company he built could not have existed but for the brilliant use of then-emerging technology, like the telephone. And he had a deep and abiding belief in the wisdom of informed crowds.

He was a giant in the news industry, personally winning a Pulitzer Prize and a Maria Moors Cabot citation for journalism in the Americas, and he built what was, in his day, the biggest newspaper company in America.

Inspired by him, we determined that our focus would be on informing communities so they could determine their own interests and act on them. Generally available, consistently reliable information, however delivered and received, guides a community's ability to make good decisions. It doesn't matter whether the subject is the environment, politics, education, nuclear policy, potholes in the streets or police union contracts. Reliable news and information are at the heart of democracy itself.

Our mission to support informed and engaged communities led us to search for ways to reach people where they are today—a world where, according to the Pew Research Center, more people in the U.S. get their news on the Web than from newspapers and presumably, soon enough, from television as well. Yet more than a quarter of Americans still lack access to a broadband Internet connection because of their poverty or rural location.

In 2008, with the Aspen Institute, we launched the Knight Commission on the Information Needs of Communities in a Democracy. The commission took a snapshot of the information landscape, assessing where it stood and what related public policies would help serve citizens. The commission concluded that among our primary goals should be universal access to broadband, media literacy and transparency in government data. Knight has provided funds for projects in those areas ever since. In our work, we also have embraced a key principle articulated by the commission: that the challenge before us today is not to preserve any particular medium or business, but to support the information needs of communities and advance the traditional public service functions and values of journalism in the digital age.

As a private philanthropic foundation, of course, we are privileged to be able to experiment without the demands for profit from the shareholders of a publicly traded company or the owners of a privately held one.

Foundations have been funding experiments on scales grand and small for most of the last century. We took inspiration from notable examples such as Carnegie's investments in libraries and public broadcasting, Rockefeller's advances in agriculture and Ford's contributions to the use of public television in the education of children. They backed ideas and leaders. They could weather some failures and learn from them. They believed that, one day, there would be breakthroughs.

For us, in this endeavor, there haven't been major ones—not yet. But there have been some lessons.

Some six years ago we started to seek out people more interested in using digital media to deliver news and information than in preserving the financial security of specific news institutions. We insisted on digital training in our journalism education programs at the university level; in one leading example, we made a grant to help NPR transform itself from a public broadcaster to a public media company through digital training intended for its entire editorial staff. An overwhelming majority of NPR's journalists took part, and we believe it has helped the organization confidently think of itself as a multimedia player.

To help break with tradition, we started using open-ended contests. Some of my colleagues drew up pages of rules for what would become the Knight News Challenge. I rejected the proposals, refusing even to look at them, on the theory that if we had three pages of rules, all we'd get back would be variations on themes we had already envisioned.

What we were looking for were precisely things we had not imagined, things that were "of" the Web, not merely journalistic ideas that were already on the Web. So we agreed to open it to ideas to deliver news and information to specifically defined geographic communities on digital platforms. We ultimately also decided we were looking more for innovation in the use of technology than tech magic itself.

A few surprises:

An amazing number of entries were appealing but ignored the geographic community focus of the contest. WikiLeaks, before its recent fame, was one of them. For many, it was unnatural to use a potentially global platform for parochial use. But we wanted to focus on ways to bend the World Wide Web to local use. It turned out to be harder than we first thought. I think we rejected the greatest number of entries on these grounds.

Sometimes we missed a good idea on the first pass. Toward the end of one year's contest process, I asked Gary Kebbel, then program director at Knight, to review a range of rejected applications to make sure we weren't missing something obvious. He came back with what has become hNews, a project proposed by the inventor of the World Wide Web, Sir Tim Berners-Lee, to write computer code to address the issue of authenticity of information on the Web. Their team created "microformats" to identify the source of important elements cited in every news story—such as its origin, date and location, and whether it had been corrected.

When Gary and I talked about it, I'm not sure whether we were happier to have found a gem of an idea or relieved we hadn't missed something so obvious.

We've had a harder time figuring out our relationship with for-profit operations and individuals who want to make profits. Once we had a project actually approved by our trustees, only to have it withdrawn by the people asking for the grant because they did not want to accept our requirement that the results be shared publicly and their Web code be open-source.

Another time, with Everyblock, the code was published in separate parts and turned out to be nearly impossible for anyone else to use. Everyblock is an aggregator now active in 16 cities. It pulls together civic information block by block—such as crime reports, school testing data, health code violations and so on—and pairs it with geographically relevant news stories and recreational information, such as movie times and restaurant reviews.

Its success caught us by surprise and taught us a lesson: Everyblock was sold to the cable news channel MSNBC. Since then, we have required ventures which we fund that become profitable to generate money for new initiatives. We've also funded two projects, one in Boston and the other in Missouri, under the title "Openblock" to make the Everyblock published code effectively usable by others.

About three years ago, we noticed that we weren't funding online news operations. The reason was that they were doing something we already understood: publishing regular news, day in and day out, online. We decided to call together several of the most promising, and that session led to our initiative to fund online news operations all over the country, including in Chicago, Hartford, Minneapolis/St. Paul, New Haven, San Diego, the San Francisco Bay Area, St. Louis and Texas.

In truth, for many of these organizations, there is relatively little, except the use of revenue, that is different from traditional ones. Interestingly, the ones that are most attentive to creating a business plan and to the use of technology have become leaders in the field and, I believe, will become examples of how to be sustainable on the Web as mission-driven operations. But each remains a work in progress.

To date, we have awarded $23 million to 56 media innovators chosen from more than 10,000 entries. Yet one of the biggest surprises has been the disappointing lack of interest and engagement displayed by newsrooms in legacy media outlets. NPR is an exception, as is American Public Media. We gave funds to aid APM's Public Insight Network, which sought to establish a wider range of expert voices in radio broadcasting.

Interestingly, one of the few applications from a newspaper came from a staffer at The New York Times, which maintains perhaps the country's best online news operation. He was supported by The Times but worked on his own time in collaboration with a staffer for the not-for-profit investigative start-up ProPublica. The duo created Document Cloud, an open platform that allows not just reporters but citizens to examine and share original source documents and link them to news stories. It is currently in use by nearly 250 news outlets.

Another surprise was the intense interest among applicants in using the Web for a greater good. We've been funding experiments at MIT's Media Lab for the past four years. Increasingly, their information experiments have focused more on the social purpose than on the ongoing delivery of news and information. We've funded them in order to learn about the use of information on digital platforms that lead to social action. As examples, several of our grantees participated in relief work in Haiti and in the coordination of social media efforts there (see http://www.knightfoundation.org/research_publications/2011 -01-haiti/kf_haiti_report_english_cx2.pdf). Another project sought to gather financial data from families in lower-income neighborhoods to enable people to press utilities for better service. Others tracked oil spills in the Gulf of Mexico.

Not all Knight-supported innovations have taken off, and that is fine. Some news experiments were overly ambitious, attempting to serve too broad an area or audience. Others overestimated people's dedication to their projects, and still others misunderstood the time and outreach required to deepen relationships with their community of users. The job of delivering news day in and day out has always been challenging. The shift to a digital platform has not changed that.

Another lesson also became clear: disappointment awaits media outlets that hope to rely on user-generated content to reproduce the scale and broad-based geographic coverage of traditional newspapers. At a very local level, it has proved too much to expect people with busy lives to contribute consequentially and consistently to citizen journalism or crowd-sourcing projects.

We found that projects made greater headway when they established an identity as part of a specific, tightly defined community or interest group to attract passionate repeat users. Journalists doing such outreach were more successful when they made themselves active members of the community, constantly asked for advice, showed that they were listening and made changes based on community input. Using technology not simply to disseminate information but to engage the audience helps new online ventures to be seen as being "of" the Web, not merely "on" the Web.

Few new ideas have surfaced that meaningfully include the reader in the news process. This seems ironic in a world where Wikipedia and blogs have become commonplace reference sources. Promising ideas and innovations predicated on audience engagement have not been adopted by traditional media. For example, Spot.us, which allows the audience to decide which story pitches to green light by virtue of their financial contributions, leaves the reporting and editing to others. The financial backing is totally transparent but few news organizations have even tried it, though the innovation itself is available for free.

That said, Spot.us serves to illustrate a pair of related points: that many ideas need simmering before they're soup, and that the Knight Foundation has the capacity and patience to support that. David Cohn first proposed Spot.us as a one-year project. I told him I liked his idea (it engaged audiences in the decision to publish without giving up editorial integrity, had total transparency in funding and also helped pay for the stories) but I would only do it if he would commit for two years, not one. "You rock!" he said. I responded, "No, it's been a while since I 'rocked' but I think you might." He has rocked it and we're now funding his fourth year. His project is still evolving and still looking for a breakthrough.

The platforms available to convey news have changed too. The world has gone mobile. According to Pew, some 85 percent of all Americans own a cell phone and 96 percent of young adult Americans own one. Mobile could be a kind of reset button for the industry, representing yet another seismic disruption—or another golden opportunity.

Too often we start with established approaches and attempt to weld them onto an emerging platform. We believe that finding new and effective ways to deliver content on mobile devices deserves the most serious attention. It surely isn't a coincidence that Google is promoting Android and that the Mexican billionaire Carlos Slim Helú, the owner of a significant percentage of the telephone access in the hemisphere, is also a major investor in The New York Times.

As it becomes easier for them to draw on location-based data automatically, rather than requiring individuals to transmit it explicitly, distributed networks may become an important resource. They may help us manage event-based news—in particular, large-scale events that affect a number of people. For example, how might applications that turn people and their smartphones into devices that can track and map radioactivity guide the response to future crises?

Despite some setbacks, game design and mechanics may yield greater insight in how we gather, deliver and share information. Early on, the Knight Foundation supported a number of games that focused on news, where the play was directly designed to help people explore topics in the headlines. In general, they have not been popular and they've been hobbled by complications in design and execution.

Yet as well as stoking competition, games can foster collaboration between individuals, because they create experiential ways to explore personal identity and social status, both online and off. We are eager to discern how that might translate to the news and information space.

From NPR to online news to gaming, the Knight Foundation has been afforded an unrivaled view of the challenges facing those who would help make sense of the world around us for our fellow citizens. It has become urgently clear through the work we've helped to finance that we must bring together those people who are passionate about news and content and the designers and developers who live to create engaging products. These are two distinct sets of skills and motivations that are not easily translatable. Both are crucial to the continued vitality of the news business, in whatever form it takes.

The questions facing anyone interested in informing communities should be familiar. It boils down to something eminently simple but deceptively hard to execute: How do we inform people to encourage engagement in their community? There is no easy route to success in this emerging digital space.

But I think these questions, taken together, hold the key:

1. Why do people need the information you provide?
2. Do you provide utility?
3. Do the things you cover matter to the community?
4. What is your point of view and how will you reflect it?
5. Where and how do people want the information?
6. How will you engage the audience?

The future will be written on the answers.

THIRTEEN

The Surprising Rise and Recurring Challenges to Public Radio

Peter Osnos

Peter Osnos is an unusual blend of journalistic professional, thinker and doer—a Young Turk who eased into the role of eminence grise. During 18 years at The Washington Post, he covered the Vietnam War and was the paper's correspondent in Moscow and London, its national editor and its foreign editor. He became publisher of Random House's Times Books Division and then founded PublicAffairs, the publisher of this book. He now serves as vice chairman of the Columbia Journalism Review. As a senior fellow for the Century Foundation, he writes a media column that appears on The Atlantic's website, and helped create the not-for-profit Chicago News Cooperative.

Osnos was a regular commentator for NPR's "Morning Edition" during its early years. In this chapter, he argues that recent scandals and turmoil at NPR News have obscured its vitality and growth. NPR's thoughtful brand of journalism has become particularly important, he writes, as other major news outlets scale back their ambition and reach.

In 1970, if some media prognosticator had said that in the 21st century public radio would be one of this country's most important, respected and, periodically, controversial sources of news and information, the reaction would have been incredulous. Radio? Broadcast television news divisions were at their pinnacle, flush with well-paid correspondents, extensive support staff and millionaire anchors attracting vast nightly audiences. Radio was widely seen as long past its heyday in nearly every respect. From the 1920s to the 1950s, most Americans spent some part of each day listening to radio news and commentary that were an essential part of the national dialogue. But by 1970, radio was much diminished. Major cities (New York City, for example) had all-news radio stations like WINS that reported headlines, weather and sports in half-hour chunks. Classical music was the core of WQXR (The New York Times–owned station that provided news updates), and there were stations like WOR and WMCA that featured soft-talk personalities in conversation with celebrities. Most of the AM and emerging FM bands were devoted to Top 40 music with religious and ethnic programming at the outer edges of the dial.

Nonprofit radio was mainly confined to university and college stations that carried the relatively esoteric music favored by their constituencies: jazz, folk, rhythm and blues. The only national nonprofit network was Pacifica Radio, founded in 1946 with a distinct tilt toward the left. Pacifica stations like KPFA in Berkeley, California, and WBAI in New York provided listener- and donor-supported noncommercial shows. Encouraged perhaps by these disparate outposts, there were stirrings of interest in a more cohesive approach to national nonprofit broadcasting along with similar moves in support of educational television. The passage of the Public Broadcasting Act in 1967 led to the creation of the Corporation for Public Broadcasting and the National Educational Radio Network in 1970. By the time its first program went on the air on May 3, 1971, it was called National Public Radio. There were a handful of employees in a small headquarters in Washington, D.C., and fewer than 100 affiliates around the country. I first became aware of the signature afternoon show "All Things Considered" in 1973 while spending a fellowship year at the University of Michigan. ATC (as it was known then and now) reflected its roots in the quirky storytelling and eclectic subject matter of the university and college stations where many of its on-air and technical staff members had their early experience.

I like to contend (more as a generalization than a provable fact) that public radio was shaped in the 1970s by people who came of age in the 1960s and believed in social activism and government support to improve a broad cross section of American life. Given the apparent official commitment to educational programming that was unavailable on the commercial stations, the concept was to link publicly supported radio and television to quasi-official entities like the CPB with mandates that were meant to instruct as well as inform. But shortly after its inception, NPR developed its own news persona and style aimed at an audience engaged in the surrounding world, near and far, which resembled the best of the BBC in Britain and the CBC in Canada. By 1980, with the launch of its second major daily show, "Morning Edition," National Public Radio was established coast to coast and had stars like Susan Stamberg, Bob Edwards, Linda Wertheimer, Nina Totenberg, Cokie Roberts, Noah Adams and Robert Siegel, most still there today. The news director, Barbara Cohen (now Cochran), was a friend and offered me a prime slot on the new show, a Q&A with host Bob Edwards, immediately following the 7 A.M. newscast on Mondays. As the national editor of The Washington Post and later the newspaper's London correspondent, I would choose a topic in the news for discussion and craft a road map for our five to seven minutes of conversation. The interview was done live in the NPR down-town studio. My wife used to say that she would not be surprised if listeners hurled their clock radios across the bedroom when they heard my full-throated energy at that early hour, but having to go into the studio ensured that I was wide awake. When we moved to London, the interviews were conducted in the BBC studios at Bush House, which still had the feeling and equipment of an earlier radio age. I much enjoyed the sense of interpreting the world like some ersatz Edward R. Murrow during the London blitz in World War II.

A considerable and professionally diverse group of listeners (from schoolteachers to moguls) comprised the faithful followers of the program. For years after I moved to Random House as an editor, I would encounter people who remembered my weekly sessions with Edwards. The NPR audience—then just a few million listeners per week—seemed to be primarily drawn from the educated baby boomer middle class who discovered NPR as FM radio became standard in cars and most portables. NPR also reflected its feisty campus and community origins in occasional flare-ups over governance and management. Local stations dominated the board of directors, and their interests sometimes collided with the ambitions and intentions of the national hub. Political criticism, mainly accusations of a "liberal" tone to the programming, was a continuing problem, since NPR substantially relied on government funding, which had to make its way through Congress. In 1983, NPR reported a multimillion-dollar deficit after a period of underfunded expansion and careened close to bankruptcy and even extinction. As a response, the CPB revamped its oversight, making NPR a program distributor that received subscriber fees from its affiliated stations. Reliance on federal grants was gradually reduced and was replaced by the system that essentially remains today: multiple revenue streams with members (and pledge drives), foundation and philanthropic contributions, and underwriting—corporate sponsorship carefully monitored to avoid becoming commercials. While the crisis in 1983 was really about fiscal discipline, the scandal left a lingering vulnerability on funding, in a way that always seemed more ideological than budgetary.

With this new structure in place, public radio providers such as WBUR in Boston, WBEZ in Chicago, WHYY in Philadelphia, WNYC in New York and the most entrepreneurial state system, Minnesota Public Radio, began to develop programming. Over time such stalwarts as "Prairie Home Companion," "Marketplace" and "This American Life" emerged from distributors like Public Radio International and American Public Media. The listening audience rarely distinguished among these production entities, ensuring NPR the primacy in branding and making it the target of most criticism, complaints and plaudits. By the 1990s, NPR and the entire public radio system had a secure place in the greater media world but were rarely included among the country's most influential news organizations: the major newspapers, magazines and networks. In Congress, the move to reduce or zero out funding for CPB, thereby eliminating the support it provided to local stations, seemed to revive whenever the GOP was in the majority, especially in the House. The cuts—invariably portrayed as saving taxpayer money— reflected a deep-seated belief among conservatives that they were underrepresented in programs and commentary. Public radio management at all levels recognized the risk of having to rely on these occasionally capricious swings in Washington's political mood. CPB grants continued to drop steadily as a percentage of budgets, particularly at NPR, where in recent years it was less than 2 percent of revenues. The federal share of member stations averaged 10 percent of their budgets, but for smaller local stations, the percentage from CPB reached as high as 40 or 50 percent, money that would be hard to replace in rural areas with more modest audiences and fewer underwriters.

It would be hard to pinpoint exactly when public radio moved from its second-tier position as a news source to the major role it has come to play in the last decade. The broadcast networks' preeminence began to recede as a result of competition from cable and increasingly deep cuts imposed by their corporate leaders. The commercial AM bands became the mainstay of talk radio where Rush Limbaugh and his outspoken (and sometimes outrageous) counterparts held forth, primarily from the right. Limbaugh and the others ensured that radio held its own among the choices Americans made as media expanded in new directions driven by digital initiatives, satellites and downloadable podcasts. As the Internet took hold, eroding the financial underpinning and circulation of newspapers and newsmagazines, the public radio audience nonetheless continued to grow. Executives responded to the September 2001 terror attacks by accelerating the network's metabolism and expanding its reportage. Around that time, more than 20 million people per week listened to public radio at least once, and the number of affiliated stations reached almost 800. In 2003, the estate of Joan Kroc, widow of McDonald's founder Ray Kroc, gave about $235 million to the NPR endowment, creating a substantial nest egg and the widespread, exaggerated notion that NPR (and the often conflated association with other public radio entities) was now rich. Endowments are a welcome source of revenue but by no means replace the continuing need to raise operating funds locally and nationally from funders of all sorts to pay for rising costs and expansion. As late as the early 1990s, public radio salaries were capped at the same level as public sector salaries. Consequently senior NPR executives and journalists, for example, could expect to be paid roughly the same as government employees. But as CPB funding was reduced and public radio was seen as increasingly important to the news ecosystem, salaries rose accordingly, although none matched the paychecks of network and cable stars.

The NPR expansion came in national and foreign bureaus, additional Washington-based beat reporters on subjects as varied as food safety, religion, race and demographics, plus investment in a Web strategy to complement its programs. The worldwide reporting staff of public radio eventually surpassed the commercial networks, with 17 permanent offices as far afield as Africa and South Asia and regional correspondents in places like Tucson and Salt Lake City. The great recession of 2007–2009 did not leave NPR unscathed, however. To meet a deficit of $23 million in its 2008 budget, several programs were canceled and there were significant staff cutbacks for the first time since the financial collapse in 1983. And yet the audience continued its upward trend. In 2010 public radio reached 34 million people a week, with over 27 million of them specifically tuned in to NPR (which, to accommodate its use of video and narrative on a robust Web site, began to use only its initials rather than being known officially as National Public Radio). In what turned out to be her final public remarks as NPR's president and CEO, Vivian Schiller told the National Press Club in March that NPR also reaches 17 million people a month across a range of digital platforms.

In the second decade of the 21st century, public radio no longer needs to justify its impact. But in keeping with its history, it continues to confront a variety of acute challenges in 2011: striking the right balance between local stations and national programmers, especially in the development of their Web sites, which are increasingly important venues for content and fundraising; complaints about the relative lack of programming aimed at minorities; and criticism about the breadth of political commentary, especially from conservatives. With the return of

Republicans to the majority in the House of Representatives and near parity in the Senate, moves to end all CPB funding of public radio and television again gained momentum. In a Wall Street Journal op-ed, Sen. Jim DeMint, a South Carolina Republican, wrote in regard to the salaries of top public media executives: "When presidents of government-funded broadcasting are making more than the president of the United States, it's time to get the government out of public broadcasting." Further on, DeMint incorporated NPR's receipt of $1.8 million from "liberal financier" George Soros' Open Society Institute as proof that it should be denied any government support.

Schiller arrived at NPR in 2009 after a career at CNN and The New York Times. Responding to congressional complaints that NPR is designed to serve elites and has become one itself, Schiller said in her speech to the National Press Club: "NPR's audience is not a left- and right-coast phenomenon. We are urban and rural, north and south, red state and blue state. Our listeners are equally distributed throughout every part of America—because of our unique network of local member stations. Rooted in their communities, locally owned, operated and staffed. These are citizens serving citizens." Schiller recognized that NPR faced implacable opponents who needed to be answered: "At a time when our industry is cutting back, when punditry is drowning real news and thoughtful analysis, NPR is moving continuously forward with quality reporting and storytelling delivered with respect for the audience—what columnist James Wolcott recently called 'the Sound of Sanity.' . . . As guardians of the public trust, we have an obligation to address the current crisis in journalism and not simply fall victim to the turbulence of these times."

Shortly after giving this speech, Schiller was forced to resign by her board of directors, ending what seemed until its final months to be a notably successful tenure. Three management mishaps had made her departure inevitable: the abrupt dismissal of Juan Williams, NPR's most prominent African American on-air personality, for inept comments he made as a contributor to Fox News; the equally precipitous firing of Ellen Weiss, NPR's top news executive, for her role in the Williams case; and finally the astounding blunder of NPR's outgoing development executive in a right-wing sting that made him and the enterprise he still represented look like a caricature of the very worst things its critics said about it. By attacking tea partiers and Republicans, the fundraiser, Ron Schiller, virtually guaranteed passage of a bill in the House mandating an end of all federal financing to NPR in any form. What so recently had seemed a golden age for public radio ended with NPR again playing defense. The outcome was unclear but NPR definitely found itself in a battle that was more about politics than money.

As bad as these problems now seem, they are no worse than those public radio has overcome in the 40 years since it was founded. And if history is any guide, NPR will devise a way to continue to serve the dedicated national audience it attracts because enough Americans all across the country rely on public radio and will, I believe, continue to find ways to support it. NPR and the other program producers and distributors in the system have achieved a stature that its founders could not have imagined. News, information, and all the daily and weekly fare on public radio are a unique asset in American life. There are many competitors to radio in our age, including those in the digital and mobile arenas that weren't even on the horizon when the concept of publicly supported, noncommercial, nonprofit broadcasting was proposed. But whatever happens in all existing realms and those yet to be invented, radio seems to have found its place and has achieved a stature equal to its reach.

FOURTEEN

Watching Al Jazeera: "You Feel Like You're Getting Real News"

Hillary Clinton

Traditional political figures are often initially wary of new figures on the media landscape. But as U.S. Secretary of State Hillary Clinton explained in her testimony before a Senate panel on March 2, 2011, she embraced them as an aid to understanding the larger world. She singled out one new media player in particular for praise: Al Jazeera. This was a strong shift from her predecessors. Defense Secretary Donald Rumsfeld repeatedly denounced the Qatar-based satellite news service for airing videos of Osama bin Laden and for "vicious, inaccurate and inexcusable" reporting, and said it served as a "mouthpiece" for the Al Qaeda leader. Clinton's assessment was quite different: "You feel like you're getting real news."

The evidence is overwhelming that it is economic concern that is driving so much of what we're seeing. You know, [the] university graduate who had to work as a vegetable seller and then was harassed by corrupt police looking for a bribe. A Google employee who was fed up because a young blogger was pulled out of a café and beaten to death by security forces in Alexandria.

Time and time again we see how security and economic opportunity really collide. And it's being played out in real time in Twitter, Facebook and other social media. I started shortly [before] becoming Secretary of State kind of a little mini–think tank inside the State Department to see how we were going to play. . . . One of the first things we actually were able to do was during the demonstrations after the Iranian election, when the Iranian government tried to shut down social media, these young people were able to help keep it open, even including, you know, calling and trying to make sure that the companies doing it understood the importance of that communication network. So fast-forward. We now have a Twitter site in Arabic, a Twitter site in Farsi. I am putting a lot of our young diplomats who speak Arabic out on every media you can think of. I did a Web chat with an Egyptian Web site. On two days' notice, they went out into Tahrir Square. They gathered 7,000 questions for me. We are really trying to play in that arena as best we can.

[T]he United States did an amazing job during the Cold War. We sent our values, our culture, our inspiration across the Iron Curtain through Voice of America, Radio Free [Europe]. I mean, we were on the front lines. Berlin Wall falls, you know, we kind of said, "Okay, fine, we're done with that." We are in an information war, and we cannot assume that this huge youth bulge that exists not just in the Middle East, but in so many parts of the world really knows much about us. I mean, we think they know us and reject us. I would argue they really don't know very much about who we are. They don't have the memory of World

War II and the Cold War and you know, Jack Kennedy and all. They don't have any of that context. And what we send out through our commercial media is often not very helpful to America's story. . . . I remember early in—right after the Afghan war started, meeting an Afghan general who said he was so surprised because all he knew about America was that, you know, men were wrestlers and women wore bikinis, because all he ever saw on American—from American television was worldwide wrestling and—what's that? "Baywatch." That was it. So we do have—we have a great cultural export, but we're not competing in the way we need to compete in the information values arena.

Al Jazeera is. The Chinese have opened up a global English network and a network in other languages. Russia has opened up a global English network. We are missing in action. You know, we kind of figure, okay, well, you know, [in] our private sector we spend gazillions of dollars and we pump out all of our networks into hotel rooms around the world. The fact is, most people still get their news from TV and radio. So while we're being active in online new media, we have to be active in the old media as well. . . . Why are Americans watching Al Jazeera? Because we don't have anything to compete with it, so they're turning to Al Jazeera. . . . And so let's try to figure out how we're going to win the information war. . . .

When I became Secretary of State I was appalled to learn that the Taliban owned the airwaves in Afghanistan and in the tribal areas in Pakistan. They had little, you know, FM radio transmitters on the back of motorcycles and they were going around threatening everybody and, you know, the governments of Afghanistan, Pakistan and, frankly, the United States military and everybody else just kind of threw up their hands and, you know, they'd shut down broadcasting after dark. It made no sense to me. I mean, we're the most technologically advanced country in the world. So slowly but surely we've been trying to take back the airwaves in Afghanistan against Taliban, with the most primitive kind of communication equipment.

Now, take that as one example where I don't think we were very competitive and we have worked like crazy to change that, and then go to the most extreme, where you've got a set of global networks that Al Jazeera has been the leader in, that are literally changing people's minds and attitudes. And like it or hate it, it is really effective.

And in fact, viewership of Al Jazeera is going up in the United States because it's real news. You may not agree with it but you feel like you're getting real news around the clock instead of a million commercials and, you know, arguments between talking heads and the kind of stuff that we do on our news, which, you know, is not particularly informative to us, let alone foreigners. That's why I worry that the Chinese are starting a global network, the Russians are starting a global network. You know, we have not really kept up with the times. . . .

I'm a child of the Cold War. I believe our cultural exports, properly presented, are powerful incentives for democracy building because what it does is free people's minds. You know, there's that famous book, I think it's called "Reading Lolita in Tehran," where it's really subversive to read fiction and literature. I talked to a lot of the people who were behind the Iron Curtain; they told me our music kept their spirits up, our poetry. We used to do a lot in sending American artists around the world. So I agree, teaching democracy is important, but how do you teach democracy? I don't think if you just lecture at somebody, that necessarily is the best way. But if you inculcate the aspiration of the human soul where people want to be free, they want to think their own thoughts, as these young tech people in Tahrir Square did—you know, they were living democracy by expressing themselves. So I think we have to do both. I think we have to do a better job of getting America's message, our values, across, and we have to do a better job in the nuts and bolts about how do you put together a political party, how do you run an election, how do you put together a free and independent judiciary? So I think it has to be both in order to be really breaking through to people in ways—especially young people today who are, in our own country, sometimes hard to figure out how best to, you know, reach and touch and teach; I think it's true worldwide. We've got to be creative.

FIFTEEN

Literacy after the Front Page

Dean Miller

Dean Miller, a reporter and editor for a quarter century at papers serving the northern Rockies, has long advocated publishing unhappy truths that communities have been loath to confront. Under Miller's leadership as a top editor, the Idaho Falls Post-Register published a series of stories documenting abuse inflicted by pedophiles at Idaho Boy Scout camps. In so doing, the paper incurred the wrath of adherents of two groups: the Scouts and the Mormon Church, which supported local scouting. The paper withstood intense pressure and continued to investigate, interviewing victims and suing to obtain sealed court files to reveal a cover-up. Its reporting helped to fuel changes in state law. The Post-Register was hailed for its dedication to scrupulous reporting and careful presentation of context.

These days, Miller is the director of the Center for News Literacy at Stony Brook University in Long Island. As he explains below, Miller advocates making sure citizens are equipped to explore issues of fairness and context for themselves. And, he argues, "news literacy" is the way to do it.

At Stony Brook University, here's how we start our course in news literacy: for the 48 hours after their first class, students are forbidden to consume news of any kind. Not CNN, not TMZ, not the Weather Channel, nor ESPN. They must forswear Facebook and walk out of any room where news of any kind is being discussed or viewed. Put down that newspaper, cast aside the magazine, we tell students. Go without news.

It is a news blackout.

The first lesson they learn is that this is nearly impossible. There are TV broadcasts and graphics carrying headlines everywhere: smartphones, elevators, gyms, the seatbacks of taxis and the tops of the pumps at gas stations. Even comedy and sports shows include copious references to the news.

Students who start the course saying they are not news consumers usually discover the opposite. They are consumers in the worst way: passively, immersively and continually.

After that exercise, they have a clearer picture of their news consumption habits and the degree to which marketers have painted a target on the skull of American college students. If they aren't making choices about the news they take in, they are asked, who is in charge of what they know?

And that's part of the point of the course.

A decade and a half after insurgent news outlets—especially cable channels and Web sites—began to Pyrrhically market themselves by declaring that "the media is biased," more than two-thirds of students reflexively discount many reports as political spin or counterspin. Ironically, this is good for news literacy teachers. Students who cop that doubting pose are ready to embrace the idea that you should not believe something you are told, you should interrogate it. We like to think this would charm the philosopher Thomas Dewey, who coined the phrase "critical thinking" as the highest aim of American pedagogy.

News literacy demonstrates a method of active and reasoned examination of received truths and wisdoms—something missing in much of undergraduate education, if you believe Richard Arum and Josipa Roksa, whose research spawned the best-selling critique "Academically Adrift."

Our approach was inspired by former Newsday editor Howard Schneider's first impression as a new professor at Stony Brook University. He found that students asked to marshal material from current events fell back on two unproductive poses: unearned cynicism and dangerous credulity. Most were just lost, unsure how to find reliable information in the journalism and counterfeit journalism washing over them.

Schneider taught the first course in 2005 and refined it over several semesters, combining critical thinking with lessons that encourage students to act like citizens. The John S. and James L. Knight Foundation took note and by 2007 decided this curriculum needed to be available nationwide. It was a Knight officer, Eric Newton, who observed that what Schneider was teaching was "news literacy" and the term stuck. Knight bankrolled the nation's first Center for News Literacy at Stony Brook to refine the course and share it. By 2011, the center was more than halfway to the goal of teaching the course to 10,000 undergraduates.

Schneider was the founding dean of Stony Brook's J-School, and his experiences in the classroom and newsroom gave rise to the school's peculiar mission: Stony Brook devotes as much attention to teaching news consumers as it does to training journalists.

Schneider's syllabus, 14 weeks that draw fresh examples from journalism for exercises in critical thinking, is emphatically not limited to aspiring Dana Priests or Bob Woodwards. And it is not media criticism. There's an academic surfeit of that. Rather, news literacy marries classical rhetoric, evidence and source analysis to practical lessons about how news is gathered in hopes that students learn to find reliable information that they can use to make decisions, take action or interact socially.

With the news blackout fresh in their minds, students are pushed to make painstaking but necessary taxonomical distinctions. Instructors emphasize that verification, independence and accountability distinguish news from other "information neighborhoods."

Having found that neighborhood and paced off its perimeters, students then learn to dissect stories methodically to decide for themselves if the evidence is sufficient and if the sources are, for example, independent and authoritative enough to be trusted. They step back and think about each situation to decide whether reports should be fair to the evidence (when it is abundant and there's a consensus) or merely balanced in reporting all aspects of a debate over unknowns.

Our noisiest critics in the academy and in the press mischaracterize the role of journalist/teachers in this vibrant subset of media literacy, and indeed the very nature of our program itself. The journalists aren't there to inculcate in students a reverence for dead-tree newspapers or traditional newscasts. Rather, we believe students must master the reporter's skill of testing and sifting to find reliable information if they are to take full possession of the powers reserved to citizens under the Constitution.

That is the heart of our movement. News literacy, it turns out, revives the civics education that was chased from the public schools decades ago when Sputnik rose and with it a cry for increased science and math training. Parents who didn't love Junior mouthing off about his free speech rights didn't make much of a fuss when civics got the ax. Some had long suspected civics courses were platforms for political proselytizing anyway.

The unintended result was that television news, cable talk and television ad campaigns became the dominant sources of civic knowledge for many young Americans, sources now supplemented by ideological blogs and news aggregators.

Aware of the pitfalls of partisanship, the news literacy movement seeks to maintain an assiduously neutral ideological standpoint. And that's not hard for journalist-instructors accustomed to keeping their views to themselves.

At Stony Brook, the Center for news literacy moved into high gear when the undergraduate college accepted the course to satisfy two core graduation requirements: critical thinking and textual analysis. It was an important stage in its evolution. Now, more than 1,500 students per year take the course. Few of them are journalism majors. And that's because Howie Schneider envisioned the class as a return to the university's traditional role in shaping skillful citizens, but with a twist: training citizens to hold journalism accountable to those who rely on it. The course is taught by a cadre of about 40 adjunct professors (most of whom are professional journalists) and by graduate student news fellows from a variety of other disciplines. Adaptations of the Stony Brook model have sprung up at 21 campuses in the United States in the past two years. In March 2011, representatives of 40 colleges and universities gathered on campus for the second national conference on news literacy. That's the other half of the Center for News Literacy's mission: to provide material and moral support needed for the spread of the course, which now has outposts as far away as Istanbul and Queensland, Australia.

It is giving fresh life to a few journalists seeking meaning or employment in turbulent times for the profession. In news literacy classrooms, they show students how to think like reporters when hunting the reliable information they need in their civic lives.

The movement is spreading from the college campus to classrooms serving younger students as well. Some American high schools are adopting the course to fill the hole left by civics or to give a current events buzz to existing English or social studies programs. More than 60 teachers have attended summer training courses in recent years and are teaching news literacy at schools from Seattle to Dartmouth, Massachusetts.

In 2009, Alan Miller, a Pulitzer Prize–winning investigative reporter for The Los Angeles Times, quit his day job to recruit journalists to teach up to 10 lessons in news literacy in partnership with classroom teachers. As of this writing, his sister program was embedded in schools in Brooklyn, Manhattan, Bethesda and Chicago, reaching 1,200 students per year with lessons in source evaluation, evidence analysis and creation of responsible material online. Many traditional journalists feel disoriented right now. But people still have a strong drive to hear stories about their lives and the world, even if they question previously respected sources of news.

The journalistic impulse appears to be a defining characteristic of human nature. Some evolutionary biologists theorize humans voluntarily do good for fellow humans who may never reciprocate, in part because language—the mechanism of reputation—rewards nonreciprocal altruism. The business and practice of telling one another about one another are not going away. They are keys to our humanity.

It's hard to find the truth. Harder yet to say it clearly. And for all that, people don't always react well to it when you do. That's true from The New York Times to the neighborhood watch blog. Professional journalists have often looked askance at such amateurs.

But Americans by the tens of millions are writing and posting things on Facebook and Twitter and Tumblr that other people actually care about—often more than they care about the reports produced by journalism's most heralded stars. At times it can be banalities about the merits of balsamic versus cider vinegar. But in times of crisis, it can be soul defining: What is our obligation to, say, Libyan dissidents—especially those of the America-hating variety? Such material should be embraced as potentially enlightening—and yet scrutinized for credibility and transparency.

Journalists are well matched to the job of helping news literacy students explore and define these dynamics. Reporters know firsthand how hard powerful forces fight to control information and how fiercely people resist new facts when they have already made up their minds. And they know what it is to respond to an angry reader or viewer.

A relatively miserable minority of journalists, however, seem to understand the First Amendment is meant to protect every person's right to disseminate ideas, not to protect a profession. A journalist, we teach students, is someone who does full-time what we all can and should do: demand answers and share them with other citizens. Journalists have no special rights, but, at least traditionally, they get paid for it.

This lesson forces news literacy students to confront their own Fourth Estate responsibilities. They too should be involved in performing a watchdog role on governmental agencies and bodies. News literacy students are primed for the fundamental impulse of democracy, which is to fight city hall or at least call it to account. You can't do that if you don't get your facts straight.

But there's a corollary: merely teaching people how to find reliable information is inadequate if they can't open their minds to new information. Advances in neuroscience have documented the fragility of memory, the suggestibility of perception and the extent to which our own biases can prevent us from hearing or remembering discomfiting facts, much less seeking them out. The more we learn about these reactions to cognitive dissonance, the clearer it becomes that if we don't challenge Americans about what they believe—and how they reach conclusions—they'll never know what they don't know.

One of our relentless cheerleaders has been Jim Leach, the chairman of the National Endowment for the Humanities. A longtime Republican congressman from Iowa now serving a Democratic president, he tours the country extolling "civility." It's a polite way to ask Americans to tone down their derision of people with whom they disagree as they discuss matters of public interest. When he learned how much attention we devote to cognitive dissonance, Leach coined "Stony Brook model" as a science-inflected way of reminding people that news literacy isn't merely flag-waving wishful thinking. There's data behind the idea that a news consumer has to consciously engage with other ideas or risk falling into intellectual ruts.

A University of Maryland study of voters in the recent off-year elections suggested that a majority of Americans went to the polls badly misinformed about the economic recovery, the state of climate science and other important context to the election. News analysts seized on the correlation between degree of misinformation and media preferences and contended, without irony, that this study validated critics of ideologically driven news channels Fox News and MSNBC.

News literacy students can see critics found a way to make the study confirm their beliefs, instead of considering alternative analyses. Isn't it just as likely that highly partisan voters, who gravitate to Fox News and MSNBC, are all but uneducable on controversial topics? No matter how neutral and factual information is, partisan bias can make it fit a preconceived worldview.

That we may misinform ourselves with reliable information is a sobering irony for our students. They linger over the idea that they may already have developed such hardened beliefs they are incapable of accepting a challenging set of facts. If this impels them to embrace the habit of testing their beliefs against new facts, we have succeeded.

The early studies of news literacy suggest its warnings about cognitive dissonance stick. A year after they've left the classroom, news literacy students remain more committed than their peers to the habit of keeping up with current events and consulting multiple news outlets.

Hence my optimism. We don't yet know the truth about the information age. Ralph Waldo Emerson declared in his era that "this time, like all times, is a very good one," but only "if we but know what to do with it."

The often cited fears of information overload, for example, will likely prove to have been a distraction. Most measures of how much "information" has been created include reams of data processing code. That stuff is binary furniture, more or less, and not information any human would consciously review. If that counts as information, then so should the thousands of birdcalls primitive humans hear each day.

We have always lived with the knowledge that there is "too much" knowledge. My grandmother, a bookworm from the woods of Idaho, used to say she wished someone would send her to prison so that she'd have time to catch up on her reading. Young scholars stumbled across evidence that scholars centuries ago started fretting once Oxford University's library exceeded 100 volumes. From "Hamlet's Blackberry" to Mark Twain's pre-glued scrapbook, humans have long hoped to preserve the information they were offered but unable to retain.

But this age of overload brings with it the means of rescue. Because the Internet allows for a two-way conversation, and because people can link online to their original sources of information, false information can be countered better than ever by light-speed verification and debunking. Somewhere someone is

Googling one of my assertions and preparing to call me to account. That is an excellent, and intentional, consequence of technologies that dystopians blame for "overload."

It's a humbling environment for a journalist, and a powerful one for a reader. By the time they arrive at college, students have just enough experience with these questions that they are ready for what I'm starting to think are the signal lessons of news literacy in this age:

1. It's your First Amendment.
2. We have just as much trouble hearing the truth as we do finding the truth.

Those of us in the news literacy movement seek to accelerate these novel derivations of ancient forces. We think the best bet for improving the state of journalism in a digital era—and the best hope for sustaining righteous democracy—comes from building a news-savvy citizenry.

SIXTEEN

Arming the Audience

Frederick R. Blevens

Frederick R. Blevens was a newspaper reporter for nearly two decades at regional newspapers in Tampa, Philadelphia, San Antonio, Fort Worth and Houston. But he has found new life in journalism on campus. He obtained a doctorate at the University of Missouri's journalism school and is now a professor at Florida International University in Miami.

Blevens teaches courses on media law, history, ethics and reporting, but he is, if anything, even more passionate about news literacy, which he teaches in the honors college. He believes the news literacy movement draws on a tradition stretching back to the conclusions of the Hutchins Commission, a panel led by the president of the University of Chicago during the 1940s that examined the social responsibility of the press. At Florida International, Blevens not only teaches college students but urges them to go into the surrounding community to help residents (many unable to read or speak English fluently) navigate the media landscape to get the information they need.

At my campus in south Florida, college students wash cars and hold bake sales to pay for a citizen news literacy program they designed for a Spanish-speaking Cuban-Nicaraguan community adjacent to campus.

This is part of a formal town-gown partnership between Florida International University and the city of Sweetwater. If car washes and bake sales don't raise enough money, the students design an alternative plan on the cheap to take a specific lesson plan into a high school classroom or deliver a guerrilla-style street campaign on news literacy.

By its nature, news literacy is a subject that can be strictly planned (and well funded) or spontaneously ignited in social theater settings (low budget). We find our students develop a strong commitment to the skills and ideas of news literacy.

New Americans and international students at Florida International University have embraced the course and now we teach it to two divergent, if not mutually exclusive, groups of students.

The purest and most intense course is in the Honors College, where a 20-student News Literacy seminar lasts two full semesters. Since its inception two years ago, the course has enrolled students from more than 20 majors and at least a dozen countries.

In the first year of offering this class, an older Cuban-American student approached me to volunteer his services in surveying the Sweetwater community and reaching out to recruit citizens. He brought family members into the community and engaged dozens of residents, pastors and merchants with a zeal that was both contagious and contagion.

As a mature first-generation college student, he's not naive. But as what we call a "news literacy ambassador," he's taking his skills into every corner of south Florida's substantial Spanish-speaking community.

On a second, broader level, we offer "How We Know What We Know" as an element of the university's recent global learning initiative. It is one of several courses freshmen and sophomores can take to satisfy core requirements. In the honors course, the first semester is spent mastering dichotomous concepts such as news/commentary, truth/deceit, concealment/revelation, critical thinking/passive engagement, and actionable information/ puffery. They learn the hazards of political and business bias and the benefits that come from biases toward the audience.

The core of the critical thinking curriculum pushes students to question assumptions and expand the bounds of debate.

In one class, students watch a Jon Stewart critique of a Fox News story that uses sexually charged clips of bikini-clad students on spring break as the eyewash for a story on a serial prostitute killer running loose in Daytona Beach. By questioning the connection between dead prostitutes (the spoken narrative) and partying spring breakers (the visual narrative), they learn the difference between truth grounded in fact and Colbertian "truthiness" grounded in the artifice and fabrication of news coverage; they come away appreciating the idea of expanding their news diets and seeking corroboration.

Those concepts turn to practice in a series of experiential scenarios.

One is the 48-hour news blackout (described by Dean Miller earlier in this book). "After I went to campus, it POURED," one student wrote, "and I had no clue to take an umbrella." On the darker side, one student was emotional about discovering a murder in her hometown neighborhood as soon as the blackout had expired: "I couldn't believe how terrible I felt about not knowing."

"When I opened the computer after this 48-hour break," a Tunisian student in the class wrote, "there was no special emotion or big enthusiasm, just the discovery that all my guesses about the situation in North Africa and the Middle East were almost all wrong. Almost a hundred deaths in Libya, Bahrain's people are massacred by the army, while in Tunisia, the militias of the old so-powerful party are still disturbing the path to calm and peace. If I did continue this experience and believe in my optimistic guessing, my weekend would have been only a party. Instead, I am going to continue watching and following the news and pray to God for a happy and peaceful ending."

In "Different, Eyes, Different Ears," each student adopts the news consumption habits of another student for 48 hours. Many are shocked and struggle to abide by the admonition not to make value judgments about what their classmates consume— or how they consume it. "She's cheating her brain on cable news," a student wrote about his research partner. "If I had to do this for one more day, I would need a shrink. Sheeeeesh." Another student perhaps more introspectively observed, "I learned about a lot of things I NEED to be doing to be more informed. This was one of the most rewarding assignments of my life."

WikiLeaks loomed large in the imagination of students during an exercise that addressed the power of information. After the class examines the foundations of concealment and revelation (and, in general, the control of information), students are asked to think of a time in their lives when they kept a secret. They are asked to think about the extent to which they went to keep that secret, what kind of lies they used to prevent it from being revealed, the intimacy of relationships in which the secret was shared and, finally, how that secret was penetrated and revealed, voluntarily or involuntarily. This starts conversations about power and secrecy. "I did not know how many secrets I had," wrote one student, "or how many times I lied."

One of the harder writing assignments requires them to construct a false story with verified facts. In teams, students work through a task we call "Just Because It's Correct, Doesn't Mean It's Right." To satisfy this assignment, they can, for instance, put unrelated facts together in ways that suggest causality: "A rare orbit of the moon especially close to Earth was followed the next day by twice the average number of accidents on I-95." It's a memorable way to register the power—and improbability—of context and the impossibility of objectivity when choosing it.

The success of the Honors College course laid the groundwork for news literacy to become an essential element of the university's "global learning" curriculum.

"How We Know What We Know" fulfills a writing-intensive humanities requirement and enrolls 120 students. The balance of nationality and majors is consistent with the course in the Honors College, but the curriculum is quite different and students are required to blog most of their assignments.

In this transdisciplinary humanities course, the content focuses on how information gets made, manipulated, suppressed and exploited in global environments. News literacy serves as one common thread throughout. Several of the assignments are identical, but the instructors take different approaches with similar content.

In one assignment, students are instructed to select one of WikiLeaks' U.S. State Department cable postings and place themselves as a diplomat in the country from which the cable originated. They must respond with a rationale for the communiqué and critique the release of the document using the philosophical and conceptual foundations of concealment and revelation.

In many ways, what we at Florida International and dozens of other universities are trying to do is put in the hands of the audience the tools to see coverage for what it is—and to challenge the news industry to set a higher bar. In our classrooms and communities, there may be no nobler mission.

SEVENTEEN

The News Belongs to the Public

Geneva Overholser

After graduating from Wellesley College in 1970, Geneva Overholser was told by a Boston Globe editor that the only newsroom job awaiting her involved fetching coffee. Instead, she put in a stretch as a freelancer in Paris and Kinshasa and then wrote editorials for the Des Moines Register and The New York Times.

After Overholser returned to the Register as its top editor, she concluded that newspapers should reconsider withholding the names of rape victims. "As long as rape is deemed unspeakable—and is therefore not fully and honestly spoken of—the public outrage will be muted as well," she wrote in a 1990 column. One victim came forward and the Register's resulting series catalogued her ordeal, by name.

As ombudsman for The Washington Post, Overholser questioned the political press corps's reliance on off-the-record and anonymous sources. Now, as director of the school of journalism at the University of Southern California's Annenberg School, Overholser writes that the key to the future of journalism lies in choices made by citizens.

If you saw the documentary "Page One: A Year Inside The New York Times," you likely are already someone who believes that substantive journalism is critical to the health of democracy and to the enrichment of your daily life. It's likely, too, that you consider The Times indispensable, perhaps even heroic, as it fends off brutal challenges. But that's an incomplete way to think about what lies ahead for the profession and practice that the paper has helped to define.

Although journalism is a crucially important topic, the conversation about it tends to be narrow and unproductive. It's conducted primarily by journalists inclined toward defensiveness and critics inclined toward argument. It is attended by citizens (perhaps much like yourself) who are frightened about the future of their newspaper (or of their favorite television or radio news source). As "Page One" showed—and the news in recent years has made clear—there is plenty of cause for concern, from repeated large-scale layoffs to multiple bankruptcies.

But even as we lament the changes and slog along in this limited conversation about the future of news, others are busily *creating* it. People are tweeting and blogging, collaborating and forming social networks, posting about goings-on in their own neighborhoods here or abroad, and generally using new technologies and emerging communities to share information in the public interest. This emerging media ecology is essentially defining the future of news. The role that journalists play in this whirlwind of activity is too often limited to taking aim at it from the sidelines—which holds no evident promise of stopping it. Meanwhile, the emerging-media world of frenzied activity is lacking in the kind of reflection and direction and participation that could make it more promising for public life.

In other words, we could use a richer debate. And you could help foster it.

* * *

Let us pull back from the specific story of The Times, and look at a much more complex picture of change, much of it frightening, much of it promising. Media and messages overwhelm us; they are everywhere we go, at every moment of our lives. We no longer consume news as a matter of routine: the ritual of reading the morning newspaper or watching the evening news is gone by the wayside for many. Even those of us who remain devotees of The New York Times or The Washington Post, The Los Angeles Times or "All Things Considered," are likely to get a good deal of our news, throughout the day, from the Huffington Post or Google News or the Drudge Report or countless other sources. Our expectations of speed have risen. Our tolerance for—or perhaps appreciation of—informed opinion, analysis, interpretation, in addition to "straight" news, has increased. In short, our attention is a precious commodity that is harder and harder to command.

This year, for the first time, more people report getting their news from the Web than from newspapers, according to the "State of the News Media 2011" from the Pew Research Center's Project for Excellence in Journalism. Even as other media experienced economic recovery, newspapers continued to see revenue declines last year, "an unmistakable sign that the structural economic problems facing newspapers are more severe than those of other media," said the report.

Young people are getting their news in original ways and even define it differently. A recent study from the International Center for Media and the Public Agenda shows that college students the world over look to Facebook, Twitter and other social network platforms for their news, whether personal or global—and they often blend these two in their minds.

The prevailing sentiment is that "we no longer search for news, the news finds us." That's unnerving for those of us raised on traditional news models. And it's beyond unnerving for The

New York Times and other legacy media outlets. In their heyday, reliable information was scarce; traditional media had great authority.

In many ways those times were easier for consumers because the guidance was strong. Now information is abundant, as my USC Annenberg colleague Kjerstin Thorson notes, but guidance is weak. As a result, many consumers cast about for tools to determine what is credible, while others, particularly young people, resist the whole notion of the "filter." Newspapers' role as gatekeepers is over; they are no longer in control of what people know.

What is most striking, however, is the abundance of possibility before us. News that comes with a rich menu of sights and sounds, inviting our interaction, offers us a sense of community, engages us and enables us to act. News as a social experience. News that fully immerses us.

Consider a few examples of the potential made visible. In Kenya, tech nonprofit Ushahidi enables citizens to report incidents of violence on their cell phones. Nonprofit aggregator Global Voices brings together thoughtful blogs of citizens around the world, sharing the experiences of people in countries rarely visited by traditional media, in a style more affecting for many readers than the traditional foreign report. And this: according to the Web Ecology Project, in just 18 days in June 2009 there were more than 2,024,166 tweets about the election in Iran.

The point is not that social networks do or don't make revolutions, but rather that more than 480,000 Twitter users connected with events in Iran. This is the kind of information consumption that causes people to engage in community. To be collaborative. To make things happen. Or, as my colleague Henry Jenkins, exulting in all things transmedia and transformational, would say, "Geek out for democracy!" It's a messy, fast-changing, still-unclear world, full of destructive potential. It's also inclusive, engaging, capable of creating trust and initiating action. The opportunities in this participatory culture are endless: in games, in collective intelligence, in the renaissance in knowledge being enabled by ever richer search tools.

Bill Keller, executive editor of The New York Times, is typical of newspaper editors in viewing many of these changes with skepticism. His March 10, 2011, column, "All the Aggregation That's Fit to Aggregate," spurned everything from live blogging to what's "trending" on Twitter to Arianna Huffington's "instinctive genius for aggregation." This is not a hopeful sign for The Times. The next day his own paper carried a piece on the magazine The Week, attributing its growth and profitability to its "giving [readers] a perspective on last week's news." How does it do this? By aggregation—a function that is much appreciated by many news consumers. They turn to aggregation because it helps them navigate the overwhelming media offerings. It gives them access to a variety of news sources, which many prefer to a reliance on one or a few.

Of course, newspapers and other legacy media are on the Web as well as in print, and some are doing groundbreaking work in the use of social media and other digital tools. Indeed, The Times is among their leaders. But are they optimizing their chances of prevailing in this fast-changing new media landscape? In a world of risk taking, experimentation, declining institutions and empowered individuals, are they doing all they need to do to go to people where they are, to engage them as they wish to be engaged? When the future is so uncertain and short-term economic incentives hamper innovation, it is both tempting and easy to focus on the audience who like you as you are, doing mostly what you've always done, with the requisite nods to forward progress. But this is a recipe for slow death for these organizations.

It's also worrisome for us as engaged citizens. The finest of our legacy institutions (like The New York Times) are critically important to this emerging ecology. Despite promising new media advances, we have not yet approached replacing these engines of investigative reporting. The crucial work of watchdog reporting continues to be done by newspapers in many communities across the country. NPR, for all its management difficulties, provides its substantial news report to an ever larger audience. Whatever their reduced states, traditional news organizations are very much alive and essential to civic life.

But if they are to thrive—indeed, if they are to survive—the legacy media and their consumers (and boosters) must more fully open their minds to the potential in the changes occurring around them. A good way to begin is to acknowledge that the "golden era"—the time of their supremacy—had its weaknesses. Take the matter of giving voice to a wide range of people, and visibility to a broad spectrum of views. Or consider what the communications scholar Pablo Boczkowski calls the "spiral of sameness," leading to increasing news homogeneity. Or what sociologist Herbert Gans calls the "class bias" of the news and of the profession, favoring reporting of the powerful, hewing to the paths of conventional thinking, narrowing the public debate.

The public perhaps felt this more keenly than we journalists did. It's little surprise, then, that the public feels the promise in the change more quickly, too. We traditionalists understand the value of authoritative voices. But can we not also appreciate the promise in having more voices heard? Or the power inherent in collaborative networks? It's easy to denigrate Twitter. But here's the question: Is quoting official sources in lengthy stories by definition more or less valuable than sending forth short bits of information from the public as well as from authorities? Can both be valuable and mutually enriching?

We are at the beginning of this media revolution. There is an enormous growth potential ahead—new audiences for news in tapping into social networks, in offering information in the public interest in games, in collaborating with emerging providers of news. To embrace these changes offers huge promise. These new news consumers may be reading news as headlines. They may be receiving it from friends rather than directly from institutions. But they are doing it 24/7. And many of them want to create news as well as exchange it among themselves. (Nor is their reliance on headlines new. I recall people thanking The Wall Street Journal for its elegantly information-rich multiple decks of headlines back in the day, sufficient to keep them from embarrassing themselves at cocktail parties.)

Whether all the changes represent a lesser thing or a greater thing is not the point. They are the *coming* thing, and we will benefit from having the strongest providers of news be richly a part of the changes. Each of us who loves certain institutions may hope that they will thrive, but the greater democratic goal is that the public they *serve* will thrive, to build richer lives and a stronger democracy.

Democracy is a collaborative process. Journalism as we know it has been anything but. Legacy media are top-down institutions in an increasingly bottom-up world. To play in this world doesn't require journalists to sell their principles short. Verification, comprehensiveness, proportionality, fairness, an emphasis on the public service: these will always distinguish journalism as an invaluable kind of communication. The challenge to media today is in part economic—a huge challenge indeed—but it is more complex than that. Any institution now operating from on high, feeding the masses in the same time-honored way, delivering exactly what it alone believes they need and failing to engage their audience will surely lose them.

As the British media scholar Charlie Beckett has put it, "Journalism has to make a new contract with the citizen. In the past the deal was that journalism was allowed to do some good and much poor work in return for advertising or tax subsidy.

"Now it has to make a case for journalism as an agent of public value and a part of people's lives in an age where people have shown that they want media to act on their behalf, not that of media shareholders or professional cliques. In return they will support what we do."

* * *

In "Page One," we observe a year in the life of The New York Times, an institution instrumental in shaping our views, even our lives. And an important year for media it was, from WikiLeaks to the launch of the iPad. Director Andrew Rossi has said he felt the journalists of The Times were "struggling to understand what their place is" in the current historic moment. He said he hopes we come away from the documentary saying to ourselves, "I should support The Times or my local paper."

The best kind of support from fans of this or any other important news institution is to encourage in them an understanding of the different roles they now must play. We must urge them to be more fully engaged with, and enriched by, the emerging possibilities and relationships. Then we can in turn be more hopeful that the fast-emerging new media ecology will be more enriched by the values and contributions of The Times and other legacy institutions.

This will not happen automatically. As Keller's column so clearly showed, it is hard for institutions that have been in control for so long to understand that they have lost it and thereby recognize the new possibilities before them.

What can you do about it? Inform yourself deeply, as you clearly are seeking to do. Support your newspapers with your subscriptions and your contributions—and also urge them to embrace the future more effectively than they have done so far.

Find digital news sources that serve your own community (be it defined by interest or geography) and support them, too. Pay for their work online or attend their events or make regular contributions to their trove of information on subjects you know well. Call attention to the best work you see being done by nonprofits. Encourage your community foundation to view the continued flow of high-quality information in the public interest as a goal as worthy of philanthropic support as the arts or education or open space.

Also, seek to broaden the narrow debate on journalism by the simple act of participating. You can bring nuance to the dialogue that automatically dismisses (or embraces) paywalls. You can remind those who inveigh against any government role in support for media that the government has always been involved, from postal subsidies to the publication of legal notices. Conversely, you can remind those who say government support is *the* solution that many different solutions offer greater promise for sustaining a free and healthy press.

As the revolution rolls on, we must bring the principles and dispositions of journalism into the fast-changing media environment, *as well as* fully and finally open the minds of journalists to the astonishing developments around them. As news organizations continue to provide them with the news, engaged citizens need to play a pivotal role in helping journalists to perceive the changed landscape around them.

INDEX

David Folkenflik is the media correspondent for NPR NEWS. His stories are broadcast on NPR's newsmagazines, including "Morning Edition," "All Things Considered," and "Talk of the Nation." Folkenflik's work has received many recognitions; he is a four-time winner of the National Press Club's Arthur Rowse Award for Press Criticism. He also appears frequently as a media analyst on U.S. and British television news programs. Previously, Folkenflik covered politics and the media for The Baltimore Sun. He lives in New York City with his wife, the journalist Jesse Baker.

I believe that a good story well told can truly make a difference in how one sees the world. This is why I started Participant Media: to tell compelling, entertaining stories that create awareness of the real issues that shape our lives.

At Participant, we seek to entertain our audiences first, and then invite them to participate in making a difference. With each film, we create social action and advocacy programs that highlight the issues that resonate in the film and provide ways to transform the impact of the media experience into individual and community action.

Thirty-two films later, from GOOD NIGHT, AND GOOD LUCK to AN INCONVENIENT TRUTH, and from FOOD, INC. to WAITING FOR "SUPERMAN," and through thousands of social action activities, Participant continues to create entertainment that inspires and compels social change. Now through our partnership with PublicAffairs, we are extending our mission so that more of you can join us in making our world a better place.

Jeff Skoll, Founder and Chairman
Participant Media

PublicAffairs is a publishing house founded in 1997. It is a tribute to the standards, values, and flair of three persons who have served as mentors to countless reporters, writers, editors, and book people of all kinds, including me.

I. F. Stone, proprietor of *I. F. Stone's Weekly*, combined a commitment to the First Amendment with entrepreneurial zeal and reporting skill and became one of the great independent journalists in American history. At the age of eighty, Izzy published *The Trial of Socrates*, which was a national bestseller. He wrote the book after he taught himself ancient Greek.

Benjamin C. Bradlee was for nearly thirty years the charismatic editorial leader of *The Washington Post*. It was Ben who gave the *Post* the range and courage to pursue such historic issues as Watergate. He supported his reporters with a tenacity that made them fearless and it is no accident that so many became authors of influential, best-selling books.

Robert L. Bernstein, the chief executive of Random House for more than a quarter century, guided one of the nation's premier publishing houses. Bob was personally responsible for many books of political dissent and argument that challenged tyranny around the globe. He is also the founder and longtime chair of Human Rights Watch, one of the most respected human rights organizations in the world.

.   .   .

For fifty years, the banner of Public Affairs Press was carried by its owner Morris B. Schnapper, who published Gandhi, Nasser, Toynbee, Truman, and about 1,500 other authors. In 1983, Schnapper was described by *The Washington Post* as "a redoubtable gadfly." His legacy will endure in the books to come.

Peter Osnos, *Founder and Editor-at-Large*